DICTIONARY OF SPORTS IDIOMS

Robert A. Palmatier
Harold L. Ray

National Textbook Company
a division of *NTC Publishing Group* • Lincolnwood, Illinois USA

DICTIONARY OF SPORTS IDIOMS

To
Our
Wives,
Marion
and
Shirley,
and
Our
Families

CONTENTS

PREFACE

Late in the 1970s, without warning, radio and television weatherpersons in America began to estimate the size of hail—and surgeons to gauge the size of tumors—in terms of the missiles of sport (marble-size, golf ball-size, baseball-size, softball-size) rather than in the previous terms relating to natural or household objects (pea-size, mothball-size, walnut-size, grapefruit-size). This development marked the return to respectability of the ''sports metaphor'' in America.

That respectability had been lost during the Watergate Hearings of 1974, according to Francine Hardaway, author of ''Foul Play: Sports Metaphors as Public Doublespeak'' (*College English*, 1976). Following the ''innocuous'' use of sports imagery by such presidents as Wilson, Truman, and Kennedy, President Nixon (on audiotape) and his defenders (on television) bombarded the airways with ''sports doublespeak'' intended to ''manipulate its audience.''

Such misuse of the sports metaphor continues in politics, business, and advertising, of course, but the weatherpersons—and surgeons—had no intention of manipulating *their* audience. They simply made an unconscious switch to a terminology that has become ''ubiquitous'' (Hardaway's word) in America. Everybody knows the size of a baseball, but not everyone knows that there are *two* kinds of walnuts—American and English—and that the former come either ''shucked'' or ''unshucked.''

Sports metaphors in the public domain are not really metaphors: they are ''idioms.'' They start out as metaphors when someone intimately familiar with a sport (or game) applies sports terminology to something analogous *outside* the sport. When the metaphors begin to be used by people who, like Howard Cosell, ''never played the game,'' they become idioms. And when they have outworn their welcome, they become clichés. Some sports metaphors, such as ''pass the buck,'' are regarded as slang throughout their careers. Others, such as ''wrestle with a problem,'' gain legitimacy almost immediately.

''Athlete's foot'' is a sports metaphor that exemplifies this progress. It develops in the locker room of a gymnasium, is carried home to the athlete's residence, and is spread to the athlete's family, neighbors, schools, and places of work. Eventually everyone forgets that athlete's foot is a metaphor for "ringworm of the foot" and adopts it in place of the medical expression. The term has now reached the status of an idiom. Athletes can still get athlete's foot, but so can everyone else.

The definition of "sports metaphor" in this work is necessarily broad because this is the first American dictionary to focus on this particular figure of speech. The coverage includes popular words and expressions in American English that derive from terms associated with sports, games, and recreation. That is to say, the more than 1,700 sports metaphors are not all from "sports," in the strictest sense. Many of them derive from "games" of all sorts, including animal games, children's games, and confidence games; and some of them come from such forms of amusement as the carnival, the circus, and the country fair.

Each entry in the dictionary consists of an entry heading, in the full, popular form of expression of the metaphor; an illustration of the correct grammatical usage of the metaphor; a definition of the popular meaning of the metaphor; the date of earliest attested use of the metaphor (where possible); the probable source of the metaphor—i.e., the sport or game from which it originated; the date of the earliest attested use of the term from which the metaphor derived (where possible); a definition of the meaning of the original term; a coded citation of other works that recognize the source of the metaphor; and comparative and contrastive cross-references to other entries in the dictionary (where appropriate).

The entry for "A-number-one" illustrates this format. A-NUMBER-ONE is the metaphor. *An A-number-one job (etc.)* characterizes the metaphor as a prenominal modifier. A first-class job (etc.) defines the meaning of the metaphor. DA: 1886 is the earliest attested date of the metaphor, according to the *Dictionary of Americanisms*. Source: SAILING identifies the sport of origin of the metaphor. DA: 1835 is the earliest attested date of the term from which the metaphor derives, also from the *Dictionary of Americanisms*. A first-class sailing vessel defines the term's original meaning. HTB cites another work, *Heavens to Betsy*, in which the source of the metaphor is discussed. These abbreviations are delineated in the Key to Works Cited. *Compare* Number One refers the reader to an entry in the dictionary that is similar but has a different meaning.

The metaphors have been gleaned from many different sources: from conversations and speeches, from radio and television, from newspapers (see SFS in Key), from magazines (see FP in Key), and from books (see LTA, OL, and SOE in Key). Once encountered, they have been checked out in the standard reference works cited in the Key to Works Cited. These works include (1) general dictionaries (the SOED, which supplied many dates; WNCD, which also supplied many dates and was the authority for the spelling of the metaphors; and WNWD, which suggested many origins and was the work most often consulted for meanings); (2) dictionaries of American English (DA and DAE) and American slang (NDAS); and (3) dictionaries of clichés (DOC), euphemisms (EOD), idioms (CI), political expressions (SPD), sports terms (LOS), and word and phrase origins (DPF, HF, HOI, HTB, THT, and WPO). Appended to the dictionary is a Classification of Metaphors According to Sport.

The dictionary should prove useful to teachers, journalists, historians, linguists, etymologists, students of Amerian culture, coaches, and aficionados of sport, as well as to those whose interest is merely one-upmanship. A provocative sports metaphor, thrown into the fray at a class meeting, bridge group, office party, or corporate board meeting can produce surprising results. As Hardaway says, the sports metaphor "operates on . . . irrational levels, manipulating its users as well as its audiences." A study of "Metaphors and Values in Higher Education" by David Deshler (*Academe,* November–December 1985) recognizes that metaphors are useful tools for "perceiving organizational culture." Deshler asserts that "imagery and metaphor play a central role in guiding decisions at both organizational and individual levels." With the potential for affecting growth in both education and corporations, we have a powerful incentive for welcoming, if not mastering, the metaphoric imagery of sports. If sports metaphors pervade all aspects of our lives, as Hardaway claims, this dictionary should help us cope.

ACKNOWLEDGMENTS

We wish to thank the Department of Languages and Linguistics at Western Michigan University for their generous support of this project. The support amounted not only to the use of the department's excellent facilities but to the personal encouragement provided by the Chairman, Peter Krawutschke, and department secretaries Helen Cummings, Ann Phillips Browning, Beverly Block, and Patricia Duzan. Several faculty members of the department assisted us by suggesting or clarifying metaphors. Of these we single out the following for special recognition: Jorge Febles (Spanish); Robert Griffin (Classics and Spanish) and his wife, Tina; Daniel Hendriksen (Linguistics); and George Osmun (Classics).

In addition, we recognize the contributions of the Department of Health, Physical Education, and Recreation at Western Michigan University. The consistent support of Chairman Roger Zabik has been especially heartening.

Dean Emeritus Marvin H. Eyler, of the University of Maryland (Department of Physical Education), graciously furnished us with his unpublished dissertation, *Origins of Some Modern Sports* (1956). This is a useful source, and we appreciate his assistance.

Finally, we wish to thank the reference librarians of Waldo Library at Western Michigan University for maintaining such excellent resources, for assisting us in their use, and for expediting interlibrary loans. Their expertise was essential to the project.

ABBREVIATIONS

adj.	adjective
adv.	adverb
Amer.	American
approx.	approximately
Brit.	British
ca.	*circa* (''around'')
cent.	century
Eng.	English
esp.	especially
Fren.	French
Ger.	German
Ital.	Italian
Lat.	Latin
M.E.	Middle English
mid	middle
M.Fren.	Middle French
n	noun
neg.	negative
O.E.	Old English
O.Fren.	Old French
orig.	originally
p.a.	predicate adjective
q.v.	which see
Span.	Spanish
usu.	usually
v	verb

KEY TO WORKS CITED

CI   E. M. Kirkpatrick and C. M. Schwarz, eds., *Chambers Idioms* (Edinburgh: W & R Chambers, 1982).

DA   Mitford M. Matthews, ed., *A Dictionary of Americanisms* (Chicago: University of Chicago Press, 1951).

DAE   William A. Craigie and James R. Hulbert, eds., *A Dictionary of American English on Historical Principles* (Chicago: University of Chicago Press, 1938).

DOC   James Rogers, *The Dictionary of Cliches* (New York: Facts on File, 1985).

DPF   Ivor H. Evans, ed., *Brewer's Dictionary of Phrase and Fable*, Centenary ed., Rev. (New York: Harper & Row, 1981).

EOD   Hugh Rawson, *A Dictionary of Euphemisms and Other Doubletalk* (New York: Crown Publishers, 1981).

FP   Francine Hardaway, "Foul Play: Sports Metaphors as Public Doublespeak," in *Sports Inside Out: Readings in Literature and Philosophy*, eds. David L. Vanderwerken and Spencer K. Wertz (Fort Worth: Texas Christian University Press, 1985), 576–582. First published in *College English* 38 (September 1976), 78–82.

HF   Charles Earle Funk, *Horsefeathers and Other Curious Words* (New York: Harper & Row, 1958; reprint, New York: Perennial Library, 1986).

HOI   Charles Earle Funk, *A Hog on Ice and Other Curious Expressions* (New York: Harper & Row, 1948; reprint, New York: Harper Colophon Books, 1985).

HTB   Charles Earle Funk, *Heavens to Betsy and Other Curious Sayings* (New York: Harper & Row, 1955; reprint, New York: Perennial Library, 1986).

LOS   Tim Considine, *The Language of Sport*, Introduction by Jim McKay (New York: Facts on File, 1982; reprint, New York: World Almanac Publications, 1983).

LTA   Stuart Berg Flexner, *Listening to America* (New York: Simon & Schuster, 1982).

NDAS   Robert L. Chapman, ed., *New Dictionary of American Slang* (New York: Harper & Row, 1986).

OL   William Safire, *On Language* (New York: Times Books, 1980).

SFS   Tim Considine, ''On Language: Starting from Scratch,'' *New York Times Magazine* (27 July 1986), 6.

SOE   Robert McCrum, William Cran, and Robert MacNeil, *The Story of English* (New York: Viking, Elisabeth Sifton Books, 1986), 249–250.

SOED   C. T. Onions, rev. and ed., *The Shorter Oxford English Dictionary on Historical Principles,* 3d ed. (London: Oxford University Press, 1944).

SPD   William Safire, *The New Language of Politics: Safire's Political Dictionary,* 3d ed. (New York: Times Books, 1978).

THT   Charles Earle Funk, *Thereby Hangs a Tale: Stories of Curious Word Origins* (New York: Harper & Row, 1950; reprint, New York: Harper Colophon Books, 1985).

WNCD   Frederick C. Mish, Editor in Chief, *Webster's Ninth New Collegiate Dictionary* (Springfield, Mass.: Merriam-Webster, 1983).

WNWD   David B. Guralnik, Editor in Chief, *Webster's New World Dictionary of the American Language,* 2d college ed. (New York: Simon & Schuster, 1982).

WPO   William Morris and Mary Morris, *Morris Dictionary of Word and Phrase Origins,* Foreword by Edwin Newman (New York: Harper & Row, 1977).

DICTIONARY OF SPORTS IDIOMS

A

ABACK *See* Taken Aback.

ABET *to aid and abet someone.* To assist someone, especially in committing a criminal act. SOED: 1779. Source: SPORTS. To urge on a dog to attack a tethered bear—in bearbaiting, a sport dating back to the 10th century. Abet came into English from the Old French *abeter,* "to hound on." THT.

ABOARD *See* All Aboard; Welcome Aboard.

ABOVEBOARD *to be aboveboard with someone.* To be open and honest with someone. SOED: 1616. Source: CARD GAMES. To hold your "hand"— and hands—above the table—the "board"—not below, where under-the-table deals are made. CI. *See also* Open and Aboveboard; Under the Table.

ABOVE YOUR HEAD *for something to be above your head.* For something to be beyond your comprehension. Source: SWIMMING. For the water to be deeper than you are tall, and you can't swim. *See also* In Over Your Head; One Hundred and Ten Percent.

ACCORDING TO HOYLE *See* Not According to Hoyle.

ACE (n) *an ace.* A top-notch professional, e.g., an ace mechanic. Source: CARD GAMES. An ace cardplayer, i.e., one who sets the standard for others. The ace is the card of the highest value. Its name derives from the Latin *as,* a unit of weight, by way of French. The word first referred to the side of the die that had only one spot and then was applied to a card or a domino with one spot. DPF. *Also:* "ace flyer," "ace golfer," etc. *See also* Ace a Test.

ACE A TEST *to ace a test.* To pass a test with a grade of *A.* Source: TEN- NIS. To ace your opponent—to serve them a ball that cannot be returned. DPF. *See also* Ace (n).

ACE IN THE HOLE *to have an ace in the hole.* To have something de- pendable in reserve. DA: 1922. Source: POKER. To have an ace card—the "hole" card—face down on the table in five-card stud poker. DOC; HTB. *See also* Ace up Your Sleeve; Down and Dirty; In the Hole.

ACE UP YOUR SLEEVE *to have an ace up your sleeve.* To have a secret weapon. Source: CARD GAMES. DOC: 16th cent. To have an ace hidden in your sleeve for use at an appropriate time. SOE. *See also* Ace in the Hole; Have a Card up Your Sleeve; Have Something up Your Sleeve.

ACROSS-THE-BOARD (adj.) *an across-the-board raise (etc.).* A raise given equally to all eligible employees. Source: BETTING. WNCD: 1945. An across-the-board bet is one that covers all of the three possible finishes that are "in the money": first ("win"), second ("place"), and third ("show"). The odds are listed on the tote board after the name of each horse in the race, in this same order. DOC. *See also* Across the Board (adv.).

ACROSS THE BOARD (adv.) *given/taken across the board.* Awarded, or assessed, to everyone, equally. Source: BETTING. To bet "across the board" is to bet that a horse will finish first ("win"), second ("place"), or third ("show")—any of the three finishes that are "in the money." The "board" that is referred to is the tote board, on which all of the horses in a race are listed, along with their odds of winning. CI; DOC. *See also* Across-the-board (adj.).

AFLOAT *See* Trying to Stay Afloat.

AFOUL OF *See* Run Afoul of.

AGAINST ALL ODDS *to succeed against all odds.* To succeed in spite of great risk and predicted failure. Source: BETTING. To win in spite of predicted failure—"odds against"—by all handicappers. *See also* Odds.

AGONY *the agony of defeat.* The pain and suffering accompanying defeat. Source: OLYMPIC GAMES; ROMAN GAMES. The thrill of victory, the agony of defeat is the motto of ABC–TV's *Wide World of Sports*. The word "agony" is from the Latin *agonia,* "a struggle" or "contest," which in turn is from the Greek *agon,* "arena," as at Olympia. DPF; SFS; THT. (Marathon runners joke about "the agony of de feet.") *See also* Arena; Snatch Defeat from the Jaws of Victory.

AHEAD ON POINTS *to be ahead on points.* To have a slight, and perhaps temporary, lead on your opponent. Source: BOXING. To have accumulated more points, awarded by the judges at the end of a particular round, than your opponent. The referee also used to score the fighters, and the scoring was once done by number of rounds won rather than by number of points per round. *Compare* Score Points; Stay Ahead of the Game.

AIM HIGH *to aim high.* To have high aspirations. Source: SHOOTING. SOED: 16th cent. To aim for a distant target, which requires raising the tip of the arrow or the barrel of a firearm above parallel. *See also* Set Your Sights High; Take Aim.

ALL ABOARD   *All Aboard!* It's time to get on the train. DA: 1837. Source: SAILING. It's time to get on board—on deck—the ship or boat. *See also* On Board; Welcome Aboard.

ALL-AMERICAN   *an all-American boy/girl.* An ideal boy or girl. Source: FOOTBALL. DA: 1920. A young man or woman who is selected for national recognition in a sport—originally football. SFS.

ALL AT SEA   *to be all at sea.* To be confused or disoriented. LTA: 1890. Source: SAILING. For a ship to be on the open sea, without landmarks or points of reference. WNWD.

ALL BETS ARE OFF   *All bets are off!* Conditions have changed: our agreement is canceled. Source: GAMBLING. All bets are canceled, due to conditions beyond our control, such as the "leveling" of the odds.

ALL IN THE SAME BOAT   *We're all in the same boat.* We're all in this mess together. HTB: 1850s. Source: BOATING. We're all going to sink or swim together.

ALL THE RIGHT MOVES   *to have, or make, all the right moves.* To make all the right decisions, take all the right actions, and have the reputation for doing so. Source: CHESS; CHECKERS. To make all the right moves on the chessboard or checkerboard, and to have the reputation for doing so. Used in many sports. *See also* Move.

ALSO-RAN   *an also-ran.* A candidate who is not one of the top vote getters: a loser. Source: HORSE RACING. WNCD: 1896. A horse that finishes a race out of the top three—i.e., "out of the money." CI; HTB. *See also* Finish out of the Money.

ANCHORMAN   *an anchorman, or anchorperson.* A television personality who coordinates the segments of a news program. Source: TUG OF WAR. The person who wraps the end of the rope around their body and serves as the "anchor" of the team. FOOT RACING. The final runner on a relay team. WNCD. The ultimate source is SAILING. *See also* Tug of War; Weigh Anchor.

ANSWER THE BELL   *to answer the bell.* To respond to a challenge. Source: BOXING. To respond to the bell that signals the start of a round or match by moving from the corner to the center of the ring. LOS; SFS. *See also* Come Out Fighting at the Bell.

ANTE UP   *to ante up.* To contribute to a cause; to pay a bill or debt. Source: POKER. DA: 1845. To deposit the agreed-upon amount of money, or chips, in the pot—to chip in—in order to be eligible to receive cards for the next hand. *Ante-*"before": before the game starts. *See also* Penny Ante; Raise the Ante; Up the Ante.

A-NUMBER-ONE *an A-number-one job (etc.).* A first-class job (etc.). DA: 1886. Source: SAILING. DA: 1835. A first-class sailing vessel: "A": the top class; "1": the best in that class. HTB. *Compare* Number One.

ANY PORT IN A STORM "Beggars can't be choosers." An adage. Source: SAILING. Any haven is suitable if it can protect the vessel from the elements.

ARENA *an arena.* The setting for major events before a large audience. SOED: 1798. Source: ROMAN GAMES. WNCD: 1600. The *arena,* Latin for "sand," was the central portion of the Roman amphitheater, the site of chariot races, gladiatorial contests, and other "games" since the 4th century B.C. SPD; THT. *See also* Agony; Political Arena.

ARMCHAIR QUARTERBACK *an armchair quarterback.* An unqualified critic. Source: FOOTBALL. A nonparticipant at, or even not at, a football game who offers advice and criticism, usually after the fact. *See also* Monday-morning Quarterback; Quarterback.

AS EASY AS FALLING OFF A LOG Extremely easy. LTA: 1840. Source: BURLING. As easy as falling off a log that is rolling in the water. CI. The reference could also be to the CHILDREN'S GAME of "king of the hill (or log)." DAE: "as easy as *rolling* off a log," 1889.

AT BAY *See* Hold at Bay.

AT EACH OTHER'S THROATS *to be at each other's throats.* To be engaged in a violent argument. Source: DOG FIGHTING. For two dogs, such as pit bulls, to be alternately seizing each other's throats in a dogfight, planned or unplanned.

AT FAULT *to be at fault.* To be responsible for causing something. SOED: 1833. Source: FOX HUNTING. SOED: 1592. For the hounds to have lost the scent of the fox because of its evasive actions. DPF. Once used in tennis. *See also* Red Herring.

AT FULL TILT *to do something at full tilt.* To do something at peak energy and speed. Source: JOUSTING. To joust, or tilt, at the top speed of your charger. CI. *See also* Go Full Tilt; Tilt at Windmills.

ATHLETE'S FOOT Ringworm of the feet. Source: ATHLETICS. DA: 1928. An infectious fungus associated with the locker room of a sports arena.

AT LOGGERHEADS *to be at loggerheads with someone.* To have a strong disagreement with someone. Source: GAMES. DA: 1871. To be engaged in a game of "loggerheads" with someone, tossing long, pestlelike objects at a mark—similar to horseshoes. The game is obsolete, as is the metal "logger-head" once used to heat a vat of tar on a ship. WPO.

AT ODDS *to be at odds with someone.* To have a disagreement with someone. Source: CHESS. To play a game of chess "at odds," i.e., with one player giving an advantage (odds) to the other, e.g., surrendering an early move to the opponent or giving up one or more pieces at the start of the game. *See also* Handicap (n).

AT RINGSIDE *to be at ringside.* To be in personal attendance at an event. Source: BOXING. LTA: 1866. To be in the first row of seats, at one side of the ring. LOS. *See also* Have a Ringside Seat.

AT SEA *See* All at Sea.

AT SIXES AND SEVENS *to be at sixes and sevens.* To be confused and disoriented. DOC: 1631. Source: DICE GAMES. The technical expression dates from Chaucer (*Troilus and Criseyde,* late 14th cent.), but the nature of the particular dicing game is uncertain. CI; DPF; THT; WPO. A case can be made for a transfer from the CHILDREN'S GAME of "jacks": Am I at "sixes" (required to pick up six jacks) or "sevens" (required to pick up seven)? Jacks is usually played with a maximum of eight "jacks."

AT STAKE *A lot is at stake.* A lot of money—energy, time—has been invested in something. Source: GAMBLING; BETTING. A lot of money has been wagered on a race or a hand of cards. This phrase is older than Shakespeare's "I see my reputation is at stake" (*Troilus and Cressida,* 1602).

AT THE DEATH *See* In at the Death.

AT THE DROP OF A HAT Instantly, without hesitation or delay. Source: BOXING. DOC: 19th cent. Early in the last century it was customary to start a boxing match by dropping a hat. DPF. If a sweep can be considered a "controlled" drop, then the usage is probably older in the sport of HORSE RACING. Horses were once started by "sweeping" the hat rather than dropping it.

AT THE END OF YOUR ROPE *to be at the end of your rope.* To be helpless, without a last resort. Source: CLIMBING(?). To be hanging at the end of a rope that does not quite reach the ground. SAILING(?). To be like a mooring rope that has been paid out "to the bitter end" (q.v.). HTB.

AT THE HELM *to be at the helm.* To be in control, in charge. Source: SAILING. To be at the wheel or tiller (the rudder handle).

AT THE KILL *See* In at the Kill.

AT THE TOP OF YOUR GAME *to be at the top of your game.* To be performing at the peak of your ability. Source: SPORTS. To be playing at the peak of your ability.

B

BACK IN THE SADDLE AGAIN   *to be back in the saddle again.* To be back in charge, or back to your normal activities again, after an illness or other interruption. Source: RIDING. To be riding a horse again after a fall, an illness, or some other interruption. CI. *See also* Saddle.

BACKLASH   *a backlash.* An opposite reaction to an action or edict. WNCD: 1815. Source: FISHING. A snag or snare of the fishing line, within the reel, during a cast, resulting in the whipping back of the line—and possibly the lure—toward the angler. SPD. *Compare* Boomerang.

BACKPEDAL   *to backpedal.* To retract a statement or reverse an opinion. Immediate Source: BOXING. WNCD: 1901. To take several steps backward from your opponent. LOS. Ultimate Source: CYCLING. To pedal in reverse in order to engage the brake (on a bicycle with "coaster" brakes) or to relax your legs while coasting (on a bike with "hard" brakes). CI. Of course, on a unicycle you *have* to backpedal in order to stay in one place or simply maintain your balance. (There are no brakes on a unicycle.)

BACK THE FIELD   *to back the field.* To support an entire slate of candidates. Source: BETTING. SOED: 18th cent. To bet on all of the horses in a race except the favorite. DPF. *See also* Play the Field.

BACK THE WRONG HORSE   *to back the wrong horse.* To support the losing party or candidate. Source: BETTING. To bet on a horse that doesn't win the race.

BACK TO SQUARE ONE   *to be/go back to square one.* To start over again, reluctantly, because of the failure of a previous attempt. Source: HOPSCOTCH. To start over again, from square one, because of a failure to hop in the proper squares or to pick up the stone properly. DOC. The fact that the squares are often numbered in hopscotch makes this source more likely than the sometimes-suggested "board games." *See also* Hopscotch.

BACKTRACK *to backtrack.* To return to an earlier passage or position. Source: HUNTING. WNCD: 1904. For a hunter to track an animal in the direction that it came from rather than where it was heading (in order to find the den, etc.), or for a hunted animal to retrace its own steps (tracks), as a rabbit or fox often does. *See also* Cover Up Your Tracks; Double Back. *Compare* Track Down.

BADGER *to badger someone.* To harass or torment someone: e.g., for a lawyer to "badger" the witness. SOED: 1794. Source: BADGER BAITING. To set dogs upon a holed-up badger, drawing it out, then letting it return to its hole, then tormenting it again. DPF; HTB; WPO. The dogs were "badger hounds," or dachshunds (q.v.). *See also* Make Sport.

BAD SPORT *a bad sport.* Someone who doesn't like to be made fun of or doesn't like to play along. Source: SPORTS. A sore loser. *See also* Make Sport. *Compare* Good Sport.

BAG (n) *See* Grab Bag; In the Bag; Let the Cat out of the Bag; Mixed Bag; Punching Bag; Punch Your Way out of a Paper Bag.

BAG (v) *to bag something.* To finally find what you have worked hard looking for, e.g., a job. Source: HUNTING. SOED: 1814. To hunt down, kill, retrieve, and put in a "game bag": e.g., to bag a pheasant.

BAIL OUT *to bail out of something.* To disassociate yourself from a risky venture. WNCD: 1967. Immediate Source: FLYING. To escape from a disabled aircraft by parachuting to the ground. Ultimate Source: BOATING. SOED: 1613. To dip water out of a leaky boat. *See also* Golden Parachute.

BAIT (n) *See* Fish or Cut Bait; Rise to the Bait; Take the Bait.

BAIT THE HOOK *to bait the hook for someone.* To attempt to "catch" someone. (Object: matrimony.) Source: FISHING. SOED: M.E. To put bait on the hook before dropping the line in the water. *See also* Bait the Trap.

BAIT THE TRAP *to bait the trap for someone.* To prepare someone for entrapment. Source: TRAPPING. SOED: M.E. To plant the bait for luring an animal into a trap. *See also* Bait the Hook; Set a Trap.

BALL *See* Carry the Ball; Get the Ball Rolling; Have a Lot on the Ball; Have Something on the Ball; Keep the Ball Rolling; My Ball; On the Ball; Play Ball; Take the Ball and Run with It; That's the Way the Ball Bounces.

BALL GAME *That's the ball game!* That's all. That's the end of your chances or opportunities. (You lose!) Source: BASEBALL. WNCD: 1848. That's the end of the game. You don't get another chance to win. NDAS. *See also* Game Is Up; Whole New/'Nother Ball Game; Your Ball Game.

BALL IS IN THE OTHER COURT   *The ball is in the other court.* The shoe is on the other foot; the tables have been turned. Source: TENNIS. SOED: *tennis court,* 1519. The ball has been hit across the net to the opponent's side ("court"), and it is now their responsibility to handle it. Many other sports are played on separated courts, but tennis is the oldest. *See also* Ball Is in Your Court.

BALL IS IN YOUR COURT   *The ball is in your court.* It's your turn to take the responsibility. Source: TENNIS. SOED: *tennis court,* 1519. The ball is on your side of the net. It's your turn to handle it. CI. The expression could be from any game involving a ball and a separated court, but tennis is the oldest of such games. *See also* Ball Is in the Other Court.

BALLPARK   *to be ballpark.* To be close—as close as a rough estimate of cost, size, weight, etc. WNCD: 1969. Source: BASEBALL. To be as accurate as the dimensions of a baseball stadium, which differ from park to park. OL; SFS. *See also* Ballpark Figure; In the Ballpark.

BALLPARK FIGURE   *a ballpark figure.* A rough estimate of cost, size, numbers, etc.: a "guesstimate." Source: BASEBALL. A figure as accurate as the dimensions of a baseball field, which vary from park to park. OL; SFS. *See also* Ballpark; In the Ballpark.

BALLYHOO   Exaggerated promotion of a product or event. WNCD: 1901. Source: CARNIVAL. Loud, exaggerated promotion of a sideshow by a carnival barker. WPO. *Also:* "to ballyhoo something."

BANDWAGON   *See* Get on the Bandwagon.

BANDY ABOUT   *to bandy something about.* To argue something back and forth. SOED: 1589. Immediate Source: ICE HOCKEY (Bandy). The Irish game of bandy—a 16th-century precursor of modern ice hockey, but played with a ball—was the source of this metaphorical sense of hitting something back and forth. DPF; HOI. Ultimate Source: TENNIS. SOED: 1577. This expression came to Ireland from France (Fren. *bander*), the home of court tennis, in which the ball was hit not only back and forth but off the walls as well. DPF; HOI. *See also* Bandy-legged; Bandy Words; From Pillar to Post; Hockey Puck; Keep the Ball Rolling.

BANDY-LEGGED   Bow-legged. SOED: 1687. Source: ICE HOCKEY (Bandy). Having legs shaped like "bandy sticks," the instruments used to roll and hit the ball in the old Irish game of bandy, a precursor of modern hockey. HF. *See also* Bandy about; Bandy Words; Keep the Ball Rolling.

BANDY WORDS   *to bandy words with someone.* To argue vigorously with someone. SOED: 1642. Source: ICE HOCKEY (Bandy). To roll or hit the ball back and forth in bandy, the Irish precursor of modern ice hockey. The metaphorical use of "bandy" derives from the 17th century; the literal use accompanied the term when it was borrowed from French in the 16th century. DPF; HOI. *See also* Bandy about; Bandy-legged; Keep the Ball Rolling.

BANK ON *to bank on something.* To count on something. SOED: 1883. Source: POKER. SOED: 1826. To rely on your personal "stake" in a poker game or other gambling game. CI. *See also* Break the Bank.

BARB *a barb.* A cutting remark. Source: FISHING. SOED: M.E. The angled point of a fishing hook. DPF. "Barb" can also be applied to the head of a hunting arrow.

BARE-KNUCKLE (adj.) *a bare-knuckle exchange.* A rough, tough confrontation. Source: BOXING. WNCD: 1924. A boxing match without gloves, as was the custom around the end of the 19th century.

BARGAINING CHIP *a bargaining chip.* Leverage for bargaining, consisting of a concession by one side in order to encourage an equal concession from the other side, as in arms reduction agreements. Source: POKER. The term is obviously from poker, but its technical meaning is unknown. Chips are not used as "concessions" in poker, and "bargaining" is not part of the game. EOD; OL; SPD. *Compare* Chip In.

BARK UP THE WRONG TREE *You're barking up the wrong tree.* You're asking the wrong person, looking in the wrong place. DA: 1832. Source: HUNTING. Your hunting dog is mistakenly barking at the foot of a tree in which the prey—a raccoon, possum, squirrel, bear, etc.—is *not* treed. DOC; DPF; HOI; WPO.

BARREL *See* Give It to Someone with Both Barrels; Let Someone Have It with Both Barrels; Like Shooting Fish in a Barrel; Lock, Stock, and Barrel; Over a Barrel.

BASE *See* Cover All the Bases; Get to First Base; Off Base (p.a.); Off-base (adj.); Touch All the Bases; Touch Base with Someone.

BASEBALL-SIZE HAIL Large-size hail—smaller than grapefruit-size but larger than walnut-size (i.e., with the husk still on) in the old terminology. Source: BASEBALL. Hail the size of a baseball—i.e., slightly less than three inches in diameter. *See also* Golf Ball-size Hail; Marble-size Hail; Softball-size Hail.

BAT (n) *See* Get Your At-bats; Get Your Turn at Bat; Go to Bat for; Off at the Crack of the Bat; Right off the Bat.

BAT AN IDEA AROUND *to bat an idea around.* To brainstorm an idea among a group of people. Source: BASEBALL. To bat a *baseball* around. To practice batting and fielding by playing "pepper" before a game: one bunter, two or more fielders. That's what the No Pepper signs on the infield walls mean. *See also* Toss Something around.

BAT CLEANUP *to bat cleanup.* To appear fourth on a program, capping the efforts of the three persons who preceded you. Source: BASEBALL. To bat fourth in a starting lineup, with the expectation that you will "clean up" on the opposing pitcher by driving in the three preceding batters. LOS.

BATTING A THOUSAND *to be batting a thousand.* To be enjoying a streak of good luck. Source: BASEBALL. To be hitting successfully in every turn at bat. LOS. *See also* Batting Average.

BATTING AVERAGE *a good batting average.* A good record of achievement. Source: BASEBALL. WNCD: 1867. A good percentage of hits in relation to number of "at-bats." At one time, .400 (to be read as "four hundred," not "forty percent") was considered to be good; now, .300 is. LOS. *See also* Batting a Thousand.

BATTLE ROYAL *a battle royal.* A king-size altercation, involving many participants. DOC: 1670s. Source: COCKFIGHTING. The culmination of an elimination process in cockfighting that was the basis for the modern championship playoffs in tennis. The cockfighting elimination started with 16 participants (in tennis, the "sweet sixteen"), then was reduced to 8 (in tennis, the "quarterfinals"), then to 4 (in tennis, the "semifinals"), then only 2 (the "battle royal" in cockfighting, the "finals" in tennis). DOC; WPO. "Battle royal" is also used to describe the fight to the death of two queen bees in the same hive. *See also* -Off; Top-seeded.

BEAD *See* Draw a Bead; Get a Bead On.

BEAN (v) *to bean someone, be beaned by someone.* To hit someone in the head (the "bean") with a blunt instrument; to be hit in the head with such. WNCD: 1910. Source: BASEBALL. To hit a batter in the head with a pitched ball (a "bean ball"); for a batter to be hit in the head by the pitcher. LOS; LTA.

BEARING DOWN ON *for something to be bearing down on you.* For something, e.g., a car or a truck, to be heading directly toward you. Source: SAILING. For a sailing ship or boat to be heading directly toward you, with the wind at its back. CI. *See also* Get Your Bearings; Lose Your Bearings.

BEAT AROUND THE BUSH *to beat around the bush.* To approach a topic indirectly, with circumlocution. LTA: 1850. Source: HUNTING. To scare game out of hiding so that it can be shot by the hunters. The job was once done in England by "beaters" (of the bushes), and the expression was originally "beat *about* the bush." CI; DOC; DPF; WPO. HOI says that the origin is "batfowling," the hunting of birds at night with a light and a stick. *See also* Beat the Bushes.

BEAT SOMEONE AT THEIR OWN GAME *to beat someone at their own game.* To outclass someone in their own field of expertise. Source: GAMES. To defeat someone in the game in which they, not you, are expert.

BEAT SOMEONE TO THE DRAW   *to beat someone to the draw.* To take advantage of an opportunity before someone else does. Source: DUELING (Western style). To draw your revolver from its holster, and shoot, before your opponent does. NDAS. *Compare* Beat Someone to the Punch.

BEAT SOMEONE TO THE PUNCH   *to beat someone to the punch.* To take action before your competitor can. Source: BOXING. LTA: 1823. To punch your opponent before they can punch you. LOS. *Compare* Beat Someone to the Draw.

BEAT THE BUSHES   *to beat the bushes for someone/something.* To search high and low for someone or something. Source: HUNTING. SOED: M.E. For "beaters" to disturb the "cover" (the bushes) of small animals or birds so that they will emerge and be shot by the hunters. DPF. *See also* Beat Around the Bush.

BEAT THE COUNT   *to beat the count.* To cheat fate. Source: BOXING. To get up from a knockdown before the count of ten. LOS.

BEAT THE ODDS   *to beat the odds.* To succeed in spite of great difficulty and predicted failure. Source: BETTING. For a horse to win a race in spite of the fact that the handicappers have set heavy odds against its happening (e.g., 50 to 1). *See also* Odds.

BEHIND THE EIGHT BALL   *to be behind the eight ball.* To be in a difficult or awkward position. Source: POOL. To have the "eight ball" between your "cue ball" and the "object ball" in a game of Eight Ball or Kelly Pool, making it impossible for you to take a straight shot. DOC; DPF; HOI; WPO. In a "friendly" game of eight ball, the rules are often relaxed to allow the eight ball to be hit by the cue ball into the object ball. *See also* Finessed; Snookered; Stymie; Stymied.

BELL   *See* Answer the Bell; Come Out Fighting at the Bell; Ready When the Bell Rings; Ring a Bell; Ring Someone's Bell; Ring the Bell; Saved by the Bell.

BENCH   *to bench someone.* To remove someone from active duty. LTA: 1917. Source: BASEBALL. DAE: 1846. For the manager to remove a player from the lineup and assign them to the "bench." DA; LOS. Also used in basketball, football, hockey, and many major sports. *See also* Benched; Come off the Bench.

BENCHED   *to be benched.* To be removed from active duty. Source: BASEBALL. To be removed from the lineup and assigned to the bench by the manager. LOS. Also used in basketball, football, hockey, and many other sports. *See also* Bench.

BENCH WARMER   *a bench warmer.* A nonparticipating participant: i.e., one who is prepared to perform but seldom or never does, e.g., an understudy in the theatre. Source: FOOTBALL. LTA: 1892. A reserve player—a third or fourth "stringer"—who warms the bench but not the "turf." Used also in many other sports.

BEND OVER BACKWARDS   *to bend over backwards to please someone.* To do everything possible to please someone. Source: GYMNASTICS; ACROBATICS. To bend backward until your hands touch the platform, as on the balance beam or in the floor exercises.

BESIDE THE POINT   *to be beside the point.* For a remark to lack relevance. Source: ARCHERY. For an arrow to miss the target, the "point" or "mark." DOC. *See also* Come to the Point; Have a Point; Make a Point.

BET (n)   *See* All Bets Are Off; Good Bet; Hedge Your Bets.

BET THE RANCH   *Don't bet the ranch on it.* Don't get your hopes too high. Source: GAMBLING; BETTING. Don't bet everything you own. *See also* Don't Bet on It; You Bet; You Bet Your Life; You Wanna Bet. *Compare* Bet Your Boots; Bet Your Bottom Dollar.

BETWEEN THE DEVIL AND THE DEEP BLUE SEA   In trouble on both sides: between a rock and a hard place. Source: SAILING. Between the lowest underwater seam (the "devil") and the "blue" waterline on the hull of a ship or boat. DPF; HTB. WPO: The "devil" is the "gunwale," a gun plank extending from the side of a large warship. *See also* Devil to Pay.

BET YOUR BOOTS   *You can bet your boots on it.* You can be absolutely certain of that. DA: 1868. Source: POKER. You can bet the most valuable thing you own, your boots, on that: it's a sure thing. DOC. *Compare* Bet the Ranch.

BET YOUR BOTTOM DOLLAR   *You can bet your bottom dollar.* You can risk everything. LTA: 1850s. Source: GAMBLING; BETTING. You can bet your last dollar, the only silver dollar left in the stack, because this is a sure thing. CI; DOC; LTA. *Compare* Bet the Ranch.

BICYCLE (v)   *to bicycle.* To appear in two Broadway shows or two television series at the same time. Source: CYCLING. WNCD: 1869. To ride a bicycle, i.e., to "cycle." *See also* Juggle.

BID   *to bid for something.* To make an offer for something; to attempt to get something, e.g., a higher position. Source: BRIDGE. To gamble that a particular number of "tricks" in a particular "suit" will win the "hand." *See also* Make a Bid for Something.

BIGGER THEY ARE   *The bigger they are, the harder they fall.* A proverb. The higher your position, the farther you'll fall when you leave it. Source:

BOXING. WPO: 1902. This is the sort of thing that a lower-ranked boxer might say about a higher-ranked opponent before a match. DOC indicates that the same proverb existed in classical times. (David vs. Goliath?)

BIG-LEAGUE *a big-league performance.* A first-class performance. Source: BASEBALL. LTA: 1899. A performance that is characteristic of the "big" (i.e., major) leagues of baseball (the American and National) as opposed to the minor leagues (the "farm" clubs). LOS.

BILK *to bilk someone.* To cheat someone out of their money. SOED: 1672. Source: CRIBBAGE. SOED: 1651. To spoil, or "balk," an opponent's attempt to score. DPF; WPO.

BINGO *Bingo!* Voilà! Eureka! I've got it! DA: 1937. Source: BINGO. WNCD: 1927. I've won the Bingo game! Players shout "Bingo!" when they have a line of markers on their card.

BIRD DOG (n) *a bird dog.* An investigative journalist. Source: HUNTING. WNCD: 1888. A dog that is trained to hunt birds. SPD. *See also* Bird-dog (v); Dog (v).

BIRD-DOG (v) *to bird-dog someone.* To follow someone closely. WNCD: 1943. Source: HUNTING. For a dog to hunt down birds, although it is not said to "bird-dog" them. NDAS; SPD. *See also* Bird Dog (n); Dog (v).

BIRD IN THE HAND *A bird in the hand is worth two in the bush.* A proverb. What you already have is worth more than what you are unlikely to get. Source: HUNTING. A bird that is shot and retrieved (i.e., is "in the hand") is worth more than twice that number that you might miss. *See also* In the Bag; It Ain't Over Till It's Over; Kill Two Birds with One Stone.

BITE (v) *to bite.* To fall for a trick or joke. ("What did the tortoise say to the hare?" "Okay, I'll *bite.* What did the tortoise say to the hare?") Source: FISHING. SOED: 1653. For a fish to take the bait, i.e., to strike at the bait on the angler's hook. *See also* Get a Bite.

BITTER END *See* To the Bitter End.

BLANK *to blank someone.* To defeat someone totally, as in a political primary when the opponent wins no delegates at all. Source: BASEBALL. DA: 1870. To "shut out" the other team, not letting them score even a single point. *See also* Draw a Blank; Shutout; Skunk. *Compare* Goose Egg; Lay an Egg; Love Game.

BLEACHERS *the bleachers.* The terraced benches in school auditoriums and gymnasiums. Source: BASEBALL. DA: 1889. The "bleacher seats": the unprotected wooden benches in the outfield of a baseball stadium that become bleached by the sun. LOS.

BLINDSIDE   *to blindside someone.* To deal someone an unexpected blow. Source: FOOTBALL. WNCD: 1972. To hit (block, tackle, sack) an opposing player from their "blind" side—i.e., when they're looking the other way. OL. The quarterback is the usual victim. *See also* Blindsided.

BLINDSIDED   *to be blindsided.* To be dealt an unexpected blow. Source: FOOTBALL. To be hit by an opposing player from your "blind" side—i.e., when you are looking the other way. OL. *See also* Blindside.

BLIZZARD   *a blizzard.* A violent winter snowstorm, with heavy winds and low temperatures. WNCD: 1859. Source: BOXING. DA: 1829. A flurry of blows. SHOOTING. Early 1800s. A volley of shots. The term was applied to baseball in 1881 and to the Great Blizzard of 1888.

BLOW   *See* Knockout Blow; Low Blow; Soften the Blow.

BLOW-BY-BLOW   *a blow-by-blow account.* A detailed description of an event that has already taken place. WNCD: 1933. Source: BOXING. A boxing announcer's or reporter's contemporaneous description of every blow that is thrown in a fight. In baseball it's a "play-by-play" account. *See also* Play-by-play.

BLOW SOMEONE OUT OF THE WATER   *to blow someone out of the water.* To destroy the competition completely. Source: HUNTING(?). To shoot a "sitting duck" with a shotgun—i.e., while it is sitting on the water. The military also use this expression for blowing up an enemy ship. *See also* Sitting Duck.

BLOW THE WHISTLE   *to blow the whistle on someone.* To expose someone as a violator of the law. Source: SPORTS. For a referee to blow their whistle to signal a violation of the rules and stop play immediately. NDAS. The police officer's whistle also serves these purposes, but its primary purpose is to call for help or scare off the violators. *See also* Cry Foul; Whistle-blower.

BLUE-CHIPPER   *a blue-chipper.* Someone or something of high class, e.g., a stock. Source: POKER. The blue chip is the most highly valued one in poker: above the red (second) and white (third). *See also* Blue-chip Stock.

BLUE-CHIP STOCK   *a blue-chip stock.* A safe, sound, high-priced stock. WNCD: 1929. Source: POKER. A stock as highly valued as the blue chip in poker—i.e., most highly valued. *See also* Blue-chipper.

BLUFF (n)   *a bluff.* A trick or pretense. DAE: 1889. Source: POKER. WNCD: 1859. A pretense of holding a hand with more value than it really has. Poker was originally called "Bluff." DAE: 1845. *See also* Bluff (v); Bluffing; Call Someone's Bluff; Pull a Bluff.

BLUFF (v)   *to bluff.* To pretend to be something you aren't, or to have something you don't. DA: 1893. Source: POKER. DAE: 1845. To bet as if you had a better hand than you really have—in hopes of convincing your opponents to "fold," thereby surrendering their money in the "pot." DPF; SOE. *See also* Bluff (n); Bluffing; Pull a Bluff; Outbluff.

BLUFFING *You're bluffing!* You're kidding! You're putting me on! Source: POKER. DA: 1887. You're betting as if you have a better hand then you really do. DPF; SOE. *See also* Bluff (n); Bluff (v); Pull a Bluff; Outbluff.

BOARD *See* Across the board (adv.); Across-the-board (adj.); Go by the Boards; Sweep the Boards.

BOAT *See* All in the Same Boat; Rock the Boat.

BOBBING ALONG *to go bobbing along.* To be bouncing up and down. Source: FISHING. For a cork float (a "bobber") on a fishing line to disappear below the surface of the water, then rise, then fall again—i.e., to "bob" up and down—when a fish is biting.

BODY ENGLISH A sympathetic motion of the body, usually unintentional, in imitation of that of someone attempting something difficult or dangerous. WNCD: 1908. Source: SPORTS. WPO: 1850. The conscious body movement employed by an athlete, e.g., a bowler, to "steer" the ball after it has already been released. The term "English" comes from BILLIARDS. *See also* English.

BOLT *See* Shoot Your Bolt.

BONER *a boner.* A mistake or blunder. LTA: 1912. Source: BASEBALL. NDAS: early 1900s. A stupid ("bonehead") play. *See also* Pull a Boner.

BONES *See* Make No Bones about It; Make No Bones about Something; Make No Bones about Wanting to Do Something.

BOOBY PRIZE *to get/win the booby prize.* To do something stupid. DA: 1893. Source: CHILDREN'S GAMES. WNCD: 1889. To be awarded a (usually silly) prize for being the worst player in a parlor game. *Booby* may derive from the Spanish *bobo*, "fool," or from the German *Bube*, "boy."

BOOK *See* Every Trick in the Book; Have the Book on Someone; Make Book on.

BOOMERANG *to boomerang.* To backfire: to produce an effect opposite to the one intended. Source: BOOMERANG. A boomerang is an Australian angled stick that, when thrown properly, returns to the thrower. SPD. When used by the native Australians for hunting, a return means a miss. *Compare* Backlash.

BOTTOM DOLLAR *See* Bet Your Bottom Dollar.

BOUNCE BACK *to bounce back.* To recover from a setback and return to action. Source: BALL GAMES. For a ball to spring back toward the striker after hitting a hard surface—as in handball, paddleball, racquetball, squash, etc. *See also* Take a Bad Bounce; That's the Way the Ball Bounces.

BOUT   *a bout with the flu.* A battle with influenza. Source: BOXING. SOED: 1591. A boxing match.

BOWL SOMEONE OVER   *to bowl someone over.* To astonish or overwhelm someone. WNCD: 1867. Source: BOWLING. To knock down bowling pins with a bowling ball. CRICKET. To "bowl a batsman over": to knock all of the bails off the wicket.

BOX   *See* Fast out of the Box; Knock out of the Box; Out of the Box.

BOXER SHORTS   *a pair of boxer shorts.* A pair of undershorts that are loose fitting and have short legs, as opposed to "briefs." WNCD: 1948. Source: BOXING. The type of shorts worn by boxers in the ring.

BOXING   *See* Shadow Boxing.

BOZO   *a bozo.* A person who is a little short on brains. WNCD: 1920. Source: CIRCUS. A clown. The ultimate source is unknown but may be the Spanish *bozal,* "stupid." DA.

BRAGGING RIGHTS   The right to brag about a success until the next challenge occurs. Source: FOOTBALL. The right to brag about a victory until the next game between the same two teams.

BRASS RING   *See* Grab the Brass Ring.

BREAK (n)   *See* Get a Break; Good/Bad Break; Make a Clean Break; Never Give a Sucker an Even Break.

BREAK AWAY   *to break away.* To move ahead of your competitors. Source: RACING. To pull ahead of your opponents in a race—a horse race, car race, bicycle race, etc. *See also* Break out of the Pack.

BREAK COVER   *to break cover.* To come out of hiding. Source: FOX HUNTING. For a fox, which is locked out of its den the night before a hunt and must therefore find other "cover," to break out of its temporary cover the next morning, thereby causing the foxhunt to begin. CI; DPF. *Compare* Cover Up Your Tracks.

BREAK EVEN   *to break even.* To earn as much as you spend, and vice versa. Source: GAMBLING. To win as much as you lose—and end up with as much money as you started with. *See also* Even Money.

BREAK OUT OF THE PACK   *to break out of the pack.* To pull away from the other contenders. Source: HORSE RACING. For a horse to pull away from the "field" and become the front-runner. OL.

BREAK SOMETHING/SOMEONE IN   *to break something/someone in.* To soften something up, e.g., a new pair of shoes; to train a new employee. Source: HORSE RACING. To train a young or wild horse. CI.

BREAK THE BANK   *to break the bank.* To win a fortune. Source: GAMBLING (Casino style). To win all the money that the "house" (the "bank") has on hand, at least for that game. CI. *See also* Bank On.

BREAK THE ICE   *to break the ice.* To relieve the "chilliness" of a meeting by trying to get a conversation started. DOC: 17th cent. Source: SAILING. To clear a path through the ice for other vessels to use. DOC; HTB. The lead vessel is called an icebreaker. *Compare* Cut No Ice.

BREAK THE RECORD   *to break the record.* To surpass all previous standards of achievement. Source: SPORTS. SOED: 1883. To surpass all previous records of achievement in a particular sport, e.g., most hits, most touchdowns, most baskets, most goals, etc. *See also* Record-breaking.

BREEZE   *See* Shoot the Breeze.

BRING HOME THE BACON   *to bring home the bacon.* To function as the "breadwinner" of the family. Source: CHILDREN'S GAMES (Catching a Greased Pig). To bring home the greased pig (the "bacon") that you caught at the country fair. DOC; DPF; HOI; WPO.

BRING IN A RINGER   *to bring in a ringer.* To substitute a phoney. Source: HORSESHOES. A "ringer" is a tossed horseshoe that surrounds the stake; a "dead" ringer is one that also touches it. In the metaphor, "ringer" is short for "dead ringer," a perfect throw. HORSE RACING. The look-alike sense of "ringer" is also associated with a horse that is entered in a race in place of another horse that it closely resembles. OL. *See also* Close Counts in Horseshoes; Dead Ringer; Horse of a Different/Another Color; Ringer.

BRING SOMEONE UP SHORT   *to bring someone up short.* To cause someone to stop an activity abruptly. Source: RACING; RIDING. For a rider to rein a horse in ("bring it up short") before reaching a barrier, such as a fence. CI. *See also* Pull Up Short.

BROAD IN THE BEAM   *to be a little broad in the beam.* To be a little wide hipped. Source: SAILING. For a sailing ship or boat to have a bottom that is unusually wide for its length. CI.

BRONX CHEER   *a Bronx cheer.* A "razzberry," or "raspberry": an interlabial trill. (Put tongue between lips. Blow.) WNCD: 1929. Source: BASEBALL. LTA: 1929. A sound uttered originally by fans at Yankee Stadium, in the Bronx, New York, to show their displeasure with the manager, the players, the umpires, or all of the above. HOI; LOS. The Yankees were once called the "Bronx Bombers." *See also* Cheerleader; Razz; Razzberry.

BUBBLE   *See* Burst Someone's Bubble; On the Bubble.

BUCK   *a buck.* A U.S. dollar. LTA: 1856. Source: POKER. A buckhorn knife, the original Western marker of the next dealer. The knife was later replaced by a silver dollar, which acquired the same name: "a buck." SPD; WPO. DA indicates that the origin may have been a "buckskin," used for exchange in the early 1700s. *See also* Buck Passer; Buck Sheet; Buck Stops Here; Pass the Buck.

BUCK PASSER   *a buck passer.* A person who places responsibility or blame on someone else. WNCD: 1920. Source: POKER. A poker player who passes the "buck"—the buckhorn knife or silver dollar token—to the player on the left in order to avoid the responsibility of dealing the next hand. *See also* Buck; Buck Sheet; Buck Stops Here; Pass the Buck.

BUCK SHEET   *a buck sheet or buck slip.* A "routing slip": a slip attached to a paper to indicate that it is to be read by the persons named thereon, in any order, and then checked, beside the name, to show that that person has done the reading. Source: POKER. The "buck" was originally a buckhorn knife that was passed ("routed") around the poker table, clockwise, to identify the next dealer. NDAS; WPO. *See also* Buck; Buck Passer; Buck Stops Here; Pass the Buck.

BUCK STOPS HERE   *The buck stops here.* This is the end—the "top" end—of the chain of authority or responsibility. Source: POKER. The token in front of me—a buckhorn knife or silver dollar—signifies that I am the dealer. DOC; SPD. This was the text of a sign that appeared on the desks of presidents Truman and Carter. *See also* Buck; Buck Passer; Buck Sheet; Pass the Buck.

BUILD SAND CASTLES   *to build sand castles.* To engage in a futile activity. Source: CHILDREN'S GAMES. To build castles out of sand, only to have them washed away by the tide. *See also* House of Cards.

BULL   *See* Have Someone in the Bullpen; Hit the Bull's-eye; Take the Bull by the Horns.

BURST SOMEONE'S BUBBLE   *to burst someone's bubble.* To dash someone's hopes. Source: CHILDREN'S GAMES. For a child to burst the bubble—soap bubble, bubblegum bubble—that another child has blown. *See also* On the Bubble.

BUSH (adj.)   *That's bush.* That's lacking in class. Source: BASEBALL. That's characteristic of the "bush league," a minor league of the lowest class (once *D,* now *A*). *See also* Bush-league; Minor-league; Sent Down to the Minors.

BUSH (n)   *See* Beat around the Bush; Beat the Bushes.

BUSH-LEAGUE (adj.)   *That's bush-league.* That's lacking in class. WNCD: 1925. Source: BASEBALL. LTA: 1909. A "bush" league is a "minor" league of the lowest rank or class: once class *D,* now class *A* or unclassified. DA. The bush leagues were once called "bushes." DA: 1910. *See also* Bush (adj.); Minor-league; Sent Down to the Minors.

BUTTERFINGERS *You're a butterfingers!* You can't hold on to anything! Source: CRICKET. SFS: 1800s. You're a lousy fielder!

BUT WHO'S COUNTING *But who's counting?* Not that it matters (but of course it does). Source: SPORTS. A count is kept in all kinds of sports and games. Not to do so would make it impossible to determine who won. *Also:* "But who's keeping score?" *See also* Count Me in; Know the Score.

BUY A PIG IN A POKE *to buy a pig in a poke.* To buy something sight unseen. Source: CON GAMES. DOC: 1580. To presume to buy a pig in a sack (a "poke"), only to find that the "pig" is really a cat. If the buyer opens the sack before the purchase, "the cat is out of the bag." CI; DPF; HOI; WPO. *See also* Let the Cat out of the Bag. *Compare* Jack-in-the-box.

BY ALL ODDS According to all predictions. DAE: 1866. Source: GAM-BLING; BETTING. According to all the odds makers or handicappers. *See also* Odds.

BY AND LARGE For the most part; generally speaking; on the whole. WNCD: 1669. Source: SAILING. To sail "by and large" is to sail both *into* the wind ("by") and *with* the wind ("large")—i.e. slightly "off" the wind. CI; DPF; WPO.

C

CALCULATED RISK *to take a calculated risk.* To take a chance after weighing the probabilities of success. Source: GAMBLING. To gamble on something after figuring the odds of winning and losing.

CALL (n) *See* Close Call; Hard Call; Judgment Call; Make the Right Call; Tough Call.

CALL 'EM AS YOU SEE 'EM *to call 'em as you see 'em.* To make decisions to the best of your ability, based on the evidence at hand. Source: BASEBALL. For an umpire to make a "call" on the basis of what they saw and heard. *See also* Close Call; Hard Call; Hard to Call; Judgment Call; Make the Right Call; Too Close to Call.

CALL IN A MARKER *to call in a marker.* To demand repayment for past favors. Source: GAMBLING. To demand payment of a gambling debt recorded on a "marker" (a sort of I.O.U.).

CALL OFF YOUR DOGS *Call off your dogs!* Cancel the attack. Source: FOX HUNTING. Call the dogs off the chase—they're on the wrong track or have lost the scent. Said to the huntsman. DPF; HTB.

CALL SOMEONE'S BLUFF *to call someone's bluff.* To challenge someone to carry out a threat or produce evidence for a claim. Source: POKER. DA: 1896. To "call" another player—i.e., to match their raised bet—because you believe that they are "bluffing" (pretending to have a better hand than they really do). CI; DPF; SOE. *See also* Bluff (n).

CALL THE SHOTS *to call (all) the shots.* To give (all) the orders. Source: POOL(?). To name the pocket into which you intend to shoot the next ball. If you are successful in the attempt, you get to "call" the next shot. The ultimate source is probably target SHOOTING: to "call" the location of the shots as they are fired. CI; NDAS.

CALL THE SIGNALS *to call (all) the signals.* To give (all) the orders; to be in charge. Source: FOOTBALL. For a quarterback to call out signals to their team members: what the play will be and when the ball should be "snapped."

CANOE *See* Paddle Your Own Canoe.

CAN OF WORMS *a can of worms.* A potentially messy problem. WNCD: 1969. Source: FISHING. A tin can full of worms that will be used as bait for fishing. Any child who had fished on a hot day with a cane pole and a can of worms knows just how messy this process can be. *Also:* "to open up a can of worms."

CAN'T MAKE HEADS OR TAILS *can't make heads (n)or tails of something.* Can't figure something out; can't decipher something. Source: COINS (Flipping Coins). Can't tell the "head" side (often a human head) from the "tail" side (often an animal or object), perhaps because the coin is old and worn down. DPF. HTB: the "head" or "tail" of a story. *See also* Heads I Win, Tails You Lose.

CAN'T WIN FOR LOSING *You can't win for losing.* You fail so much that there's no room for success. Source: GAMBLING. You lose so much that there's no room for winning. (If you *stopped* losing, you *could* win.) *See also* Win a Few, Lose a Few; You Can't Win 'Em All.

CARD *a card.* A "cutup"; a "joker." LTA: 1835. Source: CARD GAMES. The "card" is the "joker." *See also* Have a Card up Your Sleeve; Hold the Trump Card; Play Your Trump Card; Show Your Hole Card.

CARDS *See* Cards Are Stacked against You; Holding All the Cards; House of Cards; Lay Your Cards on the Table; Not in the Cards; Not Many Cards Left to Play; Play Your Cards Right; Put Your Cards on the Table.

CARDS ARE STACKED AGAINST YOU *The cards are stacked against you.* You have no chance of winning. Source: POKER. The cards have deliberately been stacked in such a way that you will receive a bad "hand" and cannot possibly win. CI; SOE. *See also* Play a Losing Game.

CAROM (n) *a carom.* A bouncing of one object off another, as when a car bounces off another car in an automobile accident. Source: BILLIARDS. WNCD: 1860. A shot in which the "cue ball" hits two "object balls" in succession. In pool, it is the colliding of any two balls. DPF. Carom is the registered name of a board game, played on a miniature pool table, having four pockets and using rings instead of balls. *Compare* Kiss (n).

CAROM (v) *to carom off something.* To bounce or glance off another object—e.g., for a car to carom off another car in an automobile accident. WNCD: 1860. Source: BILLIARDS. For a billiard ball to bounce or glance off another billiard ball, particularly as the "cue" ball hits two "object" balls in succession. DPF. Also spelled and pronounced *careen*. *Compare* Kiss (v).

CAROUSEL   *a carousel (or carrousel).* A merry-go-round. Source: JOUSTING. SOED: 1650. A medieval tournament (Fren. *carrousel,* from the Ital. *carosello,* "little chariot") in which the mounted contestants threw lances at a target, among other things. The modern merry-go-round retains the horses but substitutes grabbing a brass ring for throwing lances. THT. *See also* Grab the Brass Ring.

CARROT-AND-STICK   *a carrot-and-stick approach.* The use of an unattainable enticement. Source: RIDING. The dangling of a carrot, hanging from the end of a stick, in front of the nose of a horse (or mule or donkey) to entice it to move—or move faster. WPO agrees with the carrot but says that the stick was applied to the animal's rear. WPO: 1930.

CARRY A LOT OF WEIGHT   *to carry a lot of weight.* To have a lot of influence. Source: HORSE RACING. For a horse to carry more than the normal amount of weight in a race, either because of a heavy jockey or because an additional weight (a "handicap") has been assessed to a light jockey. DPF.

CARRY A/THE TORCH   *to carry a/the torch for someone.* To be deeply in love with someone who doesn't know it or won't return it. Source: OLYMPIC GAMES. To carry the Olympic torch (lit in Athens, Greece) to the site of the next Olympic Games. HOI. This practice is associated with the Modern Olympics. It was started at the Berlin Games of 1936. *See also* Pass the Torch; Torch Is Passed.

CARRY THE BALL   *to carry the ball.* To assume leadership or responsibility. Source: FOOTBALL. HTB: 1925. To advance the ball personally, rather than handing it off or passing it to a teammate. The source could also be RUGBY, but it could not be soccer.

CARRY THE DAY   *to carry the day.* To win a political election. Source: JOUSTING. To win the contest and honors for a particular day. DPF.

CARTE BLANCHE   *to have carte blanche.* To have free rein, a blank check. WNCD: 1754. Source: CARD GAMES. "Carte Blanche" ("white or blank card") was the white or blank card in the French game of piquet. CI; WPO.

CASH IN ON   *to cash in on something.* To profit from something. Source: GAMBLING. To exchange your chips for cash at the end of a gambling session.

CASH IN YOUR CHIPS   *to cash in your chips.* To die. Source: POKER. HTB: late 1800s. To exchange your poker chips for cash at the end of the game. DPF; EOD. The expression is also used in casino gambling, where "chips" of other sorts are used.

CAST ABOUT   *to cast about for something.* To search for something. WNCD: 1575. Immediate Source: FISHING. To throw out (i.e., "cast") your line in hopes of catching a fish. Ultimate Source: HUNTING. For a hunting dog that has lost a scent to smell around ("cast about") in order to recover it. DPF.

CAST IN YOUR LOT   *to cast in your lot with someone.* To enter into an alliance with someone. Source: LOTTERY. To put ("cast") your "lot" into the hat or bowl with the others and take a chance on "the luck of the draw." *See also* Lot.

CAT   *See* Cat and Mouse Game; Let the Cat out of the Bag; Look What the Cat Dragged in; More Than One Way to Skin a Cat; Play Cat and Mouse; Room to Swing a Cat in; When the Cat's away, the Mice Will Play.

CAT AND MOUSE GAME   *a cat and mouse game.* A situation in which one person "toys" with another—keeps them "on a string." WNCD: 1923. Source: ANIMAL GAMES. A game that is participated in willingly by the cat but unwillingly by the mouse. The cat "toys" with the live mouse that it has caught, pretending to ignore it, letting it get a foot or so away, and then catching it again. The mouse is not in a lot of danger as long as the game continues. CI; DPF. *See also* Play Cat and Mouse. *Compare* When the Cat's away, the Mice Will Play.

CATBIRD SEAT   *See* In the Catbird Seat.

CATCH AS CATCH CAN   *to do something catch as catch can.* To accomplish something any way you can. WNCD: 1764. Source: WRESTLING. To wrestle "freestyle," with no holds barred. DOC; DPF. The expression was apparently also the name of an earlier children's game, about which little is known, although presumably one child was to catch another child any way they could.

CATCH ON   *to catch on.* To grasp the meaning or get the knack of something. WNCD: 1833. Source: CHILDREN'S PLAY. To catch a ride on the back of a horse-drawn wagon. DAE.

CATCH SOMEONE FLAT-FOOTED   *to catch someone flat-footed.* To catch someone unprepared or unaware. Source: FOOTBALL. HOI: 1846. To tackle a ballcarrier before they have a chance to advance the ball. DPF.

CATCH SOMEONE OFF GUARD   *to catch someone off guard.* To take someone by surprise. Source: FENCING; BOXING. To make a thrust or land a blow when your opponent is unprepared. CI. *See also* Drop Your Guard; Off Guard; On Guard; On Your Guard.

CATCH SOMEONE RED-HANDED   *to catch someone red-handed.* To catch someone with a "smoking gun"—the evidence in hand. SOED: 1805. Source:

HUNTING. To catch a poacher—someone who hunts out of season or takes more than the law allows—with the blood of the slaughtered game on their hands. CI and WPO indicate "murder." *Also:* "to be caught red-handed." *See also* Red Herring.

CATCH THE WAVE   *to catch the wave.* To seize the opportunity. Source: SURFING. To enter a wave at just the right time and just the right place for a thrilling ride. *Note* Shakespeare's "There is a tide in the affairs of men, which taken at the flood, leads on to fortune" (*Julius Caesar,* 1599). *See also* Ride the Crest of a Wave.

CATCH UP   *to catch up.* To make up for lost time; to make up ground on a competitor. Source: RACING. To move closer to, or even with, the leader of the race. *See also* Play Catch-up.

CAUGHT NAPPING   *to be caught napping.* To be caught unprepared or unaware. Source: BASEBALL. DAE: 1868. To be caught off base. The ultimate source may be hunting: for a quarry to be caught sleeping. *Also:* "to catch someone napping." *Compare* Caught off Base.

CAUGHT OFF BASE   *to be caught off base.* To be caught unprepared or unaware. Source: BASEBALL. For a runner to be tagged out when taking such a big "lead" that they can't return to the base before the ball does. *See also* Off-base (adj.); Off Base (p.a.). *Compare* Caught Napping.

CHALK SOMETHING UP TO EXPERIENCE   *to chalk something up to experience.* To write something off as learning; to regard a failure as part of your education. Source: POOL(?). A pool player applies chalk to the tip of the cue after making a "miscue." BASEBALL(?). A zero is "chalked up" on the scoreboard when no runs are scored in a half-inning. FOOTBALL(?). Before and during the game, the coach diagrams plays on a chalkboard.

CHALK TALK   *a chalk talk.* A talk accompanied by drawings or diagrams on a chalkboard. Source: FOOTBALL(?). A demonstration of plays by means of diagrams on a chalkboard. LOS; SFS. The ultimate source may be the use of a chalkboard when lecturing to a large audience. DA: 1881.

CHAMPION   *a champion.* A defender of something. Source: ROMAN GAMES. A winning gladiator. LOS. The term is also applied to animals: e.g., a "grand champion hog."

CHAMPIONSHIP PERFORMANCE   *a championship performance.* A performance that is unexcelled. Source: ROMAN GAMES. SOED: 1825. The performance of a champion: a victorious gladiator in a Roman "circus."

CHANCE   *See* Fighting Chance; Game of Chance; Outside Chance; Snowball's Chance in Hell; Sporting Chance.

CHANGE OF PACE   *a change of pace.* A departure from your usual routine. "For a change of pace, I think I'll have tea." WNCD: 1912. Source: BASEBALL. A slow pitch that is thrown with the same motion as the preceding fast one. Also called a "change-up." WNWD. The ultimate source may be riding or running. *See also* Keep Pace with; Off the Pace; Pacemaker; Put Someone through Their Paces; Time for a Change.

CHANGE SIDES   *to change sides.* To reverse your allegiance. Source: TENNIS(?). To change ends of the court after the completion of an "odd" number of games: one, three, five, etc. This practice also occurs, in modified forms, in football, basketball, ice hockey, soccer, etc. *See also* Choose Up Sides; Side with; Take Sides with.

CHARLEY HORSE   *a charley horse.* A cramp in the upper leg. WNCD: 1888. Source: BASEBALL. A cramp in the upper leg of a baseball player. The name may have come from the nickname for one of the broken-down horses that were once used by grounds keepers to roll the dirt portion of the infield. HTB; LOS.

CHART A COURSE   *to chart a course.* To draft a plan of action. Source: SAILING. SOED: 1842. To map out a course for navigation or aviation (a "flight plan"). *See also* Course.

CHATTERBOX   *a chatterbox.* A child who never stops talking. WNCD: 1774. Source: CHILDREN'S TOYS. A child who talks like a "chatterbox," an earlier name for a type of child's rattle.

CHEAP SHOT   *a cheap shot.* An unfair action or remark. Source: FOOTBALL(?). WNCD: 1971. A late hit—a block or tackle—after the whistle has blown to end the play. OL. BOXING(?). An unfair blow, at an illegal place (e.g., "low") or time (e.g., after the bell), which is not noticed by the referee and therefore costs no points to the perpetrator.

CHECK (n)   *a check.* A restraint or control. SOED: 1515. Source: CHESS. WNCD: 14th cent. "Check!" is the announcement that you have put your opponent's king in danger of being captured: "in check." THT. All modern senses of "check" derive from the Persian word *shāh*, "king," which was applied to the chesspiece of that rank in the game that the Persians borrowed from India in the 8th century. *See also* Check (v); Checkered Past; Checkmate; Hold in Check; Rubber Check; Take a Rain Check.

CHECK (v)   *to check someone/something.* To restrain someone or gain control over something, e.g., a flood. SOED: 1581. Source: CHESS. WNCD: 14th cent. To put your opponent's king in danger: "in check." The term is used in this exact sense in ice hockey: to "check" an opposing player. *See also* Check (n); Hold in Check.

CHECKERED PAST *a checkered past, background, career, life, etc.* A past (etc.) that contains both successes and failures, with the failures probably outnumbering the successes. SOED: 1856. Source: CHECKERS. WNCD: 15th cent. In checkers, the board has alternating squares of two different colors, often red and black. The same is true for chess, the parent of checkers, where the colors are more variable, including brown and white, black and white (or silver), etc. DOC. A "checkered tablecloth" is patterned after this alternation, as are the design and home of the Ralston Purina Company: "Checkerboard Square." *Also:* "to take the checkered flag." *See also* Check (n).

CHECKMATE *Checkmate!* You lose! Source: CHESS. WNCD: 14th cent. You lose the game! Your king *(check)* is dead *(mate),* i.e., cannot avoid capture. From the Persian *shāh māt,* "The King is dead," by way of Arabic and Spanish. DPF; OL. *See also* Check (n); Stalemate.

CHEERLEADER *a cheerleader.* An extroverted person who encourages their colleagues to succeed. Source: FOOTBALL. WNCD: 1903. A leader of cheers at a football game. *See also* Bronx Cheer; Root for.

CHESS *See* Game of Chess.

CHICANERY Trickery. WNCD: 1609. Source: GOLF. From the French *chicanerie,* the name of an earlier and presumably craftier version of golf. WPO.

CHILD'S PLAY *That's child's play.* That's a piece of cake. Source: CHILDREN'S PLAY. DOC: 1580s. That's so easy that a child could do it. *See also* Duck Soup; Pushover. *Compare* Cinch.

CHIP (n) *See* Cash in Your Chips; Have a Chip on Your Shoulder; In the Chips; Throw in Your Chips; Time to Put Your Chips on the Table; When the Chips Are down.

CHIP IN *to chip in.* To help out. DA: 1861. Source: POKER. DA: 1876. To "ante up"—contribute to the "pot"—in order to take part in the next "hand." DPF. The term is also used in golf—to roll the ball into the hole from just off the green—but that use lacks the sense of helping out, although it does help out the score of the chipper. *Compare* Bargaining Chip.

CHOCK-FULL *to be chock-full of something.* To be full to the brim with something. WNCD: 15th cent. Source: SAILING. For the lower pulley of a block and tackle to be drawn as far as it will go toward the upper one. *Also:* "chock-a-block."

CHOKE *to choke.* To fail at a crucial time. Source: BASEBALL. To fail to get a hit, make a play, record a strikeout, steal a base, etc. in a critical situation. The image is of an invisible hand reaching out and choking the player at this moment, and in fact, the hand to the throat is the gesture used by a player to admit their failure. Used also in other sports, especially golf. *See also* Clutch.

CHOOSE UP SIDES *to choose up sides.* For a group of people to sort themselves out as to positions on an issue or a candidate. Source: CHILDREN'S GAMES. WNCD: 1925. For two children to choose the members of their teams (their "sides"), in alternating fashion, one choice at a time, from the group assembled for a game of football, baseball, basketball, ice hockey, etc. *See also* Change Sides; One Sided (p.a.); Side with; Take Sides with.

CINCH *a cinch.* No trouble at all. SOED: 1888. Source: RIDING. DA: 1859. A saddle girth. From the Spanish *cincha. Compare* Child's Play.

CIRCLE *See* Come Full Circle; Run Circles around; Stake Circles around.

CIRCUS *See* Three-ring Circus.

CLAY PIGEON *a clay pigeon.* An easy mark; a sitting duck. Source: SKEET. WNCD: 1888. A clay pigeon is a disk made of clay that is propelled aloft from a "trap" for persons to shoot at with shotguns. Skeet is also called trapshooting. *See also* Pigeon; Stool Pigeon.

CLEAR SAILING *It was clear sailing all the way.* It was a trouble-free experience. Source: SAILING. The sailing was done under clear skies, with no misfortunes. *See also* Sail through; Smooth Sailing.

CLOSE, BUT NO CIGAR Close to success, but not quite there. Source: CARNIVAL. Close to winning a prize, such as a cigar, but not quite succeeding. Said by operators of carnival games such as the one where you try to ring a bell on a board by striking a platform with a heavy mallet. NDAS. *See also* Give That Man a Cigar.

CLOSE CALL *a close call.* A near tragedy; a narrow escape. DA: 1881. Source: BASEBALL. An umpire's decision that could have gone either way: safe or out, fair or foul, etc. DOC. *See also* Call 'Em as You See 'Em; Judgment Call; Too Close to Call. *Compare* Hard Call; Hard to Call.

CLOSE COUNTS IN HORSESHOES Almost succeeding may count in horseshoes, but it doesn't count here. Source: HORSESHOES. Next to a "ringer," which surrounds the stake, and a "leaner," which leans against the stake, the horseshoe closest to the stake wins. British quoits is similar to horseshoes, but it is played with closed rings of metal or, on board ship, rope. *See also* Bring in a Ringer; Dead Ringer; Ringer.

CLOSE ON THE HEELS *to be close on the heels of someone.* To be in hot pursuit of someone, e.g., a wanted criminal. Source: FOX HUNTING. For the hounds to be in hot pursuit of a sighted fox. DOC.

CLOSE RACE *a close race.* A close campaign between two or more evenly matched opponents. Source: RACING. A race in which the second-place finisher comes in immediately behind the winner. SFS.

CLOSE TO THE VEST *to play it close to the vest.* To proceed carefully and discreetly. Source: CARD GAMES. To hold your cards close to your body so that the opposing players can't see them. WPO. *Also:* "close to the belt," because vests aren't worn that much anymore.

CLUTCH *to clutch.* To fail in a critical situation. Source: BASEBALL. To fail to perform—hit, pitch, field, run, etc.—in a critical situation: to "choke." Used also in many other sports. *See also* Choke; In the Clutch. *Compare* Good in the Clutch.

CLUTCH-HITTER *a good clutch-hitter.* A good performer in a critical situation. Source: BASEBALL. A batter who can be counted on to get a hit in a critical situation, e.g., when their team is behind, there are two outs, and there is at least one runner on base. *See also* Good in the Clutch; In the Clutch.

COAST *to coast the rest of the way.* To take it easy the rest of the way. DA: 1889. Source: CHILDREN'S GAMES (Sledding). DA: 1836. To slide down a hill on a sled, with gravity furnishing the power.

COCKEYED Cross-eyed; crooked (as with a picture); crazy (as of a scheme). WNCD: 1821. Source: COCKFIGHTING. Tilted like the head of a gamecock—or other fowl—when it is attempting to see or hear better what is on the ground, e.g., its opponent. *See also* Cocky.

COCKFIGHT *a real cockfight.* "It turned into a real cockfight." A vicious fight between two persons who are probably incapable of doing much harm to each other. Source: COCKFIGHTING. SOED: 1494. A vicious fight between two fighting cocks, who *are* capable of killing each other. Cockfighting was practiced in ancient Greece, Rome, and Roman Britain. DPF.

COCK OF THE WALK *the cock of the walk.* The most important person around. DAE: 1835. Source: COCKFIGHTING. SOED: 1615. The gamecock that is bred and raised in a place called a walk. CI. *See also* Cocky.

COCKPIT *a cockpit.* An enclosure in an airplane or boat where the pilot sits. Source: COCKFIGHTING. SOED: 1587. The pit in which cockfights are held. DPF; WPO. *See also* Pit Stop.

COCKSURE *to be cocksure of something.* To be stubbornly certain of something. Source: COCKFIGHTING. SOED: 1520. To be as confident as a gamecock. All senses of "cock" derive from the name of the fowl. *See also* Cocky.

COCKY *to be cocky.* To be conceited and arrogant. SOED: 1768. Source: COCKFIGHTING. To be as overbearing as a gamecock. *See also* Cockeyed; Cock of the Walk; Cocksure. *Compare* Have a Chip on Your Shoulder.

COIN   *See* Other Side of the Coin.

COLDCOCK   *to coldcock someone.* To knock someone unconscious. WNCD: 1927. Source: HUNTING; TRAPPING. To render a quarry unconscious, or dead, by hitting it with the butt of your firearm, rather than shooting it. NDAS: "to cold *caulk* a ship."

COME A CROPPER   *to come a cropper.* To have an accident or experience a failure. Source: HORSE RACING; POLO. SOED: 1858. To fall off a horse during a race or match, especially by being thrown over the horse's neck (or "crop"). CI; DOC; WPO. *Compare* Riding for a Fall.

COME AWAY EMPTY-HANDED   *to come away empty-handed.* To have nothing to show for your efforts. SOED: 1613. Source: HUNTING. To return from a hunting trip without any game. *Compare* Left Holding the Bag.

COME BACK TO THE FIELD   *to come back to the field.* A euphemism. To lose your lead. Source: HORSE RACING. For a horse in the lead to "fade" and allow the pack of contenders to catch up—rather than for the contenders to overtake the leader. *Compare* Run away from the Field.

COME-FROM-BEHIND (adj.)   *a come-from-behind victory.* A victory, e.g., in a political race, in which the candidate moves up from second place or lower, possibly last, to become the winner. Source: RACING. A victory in which the racer moves up from second place or lower, possibly last, to become the winner.

COME FROM BEHIND (v)   *to come from behind.* To move from a lower position, possibly last, to a higher position, possibly first, in a political race. Source: RACING. For a racer to take the lead after being behind for most of the race.

COME FULL CIRCLE   *to come full circle.* For a cycle of events to return to where it started. Source: WHEEL OF FORTUNE. For the (medieval) wheel of fortune to complete its cycle, meaning that those who have just experienced bad fortune can now expect good. CI. Alluded to in Shakespeare's *King Lear,* 1606. *See also* What Goes around, Comes around.

COME IN FIRST   *to come in first, second, third, etc.* To finish first (etc.) in a competition. Source: RACING. To finish first (etc.) in a race—i.e., to be the first (etc.) to cross the finish line.

COME INTO PLAY   *to come into play.* For something to become a relevant factor in an activity. Source: SPORTS; GAMES. For a previously ignored factor, such as time or the weather, to become important in a sport or game.

COME IN WITH FLYING COLORS   *to come in with flying colors.* To score a huge success. Source: SAILING. To return to port safely, with flags ("colors") flying. NDAS.

COME OFF SECOND BEST   *to come off second best.* To lose. A euphemism. Source: BOXING; WRESTLING. To get up off the canvas after losing a match. CI. *Compare* Second to None.

COME OFF THE BENCH   *to come off the bench.* To be called on to substitute for someone. Source: BASEBALL. To be called on by the manager to leave the "bench" and substitute for a player in the lineup. The expression is used in many other sports, including football, basketball, soccer, and ice hockey.

COME OUT FIGHTING AT THE BELL   *to come out fighting at the bell.* To plunge into an activity eagerly and enthusiastically. Source: BOXING. To move quickly from your corner toward your opponent at the sound of the bell signaling the start of the fight or round. *See also* Answer the Bell; Saved by the Bell.

COME OUT OF LEFT FIELD   *to come out of left field.* To come out of nowhere. Source: BASEBALL. For a sidearm pitch from a right-handed pitcher to come in so wide that it seems to be coming from left field; for any pitch to be thrown in such a way that it seems to be coming out of nowhere. SFS. *See also* Out in Left Field.

COME OUT SMOKING   *to come out smoking.* To attack an opponent vigorously from the outset. Source: BOXING. To throw a flurry of punches from the very beginning of a fight or round. LTA. *Compare* Come Out Swinging.

COME OUT SWINGING   *to come out swinging.* To attack your opponent from the outset. Source: BOXING. To leave your corner quickly, at the sound of the bell, and start throwing punches at your opponent. FP. *See also* Swing from the Heels. *Compare* Come Out Smoking.

COME TO GRIPS WITH   *to come to grips with something.* To face reality. Source: WRESTLING. To wrestle with an opponent. Freestyle wrestling usually begins with the mutual gripping of hands. *See also* Get a Grip on Yourself.

COME TO THE POINT   *to come to the point.* ("Come to the point!") To get to the heart of a matter. Source: SHOOTING. For a missile to arrive at the intended target. CI. *See also* Beside the Point; Make a Point; To the Point. *Compare* Hit the Bull's-eye; Hit the Spot.

COME TO YOUR SENSES   *to come to your senses.* To face reality. Source: BOXING. To recover consciousness after a knockout. CI.

COME UNSTRUNG   *to come unstrung.* To become unnerved, "shook up." SOED: 1692. Source: ARCHERY. SOED: 1598. For a bow to have its string slackened or removed. WNWD.

COME UP FOR AIR   *to come up for air.* To pause, while speaking, in order to "catch your breath." DOC: 1930s. Source: SWIMMING. To come to the surface of the water to get a breath of air. DOC. *See also* Surface; Surface for Air.

COM'ON IN—THE WATER'S FINE   *Com'on in—the water's fine!* Join the party! Source: SWIMMING. Come on into the water—the temperature's warm.

CONTACT SPORT   *a contact sport.* "Girl watching is not a contact sport." A potentially hazardous physical activity. Source: SPORTS. A sport that involves violent physical contact between players, e.g., boxing, wrestling, football, ice hockey, soccer, baseball, basketball, rugby, etc.

CONTENDER   *a contender.* A candidate, especially a "leading" candidate; a "top" candidate for a position or office. Source: SPORTS. A candidate, especially a superior candidate; a "top contender" for a title, prize, etc. LOS. The term probably originated in boxing. *See also* Top-ranked Contender.

CORDUROY   A ribbed fabric, nowadays usually of cotton or a blend of cotton and a synthetic material. WNCD: 1774. Source: HUNTING. The ribbed or corded fabric, of silk or velvet, worn by the kings of France while hunting: French *corde du roi,* "the king's cord." DPF; HF; WPO. Based on this weave is the term "corduroy road," a road made of logs laid crosswise to the direction of travel; it's very bumpy. SOED: 1930.

COUNT (n)   *See* Beat the Count; Down for the Count; Down for the Long Count; Go down for the Long Count; Take the Long Count.

COUNTERPUNCHER   *a counterpuncher.* A defensive person, one who fights back only when attacked. Source: BOXING. A boxer who has adopted the style of "countering" their opponent's punches rather than initiating their own. LOS.

COUNT ME IN   *Count me in!* Include me in your plans! Source: POKER. Include me in the deal for the next hand. My ante is in the pot. *See also* But Who's Counting; In.

COUNT ME OUT   *Count me out!* I don't want any part of your scheme! Source: POKER. Count out my winnings. I don't intend to ante up and play the next hand. *See also* Don't Count Me out; Out (2).

COUP   *a real coup.* A brilliant move. WNCD: 1791. Source: BOXING. A blow, especially to the side of the head: a "box" to someone's ears.

COURSE   *a course.* A direction, cycle, class, etc. Source: RACING. SOED: 1687. A measured track for racing: a racecourse or racetrack. *See also* Chart a Course; Horses for Courses; Par for the Course; Run Its Course; Stay the Course.

COURT   *See* Ball Is in the Other Court; Ball Is in Your Court; On Center Court.

COVER ALL THE BASES   *to cover all the bases.* To take all possible precautions. Source: BASEBALL. To guard all of the bases, including home plate, against an advance by the runner(s). *See also* Touch All the Bases; Touch Base with Someone.

COVER-UP (n)   *a cover-up.* A concealment of your real actions or intentions. WNCD: 1927. Source: BOXING. A covering up of your head with your arms and gloves during a fight—e.g., Muhammed Ali's "Rope-a-dope."

COVER UP YOUR TRACKS   *to cover up your tracks.* To conceal your illegal or immoral activity. DE: 1865. Source: FOX HUNTING. For the fox to conceal its scent by retracing its tracks, running in the track of another animal, running in or across a creek, etc. *See also* Backtrack; Cover-up (n).; Red Herring. *Compare* Break Cover; Make Tracks.

CRAP GAME   *a crap game.* A high-risk venture. Source: CRAPS. DA: 1843. Craps is a game of chance in which two dice are thrown to get a "natural" (a 7 or 11) or to establish a "point" (without first throwing a losing number: 2, 3, or 12) and then are thrown again in the hope of repeating that same point (without throwing a 7). Craps derives from the French game of *hasard* as modified in New Orleans in the first half of the 19th century. DPF; HF; WPO. A "floating" crap game is one that changes locations frequently in order to stay one step ahead of the law. NDAS. *See also* Game of Craps; Shooting Craps.

CRAP OUT   *to crap out.* To fail because of bad luck. Source: CRAPS. To lose at craps, i.e., to throw a losing number (2, 3, or 12) on the first throw or to throw a 7 once the "point" has been established. At its worst, to "crap out" is to throw "craps"—"snake eyes," or two "aces"—on the first throw. On the other hand, a "natural," a 7 or 11 on the first throw, is a winner. DA.

CRAPSHOOT   *a crapshoot.* A gamble. WNCD: 1971. Source: CRAPS. DAE: 1895. A roll of the dice in craps, in which a shooter (a "crapshooter") attempts to throw certain combinations of numbers on two dice in order to win the game. Much of the gambling is done in "side bets" by persons other than the shooter. The rolling of dice is ancient, perhaps as old as 5,000 years. *See also* Shooting Craps. *Compare* Game of Chance.

CRAZY LIKE A FOX   *to be crazy like a fox.* To be sly and cunning and tricky—in spite of being perceived as crazy. Source: FOX HUNTING. To be as cunning and crafty as a "sly old fox" when it is escaping its pursuers. DOC. *See also* Foxhole.

CRESTFALLEN *to be crestfallen.* To be dejected, with head bowed. Source: COCKFIGHTING. SOED: 1589. For the cock's comb (its "coxcomb") to be drooping, as from the rigors of the cockfight. The term was also once used to describe the drooping cap of the court jester. WNWD.

CRICKET *See* Not Cricket.

CROPPER *See* Come a Cropper.

CROSS SWORDS *to cross swords with someone.* To engage in angry confrontation or debate with someone. Source: FENCING. To engage in a fencing match, or duel, involving swords or sabers.

CROSS THE FINISH LINE *to cross the finish line.* To complete a task. Source: RACING. To complete a race. The term "finish line" is still used in racing, even though a line is no longer drawn in the dirt to mark the start and finish in either horse racing or foot racing. The expression probably originated in foot racing, which is more ancient than horse racing.

CROSS THE LINE *to cross the line.* To exceed the limits of decency or respectability. Source: BOXING. For boxers in ancient Greece to cross the line that was drawn on the ground between them at the start of the race—a foul. SFS. *Compare* Stop Short of Something.

CRUISE *to cruise/go cruising.* For adults to seek out sexual partners, e.g., in singles bars; for teenagers to drive slowly around town, in formation, showing off their cars. Source: SAILING. WNCD: 1651. For ships—"cruise ships"— to sail around at a leisurely pace. WNWD. *See also* Shakedown Cruise.

CRY FOUL *to cry foul.* To call attention to the violation of a rule. Source: SPORTS. To call attention to the violation of a rule of a sport or game. "Foul!" is cried out by the official in a boxing or fencing match. *See also* Blow the Whistle.

CRYING TOWEL *a crying towel.* A symbol of defeat. Source: SPORTS. A towel symbolically given to a defeated opponent for crying in over their loss—all in good fun, of course.

CRY UNCLE *to cry (or say) uncle.* To admit defeat or beg for mercy. Source: CHILDREN'S GAMES. To cry "Uncle!" as a signal of defeat in a child's wrestling match. DOC; HTB; WPO. *Compare* Throw In the Sponge/Towel.

CURVE *See* Throw Someone a Curve.

CUT A DEAL *to cut a deal.* To conclude a business arrangement with someone. Source: CARD GAMES. For a player other than the dealer to insure that a deck of cards is ready for dealing by removing any number of cards from the top and placing them on the table, face down. The dealer then places the remainder of the deck on top of the portion removed.

CUT AND RUN   *to cut and run.* To leave without warning. DAE: 1784. Source: SAILING. DAE: 1704. To cut the mooring cables or ropes and sail away as fast as possible, perhaps without even weighing anchor. *See also* Run (v). *Compare* Weigh Anchor.

CUT CORNERS   *to cut corners.* To sacrifice quality in order to reduce expenses. Source: FOOT RACING. To cheat in long-distance footraces, such as cross-country and the marathon, by taking a shortcut.

CUT ME IN   *Cut me in!* Include me in your plans! Source: POKER. Include me in the next game—i.e., allow me to cut the cards for the next deal. *See also* Deal Me in; In.

CUT NO ICE   *That doesn't cut any ice with me.* That action or argument doesn't impress me in the least. DAE: 1896. Source: ICE SKATING. The figure that you have just cut in the ice doesn't impress me in the least (says the judge). CI; DOC. *See also* Cut Quite a Figure. *Compare* Break the Ice.

CUT QUITE A FIGURE   *to cut quite a figure.* To make quite an impression on others, especially because of your appearance. DAE: 1815. Source: ICE SKATING. To execute ("cut") a near-perfect pattern, e.g., a figure eight on the ice in figure skating. *See also* Cut No Ice.

CUT YOUR LOSSES   *to cut your losses.* To avoid losing everything; to quit before things get worse; to "quit while you're behind." Source: GAMBLING. To quit gambling before you lose your original "stake."

D

DACHSHUND *a dachshund.* A dog by that name, long and low to the ground. Source: HUNTING. SOED: 1881. A "badger hound" (Ger. *Dachs,* "badger," *Hund,* "dog"), once used for hunting badgers or for "baiting" badgers when they were caught alive. HF.

DARK HORSE *a dark horse.* A candidate for office who is relatively unknown but is beginning to make quite an impression. DOC: 1831. Source: HORSE RACING. An entry in a race that is relatively unknown but is beginning to show promise. CI; DOC; DPF; FP; HTB; SPD; WPO. *See also* Shot in the Dark; Underdog. *Compare* Horse of a Different/Another Color.

DEAD AS A MACKEREL *as dead as a mackerel.* As dead as a doornail— absolutely, positively dead. Source: FISHING. As dead as a dead fish. DOC. *See also* Knock 'Em Dead.

DEAD DUCK *If you go in there, you'll be a dead duck.* If you go in there, you're sure to be shot down. DA: 1829. Source: HUNTING. You'll be like a duck that is either dead (and now duck soup) or soon will be (a "sitting duck") (q.v.).

DEADHEAD (n) *a deadhead.* A non-paying customer: a "freeloader." Source: SPORTS. SOED: 1853. A non-paying spectator at a sporting event. NDAS. *See also* Deadhead (v).

DEADHEAD (v) *to deadhead.* For a transport vehicle to return empty, i.e., without a "payload," after hauling a load. WNCD: 1911. Source: SPORTS. This verb is derived from *deadhead (n)* (q.v.).

DEAD HEAT *a dead heat.* A tie. Source: HORSE RACING. SOED: 1840. The finish of a race in which two or more contenders cross the finish line (come under the wire) at exactly the same time: a photo finish. DPF. *See also* Photo Finish; Under the Wire.

DEAD IN THE WATER   *to be dead in the water.* To be unable to take action. Source: SAILING. To be becalmed—no wind.

DEAD ON TARGET   *to be dead on target.* To be precisely correct. Source: SHOOTING. For your shot to be precisely in the center of the target. *See also* Target (v).

DEAD RINGER   *X is a dead ringer for Y.* X looks exactly like Y. Source: HORSESHOES(?). A dead ringer is a tossed horseshoe that not only rings the stake but ends up touching it, in perfect position. The metaphorical use of the term may refer to the fact that all "dead ringers" look alike. HORSE RACING(?). A lookalike horse that is substituted for one of higher quality. CI; NDAS. *See also* Bring in a Ringer; Close Counts in Horseshoes; Ringer.

DEAD SET ON   *to be dead set on something.* To be obsessed with (doing) something. DA: 1848. Source: HUNTING. "Dead set" is the position of a bird dog "at point," i.e., pointing its nose at a quarry (or its cover) and remaining absolutely motionless.

DEAL (n)   *see* Cut a Deal; Fair Deal; New Deal; One-shot Deal; Raw Deal.

DEALER'S CHOICE   *Dealer's choice!* It's your decision. Source: POKER. The dealer has the right to choose the conditions of the upcoming hand: "draw" or "straight," five or seven cards, "wild" cards or not, etc. *See also* Wheeler-dealer; Wheeling and Dealing.

DEAL ME IN   *Deal me in!* Include me in your plans! Count on me for financial support! Source: POKER. Deal me cards in the next hand! I'm joining the game! *See also* Cut Me in; Deal Yourself in; Ready to Deal.

DEAL ME OUT   *Deal me out!* Don't include me in your plans or schemes! Source: POKER. Don't deal me another hand! I'm leaving the game! *See also* Dealt out; Out (2).

DEALT OUT   *to be dealt out of an activity.* To be left out or deliberately ignored. Source: POKER (and other card games). To not be dealt a hand of cards for the next game, for various reasons. *See also* Deal Me out; Out (2).

DEAL YOURSELF IN   *to deal yourself in.* ("I'm dealing myself in!") To join in with others on a project, usually involving a commitment of funds. Source: POKER. For the dealer to include himself/herself in the hand, rather than deal cards only to the other players. *See also* Deal Me in.

DEATH TRAP   *a death trap.* An unsafe building or enclosure. WNCD: 1835. Source: TRAPPING. A trap that kills an animal rather than capturing it alive. CI. The classic mousetrap is an example of a death trap. *Compare* Pitfall.

DEBT OF HONOR *a debt of honor.* A debt unenforceable by law—and therefore enforceable only by honor. Source: GAMBLING. A gambling debt. DPF.

DEBUT *a debut.* A debutante's formal introduction to society; the opening of a new show or business; the introduction of a new product. SOED: 1751. Source: BILLIARDS. The opening shot of a billiard game. (Fren. *de but,* "from the mark.") WNWD. *See also* Gambit; Opening Gambit.

DECK (n) *See* Hit the Deck; Not Playing with a Full Deck; On Deck; Play with a Marked Deck; Play with a Stacked Deck.

DECK (v) *to deck someone.* To knock someone to the ground or the floor. Source: SAILING. To knock someone to the deck of a sailing vessel. The "boom" is often the "decker" here.

DECKED *to be decked by someone or something.* To be knocked down by someone or something. Source: SAILING. To be knocked to the deck by someone or something, e.g., the "boom."

DECKED OUT *all decked out.* All dressed up. Source: SAILING. All fitted out and polished up: "shipshape" (q.v.).

DECOY *a decoy, e.g., a police decoy.* An authorized "lure," e.g., a policewoman posing as a prostitute. Source: HUNTING. DAE: 1784. A replica of a bird or animal that is used to lure game to the hunter.

DEEP SIX *to deep six someone or something.* To bury someone six-feet deep; to render someone *hors de combat* (and probably hors d'oeuvre). WNCD: 1952. Source: SAILING. To throw something overboard, sending it to its "watery grave" six fathoms deep. NDAS. *Compare* Go Overboard.

DEKE *to deke someone.* To fake someone out. Source: FOOTBALL. To fake an opposing player out of position. (From *decoy.*) NDAS. Also used in basketball, ice hockey, soccer, and other sports. *See also* Fake Out; Juke.

DERBY *a derby.* A hat with a rounded top and a narrow brim. SOED: 1888. Source: HORSE RACING. A hat of the type traditionally worn by men at the annual race at Epsom Downs (Surrey, England), which was named after the Earl of Derby, who founded the event in 1780. WNWD; WPO.

DESIGNATED *the designated driver (etc.)* The member of a group who is picked to serve the group in some special way—e.g., to abstain from drinking and drive the others home. Source: BASEBALL. From "designated hitter" (q.v.).

DESIGNATED HITTER *a designated hitter.* Someone who is selected to act as a representative for someone else. In the Iran–Contra hearings in 1987, the designated hitter was the senator or representative selected to question the witness following the questioning by counsels. Source: BASEBALL. WNCD: 1973. In the American League: a player designated to bat, and hopefully hit, for the pitcher. *See also* Designated.

DESULTORY   Not staying long in one place, at one job, etc. WNCD: 1581. Source: ROMAN GAMES. Like a horseman or charioteer (a *desultor*) in the "Roman Circus" who was able to leap *(saltire)* back and forth from one horse, or one chariot, to another. DPF; THT.

DEVIL TO PAY   *There'll be the devil to pay.* There'll be a lot of trouble. Source: SAILING. HTB: 1821. The "devil" was the seam nearest the keel, and to caulk it with hot pitch was a headache. LTA. *See also* Between the Devil and the Deep Blue Sea.

DIBS   *to have dibs on something.* To lay prior claim to something. ("I've got dibs on the front seat!") Source: CHILDREN'S GAMES (Jacks). SOED: 1730. To lay claim to the jacks (the "dibs") for the first game. DPF; WPO. Originally, "dibs" were "dibstones"—pebbles, or the knucklebones of sheep. They were once used like modern poker chips in many gambling games.

DICE   *See* No Dice; Roll of the Dice; Shoot the Dice; Throw of the Dice.

DICE ARE LOADED AGAINST YOU   *The dice are loaded against you.* You have little or no chance of succeeding, because of someone else's dishonest actions. Source: DICE GAMES (esp. Craps). The dice have been weighted in such a way that they will almost always turn up in your opponent's favor. CI; DAE. *See also* Load the Dice; Play with Loaded Dice. *Compare* Loaded Question.

DICEY   *a little dicey.* A little risky or chancy. WNCD: 1950. Source: CRAPS; DICE GAMES. As uncertain as the combination that will turn up in a throw of the dice. WPO.

DIE IS CAST   *The die is cast.* The decision has been made; the first step has been taken; there is no turning back now. WPO: 1548. Source: DICE GAMES. The "die" (one of a pair of dice) has been thrown ("cast") and the thrower will have to live with the results. CI; DOC; HTB. This is a translation of Julius Caesar's statement before crossing the Rubicon in 49 B.C.: *Alea iacta est.*

DIG IN YOUR HEELS   *to dig in your heels.* To solidify your position on an issue. Source: TUG OF WAR. To lean backward, while holding on to the rope, with your legs straight and your heels "planted" in the earth.

DIRTY POOL   *That's dirty pool!* That's not fair! WNCD: 1940. Source: POOL. That's in violation of the rules of pool! *Compare* Not Cricket.

DISCARD   *to discard something.* To throw something away. SOED: 1598. Source: CARD GAMES. WNCD: 1591. To exchange a card in your hand for a card from the dealer, as in "draw" poker, or from the stack of cards on the table, as in gin rummy.

DISC JOCKEY *a disc jockey.* The host of a radio music program: a "rider" of the records. WNCD: 1941. Source: HORSE RACING. Jockey: a rider of racehorses. *See also* Jock.

DIVE IN HEAD FIRST *to dive in head first.* To start something without proper planning or preparation. Source: DIVING. To dive into unfamiliar waters "head" first, rather than the more judicious "feet" first.

DIVE RIGHT IN *to dive right in.* To get to work without delay, and possibly without any particular plan of attack. Source: DIVING. To dive into the water without delay, and at any convenient point. *See also* Plunge in; Take a Dive.

DOESN'T KNOW THE SCORE *X doesn't know the score.* X is ignorant or unsophisticated, or both. Source: SPORTS. X doesn't know where their team stands at any given moment during a game.

DOG (v) *to dog someone's heels/footsteps.* To follow someone persistently, as an investigator or reporter does. DAE: 1842. Source: HUNTING. SOED: 1519. To follow someone the way a hunting dog tracks a rabbit or other game. *See also* Bird Dog (n); Bird-dog (v).

DOG AND PONY SHOW *a dog and pony show.* A small-scale, portable presentation or sales pitch. WNCD: 1970. Source: CIRCUS. A small-scale circus, consisting of little more than a dog that does tricks and a pony that circles inside the single "ring." WPO.

DOGFIGHT *a dogfight.* ("It developed into a real dogfight.") A spontaneous altercation between two or more persons. DAE: 1865. Immediate Source: FLYING. An aerial battle between two or more planes. Ultimate Source: DOG FIGHTING. WNCD: 1656. A spontaneous or prearranged fight between two dogs, such as pit bull terriers. *See also* Let Slip the Dogs of War.

DOLL *You're a doll!* You're nice! Source: CHILDREN'S TOYS. SOED: 1700. You're like a perfectly mannered child's baby doll. "Doll" and "dolly" are short forms, probably shortened by children, of the name Dorothy. *See also* Dolled Up.

DOLLED UP *all dolled up.* All dressed up. Source: CHILDREN'S TOYS. All dressed up like a child's baby doll. *See also* Doll.

DOMINO EFFECT *a domino effect.* The effect of an action by one party leading to a similar action by another party. WNCD: 1966. Source: DOMINOES (as Children's Toys). The effect of all of the upright dominoes, in a row, falling down, one at a time, when the first one is tipped over. *See also* Domino Theory.

DOMINO THEORY   *the domino theory.* The political theory that if one nation turns Communist, the neighboring countries will also turn Communist. WNCD: 1965. Source: DOMINOES (as Children's Toys). When dominoes are set upright in a row, and the first one is tipped over, all of the others fall down, one at a time. EOD; SPD. The term was first applied in the 1960s to the countries in Southeast Asia. Later, in the 1980s, it was applied to the countries of Central America. *See also* Domino Effect.

DON'T BET ON IT   *Don't Bet on it!* Don't count on it! Source: GAMBLING; BETTING. Don't place a bet on that hand of cards, throw of the dice, horse race, etc. You'll probably lose. *See also* Bet the Ranch.

DON'T COUNT ME OUT   *Don't count me out!* Don't eliminate me from consideration or participation. Source: BOXING. If the referee counts to ten before the knocked-down boxer is ready to resume fighting, the boxer is said to be "counted out." *See also* Count Me out; Knockout.

DON'T LOOK A GIFT HORSE IN THE MOUTH   Don't be critical of something you got for nothing. (The apparent philosophy of the ancient Trojans.) Source: HORSE RACING. Don't examine the teeth—to determine the age, and therefore the worth—of a horse you got as a gift. CI; DOC; WPO. *See also* Long in the Tooth. *Compare* Straight from the Horse's Mouth.

DOUBLE BACK   *to double back.* To turn around and go back the way you came. Source: HUNTING. For a hunted animal, e.g., a rabbit or a fox, to stop and retrace its steps. CI. *See also* Backtrack.

DOUBLE-BARRELED   *a double-barreled attack.* A two-pronged attack. Source: SHOOTING (Firearms). SOED: 1709. A double-barreled shotgun, having two barrels: either "side-by-side" or "over-and-under." DPF. *See also* Give It to Someone with Both Barrels; Let Someone Have It with Both Barrels.

DOUBLE DARE   *to double dare someone to do something.* ("I double dare you to jump off the roof.") To goad someone into doing something foolish, and perhaps dangerous. Source: CHILDREN'S PLAY. For a child to dare another child to do something, with the promise that the first child will do it after the second child has. (Never fall for a double dare.)

DOUBLE-DEALER   *a double-dealer.* One who promises one thing but does the opposite. SOED: 1547. Source: POKER. One who deals the cards illegally: one kind of deal for the dealer, another for the other players. *Double* is used here in the sense of "duplicity." *See also* Double-dealing.

DOUBLE-DEALING   The promising of one thing but the delivering of something else. SOED: 1529. Source: POKER. Dealing one way to yourself, but another way to the other players. *See also* Double-dealer.

DOUBLE DUTCH Gibberish. Source: CHILDREN'S GAMES (Skipping Rope). A type of rope skipping that involves *two* ropes; the chant that accompanies this type of rope skipping. CI. "Dutch" is apparently to English as "Greek" was once to Latin: "It's Greek to me."

DOUBLEHEADER *a doubleheader*. Two events of a similar nature in succession. DA: 1946. Source: BASEBALL. LTA: 1896. Two baseball games on the same day—or night (a "twilight" or "twinight" doubleheader). DA; LOS.

DOWN AND DIRTY *Give it to me down and dirty*. Tell me the bad news, frankly and bluntly. Source: POKER. In seven-card "stud," the final card is dealt facedown ("down and dirty"), as are the first two cards. Also used in blackjack, or "twenty-one." *See also* Ace in the Hole.

DOWN AND OUT *to be down and out*. To be destitute, penniless, hopeless, as in the film *Down and Out in Beverly Hills*. SOED: 1889. Source: BOXING. To be knocked down and counted out. DOC; DPF. *See also* Knockout; Out (1). *Compare* Down but Not out.

DOWN BUT NOT OUT *to be down but not out*. To be down on your luck but not completely "washed up"—i.e., not hopeless. Source: BOXING. To be knocked down but not counted out—i.e., not "knocked out." LOS. *See also* Out (1). *Compare* Down and out.

DOWN FOR THE COUNT *to be down for the count*. To be soundly defeated. Source: BOXING. To be knocked down for the count of ten—a knockout. British: *"out* for the count." CI. *See also* Go down for the Long Count.

DOWN FOR THE LONG COUNT *to be down for the long count*. To be dead. Source: BOXING. To be knocked down for the count of ten and unable to get back up—i.e., to be knocked unconscious. SFS. *See also* Take the Long Count.

DOWN ON YOUR LUCK *to be down on your luck*. To be experiencing more failures than successes. Source: GAMBLING. To be losing more money than you're winning. CI. *Down* may refer to the "down" side of the "Wheel of Fortune" (q.v.). *See also* Luck of the Draw.

DOWNSIDE *The downside is. . . . The Market is on the downside*. The bad news is. . . . The Market is down. WNCD: 1946. Source: WHEEL OF FORTUNE. The "downside" of the wheel is the "bad" side, the one that is "falling." *Compare* Upside.

DOWN THE STRETCH During the most difficult or crucial part of a campaign or other long-term activity. Source: HORSE RACING. The oval racetrack has two straightaways or "stretches," the "backstretch" and the "homestretch," on which the horse is expected to stretch out its legs and go as fast as possible. The term "stretch" may be related to the fact that an oval looks like a "stretched-out" circle. *See also* In the Homestretch; Stretch a Point.

DRAGNET *a dragnet.* A police "sweep" that is designed to "net" criminals, as on the television series *Dragnet.* DAE: 1865. Source: FISHING. SOED: 1541. A net that is "dragged" behind a boat to catch fish.

DRAG YOUR FEET *You're dragging your feet (or heels)!* You're holding up the progress of the group. Source: CHILDREN'S PLAY. You're dragging your feet (or heels) on the ground (or pavement) behind the wagon, causing it to slow down.

DRAW (n) *a draw.* A tie. DAE: 1871. Source: DRAWING LOTS. A drawing of lots to break a tie. *See also* Luck of the Draw; Win, Lose, or Draw.

DRAW A BEAD *to draw a bead on something.* To focus all of your attention on, or take careful aim at, something. Source: SHOOTING (Firearms). To "sight" over the "bead"—a tiny ball—on top of the end of a rifle or gun barrel. DPF. *See also* Get a Bead On.

DRAW A BLANK *to draw a blank.* To be unable to recall something from your memory banks, such as a person's name; to fail to achieve something. Source: DRAWING LOTS(?). To draw a "lot"—in this case a piece of paper—with nothing on it ("blank": a losing draw). LOTTERY(?). SOED: 1567. To draw a losing lottery ticket. CI; DOC. Hunting(?). To "draw a bead" on a bush or brush pile and find nothing there. DPF. *See also* Blank.

DRAWBACK *The only drawback it.* . . . The only problem is. . . . Source: ARCHERY(?). The major problem with a bow is drawing the string back to its proper position. The source may simply be "recoiling" from something frightening, such as a snake (SOED: 1618); or the term may refer to the difficulty that a team of horses has to hold a wagon back from rolling downhill (DA).

DRAW THE COLLAR *to draw (or take) the collar.* To have nothing to show for your efforts. Source: BASEBALL. To strike out, i.e., to score a zero (a goose egg). "Collar" gets its name from the horse collar, which is shaped like a zero or goose egg. *See also* Goose Egg; Lay an Egg; Love Game.

DRAW THE LINE *to draw the line at (doing) something.* To decline to participate in something because it is personally offensive. DOC: 1820s. Source: CHILDREN'S GAMES. To refuse to cross the line that has been drawn on the ground by another child—and over which you have been dared to step. HTB: to plow a boundary marker.

DRAW TO AN INSIDE STRAIGHT *to draw to an inside straight.* To attempt something that is highly unlikely to succeed. Source: POKER. To replace a card in your hand (in "draw" poker) with one that you hope will complete a broken series of two cards in succession, a missing card, and two more cards that pick up the series (e.g., 5,6—8,9, and you're trying for a "7"). *See also* Fill an Inside Straight; Like Drawing to an Inside Straight; Like Trying to Fill an Inside Straight. *Compare* Play Both Ends against the Middle.

DRIFT   *Do you get (or catch) my drift?* Do you follow my line of reasoning? Source: SAILING(?). Are you aware of the lateral movement of my vessel? *See also* Give Someone Some Leeway.

DRINK LIKE A FISH   *to drink like a fish.* To drink too much alcohol too often. Source: FISHING. To drink as much alcohol as a fish drinks water. *See also* Loaded to the Gills.

DRIVE SOMEONE UP THE WALL   *to drive someone up the wall.* To drive someone crazy. Source: FOX HUNTING(?). For the hounds to drive the fox up (and over) the stone wall of the hunting grounds. The source may be simply driving someone crazy—until they start "climbing the walls."

DROPOUT (n)   *a dropout.* A student who leaves school before graduating. WNCD: 1930. Source: FOOT RACING(?). A runner who withdraws from a race that they are taking part in.

DROP OUT (v)   *to drop out of something.* To withdraw from an activity that you are taking part in—e.g., school. Source: FOOT RACING. To withdraw from a race that you are taking part in—i.e., literally to fall behind and drop from the pack.

DROP YOUR GUARD   *to drop your guard.* To leave yourself unprotected from attack. Source: BOXING. To lower your hands, especially the "lead" hand, during a fight, thereby leaving your head unprotected (unguarded) from blows by your opponent. LOS. *See also* Catch Someone Off Guard; Let Down Your Guard; Off Guard.

DUCK (n)   *See* Dead Duck; Have All Your Ducks in a Row; Lame Duck; Sitting Duck.

DUCK (v)   *to duck.* To lower your head in order to avoid a flying object— usually upon hearing the warning "Duck!" SOED: 1598. Source: SWIM- MING. SOED: 1550. To dive ("duck") underwater, while swimming, as a duck does. *See also* Juke.

DUCK SOUP   *as easy as duck soup.* Too easy: "child's play" (q.v.). LTA: 1912. Source: HUNTING. As easy as shooting a "sitting duck" (q.v.)—i.e., a duck sitting on the water—and converting it into soup. DOC; HTB. *See also* Dead Duck.

DUFFER   *a duffer.* An inexperienced or inept performer. Source: GOLF. A novice or mediocre golfer: a "hacker." NDAS. The term came into golf from commerce: a peddler of fake jewelry. WNCD: 1756. *See also* Hacker.

DUMBBELL   *a dumbbell.* A stupid ("dumb") person. Source: WEIGHT
LIFTING. SOED: 1785. A short bar, weighted at both ends, for lifting with
one arm. (THT notes that the original "dumbbell" was a weight machine for
body building.)

DUMMY   *a dummy.* A stupid ("dumb") person: a "dumbbell." SOED: 1796.
Source: BRIDGE. SOED: 1736. The nonplaying partner of the winning bidder
in a game of bridge (and, earlier, whist). The bidder plays the upturned hand
dealt to the "dummy."

E

EARN A LETTER *to earn a letter in something.* To be recognized for excellence in some activity. Source: FOOTBALL. To be awarded a cloth "letter" (e.g., *U*) for membership on a high-school or college football team. LOS. Letters can now be earned in just about any sport or sports-related activity, such as cheerleading. *See also* Letter.

EASY MARK *an easy mark.* A "sucker." WNCD: 1896. Source: CON GAMES. A person "marked" for an easy swindle by con artists.

EAT SOMEONE'S DUST *to eat someone's dust.* To trail another competitor in a competition. Source: HORSE RACING. To ride behind another horse, especially the leader, in a race—receiving the dust kicked up by the other horse. The term is also used in dirt-track car racing. *Compare* In Someone's Wake.

EGG *See* Goose Egg; Lay an Egg.

EIGHT BALL *See* Behind the Eight Ball.

END (n) *See* At the End of Your Rope; Go off the Deep End; Hold Up Your End; Play Both Ends against the Middle; Tie Up some Loose Ends; To the Bitter End.

END RUN *to make (or try) an end run.* To take an indirect approach. Source: FOOTBALL. DA: 1902. To run the ball around the left or right end of the line of scrimmage, rather than straight ahead.

ENGLISH Pressure applied, as by the media, to "steer" an issue in a particular direction. DA: 1945. Source: BILLIARDS. DA: 1869. The sideward spin put on a cue ball to cause it to move in that direction after striking the object ball or the rail. NDAS; SPD. *See also* Body English.

ENTER THE LISTS *to enter the lists.* To join a competition or controversy. SOED: 1579. Source: JOUSTING. For a challenger in a medieval tournament to enter the gate (the "lists") to the tilting ground, thereby declaring himself a participant. CI; DOC; DPF. *Compare* Make a Bid for Something.

EUCHRE   *to euchre someone.* To trick or outsmart someone. DAE: 1863. Source: CARD GAMES (Euchre). To prevent the player who declared trump from taking the minimum three tricks. WNCD; WNWD. *Compare* Snooker.

EUCHRED   *to be euchred.* To be tricked or outsmarted. Source: CARD GAMES (Euchre). To be prevented from taking the necessary three tricks after declaring trump for that hand. WNWD. *Compare* Snookered.

EVENLY MATCHED   *to be evenly matched.* To be of equal ability. Source: BOXING. To be of equal ability in the ring, based on prior experience, height, weight, reach, etc. *See also* Matchup.

EVEN MONEY   A 50–50 chance of succeeding. Source: GAMBLING. The odds are even; e.g., a $1 bet will return $1. *See also* Break Even.

EVERY TRICK IN THE BOOK   *to know/use/try every trick in the book.* To be a master at your craft. Source: CARD GAMES. To know, use, or try every move, play, or strategy in the book of Hoyle. *See also* Never Miss a Trick; Not According to Hoyle.

F

FACE-OFF (n) *a face-off.* A face-to-face confrontation. Source: ICE HOCKEY. WNCD: 1896. The dropping of the "puck" by an official between two opposing players, in a prescribed area, to start, or restart, the game. Also used in soccer.

FACE OFF (v) *to face off with someone.* To have a face-to-face confrontation with someone. Source: ICE HOCKEY. For an official to start, or restart, a hockey game by dropping the "puck" in a prescribed area, between two players who are "facing" each other. NDAS. Also used in soccer.

FADE IN THE STRETCH *to fade in the stretch.* To weaken near the end of an activity—e.g., a political campaign. Source: HORSE RACING. For a horse to weaken and slow down in the "homestretch," the straightaway of a racetrack that leads to the finish line.

FAIR DEAL *to get a fair deal.* To be treated honestly. Source: POKER. To be dealt an honest hand. SOE. *See also* Fair Dealing; New Deal; Raw Deal.

FAIR DEALING *to have a reputation for fair dealing.* To be known as an honest businessperson. Source: POKER. "Fair dealing" is the honest distribution of cards by the dealer to the players—e.g., from the *top* of the deck. *See also* Fair Deal.

FAIR GAME *to be fair game.* To be "up for grabs": available for (legal) acquisition. Source: HUNTING. For an animal to be "in season" for hunters, fishers, trappers, etc. CI. *See also* Open Season.

FAIR PLAY *See* Spirit of Fair Play.

FAIR SHAKE *to get a fair shake.* To get fair treatment from someone. DOC: 1830s. Source: DICE GAMES. To get a fair and honest "shake" of the dice. DOC; NDAS.

FAKE OUT   *to fake someone out.* To outmaneuver someone. Source: FOOT-BALL. To outmaneuver, or "deke," an opposing player. LOS. *See also* Deke.

FALL GUY   *a fall guy.* A person who is left to take the consequences of a crime: a patsy. DA: 1908. Source: BOXING; WRESTLING. A boxer or wrestler who is paid to lose a fight—i.e., to "take a fall." DPF; WPO. In the TV series *Fall Guy,* the hero was a Hollywood stuntman. The metaphorical use of the term may have been reinforced by the surname of Albert Fall, the "fall guy" of the Teapot Dome scandal in the 1920s. *See also* Take a Fall; Take the Rap.

FALL OFF A HORSE   *When you fall off a horse, the best thing to do is to get right back on again.* A maxim. When you suffer a setback, the best thing to do is to get right back into action again. Source: RIDING. The purpose of this advice is to prevent novices from becoming "horse shy" after their first fall. *See also* Riding for a Fall.

FALL SHORT OF THE MARK/TARGET   *to fall short of the mark or target.* To fail to live up to expectations or achieve a goal. Source: ARCHERY. For an arrow to fall to the ground before reaching the target, or "mark." DPF.

FALSE START   *a false start.* A premature action. Source: FOOT RACING. WNCD: 1815. A start of a race by a runner before the gun sounds, or before the word "Go!" is spoken. CI. Also used in swimming, rowing, and skating. *See also* Jump the Gun; No Go.

FAN   *a fan of someone/something.* An ardent admirer of someone or something. DAE: 1896. Source: BASEBALL. SOED: 1889. Either short for "fanatic" or alluding to the "fans" once held by spectators at a baseball game. DAE; LTA; NDAS; THT; WPO. *See also* How about That, Sports Fans; Root for.

FARM OUT   *to farm someone/something out.* To reassign an employee to a position outside the parent organization; to subcontract a job to another firm. DAE: 1845. Source: BASEBALL. To send a major-league player down to a "farm" club in the minor leagues. *See also* Sent Down to the Minors.

FAST OUT OF THE BOX   *to be fast out of the box.* To be a fast starter. Source: BASEBALL. For a batter to fly out of the batter's box toward first base after getting a hit. *See also* Knock out of the Box; Out of the Box.

FAST SHUFFLE   *to give someone a fast shuffle.* To trick someone with fast talk or sleight of hand. Source: CARD GAMES. To pretend to shuffle a deck of cards but not actually do so. NDAS; SPD. *See also* Get Lost in the Shuffle.

FAST STARTER   *a fast starter.* Someone who gets off to a fast start in a competition, e.g., a political campaign. Source: FOOT RACING. A runner who leaves the starting line, or starting "blocks," immediately upon hearing the sound of the gun or the pronouncement of the word "Go!" *Compare* Get Nowhere Fast.

FAULT   *See* At Fault.

FENCING   *See* Verbal Fencing.

FERRET OUT   *to ferret something out.* To search for and uncover something. SOED: 1577. Source: HUNTING. SOED: 1450. To use a "ferret," a weasel-like animal, to hunt rabbits in their holes.

FIELD (n)   *See* Back the Field; Come back to the Field; Come out of Left Field; Have a Field Day; Level the Playing Field; Out in Left Field; Play the Field; Run away from the Field; Trail the Field.

FIELD (v)   *to field questions.* To take, and attempt to answer, questions from the audience. Source: BASEBALL. SOED: 1824. To attempt to stop or catch batted balls in the infield or outfield. LOS.

FIELD DAY   *See* Have a Field Day.

FIGHTING CHANCE   *a fighting chance.* A fair chance to either compete or win. WNCD: 1889. Source: BOXING. A chance to win a fight, or even get a fight, with an opponent. LTA.

FILL AN INSIDE STRAIGHT   *like trying to fill an inside straight.* Like trying to do the impossible. Source: POKER. Like trying to complete a five-card sequence when you have the first two and the last two cards (e.g., 5,6—8,9). *See also* Draw to an Inside Straight; Like Drawing to an Inside Straight; Like Trying to Fill an Inside Straight. *Compare* Play Both Ends against the Middle.

FINDERS KEEPERS, LOSERS WEEPERS   What you find becomes your own property. A child's maxim. Source: CHILDREN'S PLAY. This is the children's version of "Possession is nine tenths ('points') of the law." CI. *See also* String Someone along.

FINESSE (1)   *to finesse someone.* To outsmart someone. SOED: 1778. Source: BRIDGE (Whist). SOED: 1746. To take a "trick" with the lower-valued of two cards of the same suit in your hand, in hopes of being able to take another trick with the higher-valued card later on. SPD. *See also* Finesse (2); Finessed.

FINESSE (2)   *to finesse something.* To handle something shrewdly and delicately. Source: BRIDGE (Whist). *See also* Finesse (1).

FINESSED   *to be finessed.* To be put in an awkward position. Source: CROQUET. To be forced to play your ball from a position from which it is difficult to make a shot. SPD. *See also* Behind the Eight Ball; Finesse (1); Snookered; Stymied.

FINISH *See* Cross the Finish Line; Lead from Start to Finish; Nice Guys Finish Last; Photo Finish.

FINISH OUT OF THE MONEY *to finish out of the money.* To finish behind the first three vote getters in an election. Source: HORSE RACING. To finish lower than third in a horserace. Only the top three finishes "pay off": first ("win"), second ("place"), and third ("show"). *See also* Also-ran. *Compare* Nice Guys Finish Last.

FIREWORKS Noisy excitement, e.g., of an angry confrontation. ("That's when the fireworks began.") Source: FIREWORKS. SOED: 1588. The objects that explode loudly, burn brightly, and smoke profusely, often in color, at fairs, carnivals, celebrations, etc.

FIRST OUT OF THE BLOCKS *to be first out of the blocks.* To take an early lead in a competition, e.g., a political "race." Source: FOOT RACING. To get away first from the starting line, where both feet are braced against metal or wooden "blocks." This is a 20th-century metaphor. The original brace was a "stake." *See also* Get a Head Start; Out of the Blocks; Quick off the Mark.

FIRST-STRING (adj.) *a first-string performer.* A first-class performer; a member of the first team. Source: SPORTS. WNCD: 1917. A member of the starting team: a "first-stringer." The term may have come into sports from the symphony orchestra, where the first violinist (or concertmaster) is sometimes called the first string. *Also:* "second-string," "third-string," etc.

FIRST-STRINGER *a first-stringer.* A first-class performer. Source: FOOT-BALL. A member of the starting team—i.e., not a substitute. LOS. *Also:* "second-stringer."

FIRST TEAM *a member of the first team.* A member of the top echelon of an organization; a member of the first group assigned to attack a problem. Source: SPORTS. A member of the "starting" team, as selected by the coach or manager. EOD. *See also* Team Effort.

FISH (n) *See* Drink Like a Fish; Have Other Fish to Fry; Kettle of Fish; Like a Fish out of Water; Like Shooting Fish in a Barrel; More Fish in the Ocean.

FISH (v) *to fish for something.* To attempt, indirectly, to get information or compliments (to "fish for compliments") from another person. SOED: 20th cent. Source: FISHING. SOED: M.E. To fish—for fish. *Also:* "to fish for something in a trash barrel." SOED: 1727.

FISHING EXPEDITION *to go on a fishing expedition.* To conduct an investigation without a particular goal in mind. WNCD: 1925. Source: FISHING. To go on a fishing trip. (You never know what you'll catch on a fishing trip—maybe nothing.) EOD; SPD.

FISH IN TROUBLED WATERS *to fish in troubled waters.* To take advantage of a troubled situation in order to advance yourself. Source: FISHING. To take advantage of a storm—when fish bite but most anglers flee—by remaining to fish in the rough waters. DOC; DPF; HOI.

FISH OR CUT BAIT *to fish or cut bait.* ("It's time to fish or cut bait.") To decide whether to be a spectator or a participant. DAE: 1876. Source: FISHING. Either to start fishing or prepare the bait for those who *are* fishing. DOC; WPO. The "cutting" may refer to cutting up "junk" fish to throw overboard to attack "game" fish (in deep-sea fishing). HTB.

FISH OUT *to fish something out of a container.* To extract something from a garbage can or trash bin, where it must be located by feel. SOED: 1632. Source: FISHING. To draw a fish out of the water.

FISH STORY *a fish story.* A tall tale. DAE: 1819. Source: FISHING. An exaggerated story about a huge fish that got off the hook and can't be produced as evidence. *See also* Fishy.

FISHTAIL *to fishtail.* To wiggle back and forth, the way a trailer sometimes does at high speeds. Source: FISHING. For a fish, or a fishing lure, to wiggle its tail from left to right. (Whales and porpoises wiggle their tails up and down.) WNCD: "Flying," 1927.

FISHY *to sound—or smell—fishy.* To seem exaggerated or suspicious. Source: FISHING. WNCD: 1547. To smell like a "fish story" (q.v.).

FIVE WILL GET YOU TEN *Five will get you ten that . . .* There's an excellent chance that . . . Source: GAMBLING. A five-dollar bet will earn you ten dollars—i.e., another five: you can double your money.

FIZZLE OUT *to fizzle out.* To peter out, run down, run out of gas. DA: 1848. Source: FIREWORKS(?). For the fuse of a firecracker to sputter and die without igniting the charge. The ultimate source may be the weakening of the carbonation in a drink. *Compare* Hang Fire.

FLAKE *a flake.* A "nut." LTA: 1964. Source: BASEBALL. SFS: 1950s. An eccentric baseball player. *Compare* Screwball.

FLAKY *to be flaky.* To be odd or eccentric. Source: BASEBALL. Derived from the noun "flake" (q.v.). NDAS: SFS.

FLASH IN THE PAN *a flash in the pan.* An overnight sensation, perhaps to be forgotten tomorrow. Source: SHOOTING. DOC: early 1800s. A flash of powder in the "pan" of a flintlock musket that is not accompanied by an explosion of the charge. CI; DPF; HOI; WPO. *See also* Hang Fire.

FLAT-OUT (adj.) *to be flat-out wrong.* To be totally and irresponsibly wrong. Source: CAR RACING. WNCD: 1925. To be driving "flat out," with the "pedal to the metal" (the accelerator to the floor), which makes control difficult. OL. *See also* Go Flat out.

FLIP   *to flip over something.* To go wild over something. Source: GYMNASTICS. A flip is a somersault, in which the gymnast turns over in the air. The ultimate source may be flipping coins, where the coin turns over and over in the air. WNWD.

FLIP SIDE   *the flip side.* The "other" side of a phonograph record—i.e., not the "featured" side. WNCD: 1949. Source: COINS (Flipping Coins). The "down" side of a flipped coin: the side that doesn't count. NDAS. *See also* On the Flip Side.

FLOOR   *to floor someone.* To shock or astonish someone, usually by making a startling announcement. SOED: 1840. Source: BOXING. SOED: 1642. To knock someone to the floor. *See also* Floored; Wipe the Floor with.

FLOORED   *to be floored by something.* To be shocked or astonished by some startling news or behavior. Source: BOXING. To be knocked to the "floor" (the canvas) by your opponent. Possibly also from wrestling: to be thrown to the floor (the mat) by your opponent. *See also* Floor.

FLUKE   *a fluke.* A stroke of good luck. Source: BILLIARDS. SOED: 1857. An accidentally good shot. NDAS. *See also* Stroke of Good Luck.

FLUSH OUT   *to flush someone out.* To drive someone, e.g., an escaped criminal, out of hiding. Source: HUNTING. To drive a bird from its cover. From the Middle English *flusshen,* "to fly up suddenly."

FLY BY THE SEAT OF YOUR PANTS   *to fly by the seat of your pants.* To operate by instinct; to cook without a recipe; to wing it. Source: FLYING. To fly without use of a map or instruments. WNWD. *See also* Flying Blind; Wing It.

FLYER   *See* Take a Flyer.

FLYING BLIND   *to be flying blind.* To not really know what you're doing; to be improvising, or winging it. Source: FLYING. To be flying without visual orientation, although perhaps on instruments, because of bad weather, power failure, etc. WNWD. *See also* Fly by the Seat of Your Pants; Wing It.

FLY IN THE FACE OF   *to fly in the face of danger, logic, etc.* To take an action or make a proposal that ignores danger or defies logic. Source: FLYING. To fly into the sun, as Icarus did, or into bad weather, dangerous territory, etc.

FOILED   *Curses! Foiled again!* Defeated again! SOED: 1548. Source: WRESTLING. Thrown or taken down. SOED.

FOLD *to fold*. To drop out, fail, go bankrupt. Source: POKER. To drop out of a hand of poker—by "folding" your cards back into a small pile and placing them on the table. *See also* Time to Put Your Chips on the Table.

FOLLOW SUIT *to follow suit*. To follow someone's lead or example. Source: CARD GAMES. To play a card of the same "suit" (spades, clubs, hearts, diamonds) as the one that was just played in that "trick." CI; SOE.

FOLLOW THE LEADER *to follow the leader*. To imitate someone's example. Source: CHILDREN'S GAMES. To imitate exactly the actions of the leader of the game—or else pay a penalty. DPF. *Also:* "a game of follow the leader." *See also* Wild-goose Chase.

FOOTBALL *See* Political Football.

FOOT/FEET *See* Drag Your Feet; Get Off on the Right Foot; Get Off on the Wrong Foot; Get your Feet Wet; Jump in with Both Feet; Land on Your Feet; Out on Your Feet; Put Your Best Foot Forward; Swept off Your Feet.

FOR A LARK *to do something for a lark*. To do something just for fun. Source: SPORTS. (O.E. *lac*, "contest.") DPF: ca. 1800. To do something for sport or play. *See also* Have a Lark.

FORCE SOMEONE'S HAND *to force someone's hand*. To cause someone to take an action or reveal their plans prematurely. Source: CARD GAMES. SOED: Whist, 1746. To cause your opponent to play a card that they didn't want to—or before they intended to—or to make a particular bid. CI; DPF. *See also* Squeeze Play.

FORTUNE HUNTER *a fortune hunter*. A person who is more interested in marrying for money than marrying for love. Source: HUNTING. A "hunter" is a human or animal that is searching for its natural prey.

FOUR-FLUSHER *a four-flusher*. A cheater. DAE: 1910. Source: POKER. A poker player who pretends to have five cards of the same suit (a "flush") but really has only four—e.g., four hearts and a diamond instead of five hearts. WPO.

FOUR OF A KIND *to have four of a kind*. To have four things of the same kind: e.g., four daughters, four sons, or quadruplets. Source: POKER. WNCD: 1934. To have four cards of the same "value," regardless of suit: e.g., four kings or four queens. Four of a kind beats a straight flush (five cards in a series in the same suit). *See also* Three of a Kind; Two of a Kind.

FOURSOME *See* Twosome.

FOXHOLE *a foxhole*. A hole dug in the ground for protection by a soldier. WNCD: 1919. Source: FOX HUNTING. A hole dug in the ground by a fox for protection from its pursuers. DPF. *See also* Crazy Like a Fox.

FOX-TROT *a fox-trot.* A dance in 4/4 time. DAE: 1915. Source: FOX HUNTING. DAE: 1872. A slow gait that combines features of "trotting" (the horse's front legs) and "pacing" (the horse's hind legs), presumably the gait of either the "hunted" (the fox) or the "hunter" (the horse) in a fox hunt. DPF.

FRANCHISE *X is the franchise.* X is what keeps the business afloat. Source: SPORTS. X is the player who keeps the team (i.e., the "franchise") solvent, by drawing fans to the games. *See also* Meal Ticket.

FREE AGENT *a free agent.* Someone who is not under contract—professional or marital—with someone else. Source: SPORTS (orig. Baseball). WNCD: 1955. An athlete who is free to negotiate a contract with any team that will have them. *Compare* Give Someone Free Rein.

FREE-FOR-ALL *a free-for-all.* A brawl; a donnybrook. LTA: 1902. Source: BOXING; WRESTLING. WNCD: 1881. A boxing or wrestling match that is open to all challengers. LOS. HORSE RACING. A horse race that is open to all spectators. DAE: 1881. *See also* Home Free.

FREE SWINGER *a free swinger.* An uninhibited competitor, in regard to both actions and words. Source: BOXING. A fighter who is more "slugger" than "boxer"—i.e., one who lacks discipline and finesse.

FRIENDLY CONFINES *the friendly confines.* Familiar surroundings: "home." Source: BASEBALL. Wrigley Field, the home of the Chicago Cubs. With its vine-colored walls, urban setting, neighborhood streets, small dimensions, limited capacity (39,000), and age (built 1914–1916), Wrigley Field is indeed "friendly" to players and fans alike. The phrase is attributed to Ernie Banks.

FROM PILLAR TO POST *to go from pillar to post.* To bounce around from one predicament to another. Source: TENNIS. For a tennis ball to bounce around the court (in indoor "court" tennis)—from the "pillar" (which supports the stands) to the "post" (which holds the net). Originally "from post to pillar," ca. 1400. CI; DOC; DPF; HOI; WPO. *See also* Bandy about; Tennis, Anyone.

FROM STEM TO STERN From one end to another. ("I cleaned the house from stem to stern.") Source: SAILING. From the front end of the ship or boat (the "stem" or "bow") to the rear (the "stern"). WPO.

FROM THE WORD GO *from the word "Go!"* From the very beginning. DA: 1834. Source: FOOT RACING. From the spoken signal that can be used to start a footrace. The "starter" used to say "On your mark(s)! Get set! Go!" Now they usually fire a "blank" in a starter's pistol. DOC. *See also* Get Set; Have a Go; No Go; On the Go.

FRONT-RUNNER *a front-runner*. The leader in a competition, such as a political "race." Source: FOOT RACING. The leader of a race: the one out in "front."

FULL-COURT PRESS *See* Mount a Full-court Press.

FULL CRY *See* In Full Cry.

FULL HOUSE *a full house*. Three of one kind and two of another—e.g., three sons and two daughters. Source: POKER. WNCD: 1887. A hand containing three cards of the same face value and two others of a different face value—e.g., three queens and two fours. Originally a "full *hand.*" DA: 1850.

FUN AND GAMES *just fun and games*. Just plain fun. WNCD: 1920. Source: GAMES. NDAS: early 1900s. Games played for personal enjoyment, not for money or to amuse someone else. *See also* Not All Fun and Games.

FUNCTION AS A TEAM *to function as a team*. To work together. Source: SPORTS. To function as a unit—rather than as an assemblage of individuals—during a game. The original "team" was probably a pair of oxen, who also had to learn to work together. *See also* Team Effort.

G

GAFF   *See* Stand the Gaff.

GAMBIT   *a gambit.* A bold initiative. Source: CHESS. SOED: 1656. An opening move in which one chesspiece is sacrificed for an advantageous position. Not all opening moves are "gambits." OL. *See also* Debut; Make a Play for; Opening Gambit.

GAMBLE AWAY   *to gamble away your fortune.* To squander your life savings. DAE: 1808. Source: GAMBLING. To lose all of your money at the racetrack or the gambling table. *See also* Not Worth the Gamble.

GAME (adj.)   *I'm game.* I'm willing. SOED: 1856. Source: COCKFIGHTING. I'm as ready and willing as a gamecock before a fight.

GAME (n)   *See* Fair Game; Fun and Games; Get Up for the Game; Guessing Game; Let the Games Begin; Love Game; Name of the Game; Not All Fun and Games; Numbers Game; Off Your Game; Only Game in Town; On Your Game; Play a Losing Game; Play a Waiting Game; Play Games; Play the Game; Shell Game; Skin Game; Stay ahead of the Game; Two Can Play This Game; War Games.

GAME IS UP   *The game is up.* The attempt has failed; the jig is up. Source: GAMES. The game is over. CI. *See also* Ball Game.

GAME OF CHANCE   *a game of chance.* A situation that is beyond your control, in which anything can happen. Source: GAMBLING. WNCD: 1952. A game in which winning is dependent on luck rather than skill. *Compare* Crapshoot; Game of Craps.

GAME OF CHESS   *a game of chess.* A battle of wits—slow and calculated. Source: CHESS. A chess game. FP.

GAME OF CRAPS   *a game of craps.* A high-risk venture. Source: CRAPS. A "crap game," (q.v.). *Compare* Game of Chance.

GAME OF INCHES   *a game of inches.* An activity that can tolerate only the slightest margin of error. Source: BASEBALL. A game that can be won or lost by the slightest margin: the length of the drive (over the fence, off the wall); the proximity to the foul line (fair, foul); the distance from the fielder's glove (caught, missed); etc. (Golf is a "game of *itches*" for duffers, because they spend so much time in the rough.)

GAME OF LIFE   *the game of life.* The struggle to survive. Source: GAMES. Life is a game, with established rules and with humans as players. EOD. *Also:* the "game of politics," the "game of love," "What's your game?"

GAME PLAN   *to have a game plan.* To have a plan of action. WNCD: 1970. Source: FOOTBALL. LTA: 1850s. To have a prearranged strategy—or set of plays, both offensive and defensive—to use against a particular opponent in an upcoming game. EPD; FP; SPD.

GAMER   *a gamer.* A tough, gutsy person. Source: BASEBALL. A baseball player who plays the game in spite of injuries.

GAMESMANSHIP   Skill in bargaining, negotiating, selling, etc. Source: GAMES. WNCD: 1947. Skill in playing games. EOD; FP. Formed after "sportsmanship" (q.v.).

GATE   *the gate.* The amount of money taken in (the "take"), or the number of customers in attendance, at an event. Source: SPORTS. The amount of money taken in at the gate(s) of a sporting event. (From "gate money," DAE: 1868.)

GAUNTLET   *See* Throw Down the Gauntlet.

GENTLEMEN, START YOUR ENGINES   *Gentlemen, start your engines!* You're about to be entertained (presumably by dancing girls). Source: CAR RACING. This is the command given by the starter at the annual Indianapolis 500 race to instruct the drivers—actually, their mechanics—to start the engines of the race cars that are lined up in preparation for the beginning of the race.

GET A BEAD ON   *to get a bead on something.* To focus in on something. Source: SHOOTING. To take aim at something by lining it up with the BB-size "bead" on the top of the end of the barrel of the firearm. WPO. *See also* Draw a Bead.

GET A BITE   *to get a bite.* To get a response to an offer. Source: FISHING. SOED: 1653. To get a nibble on a baited hook. *See also* Bite (v); Get a Nibble.

GET A BREAK   *to get a break.* To get a fair chance; to get lucky. DA: 1911. Source: POOL. To get a lucky "break" of the rack of balls, with at least one of the balls going in the pocket, which permits the "breaker" to continue shooting. The winner of the game also "breaks" first in the next one. WPO. *See also* Good/Bad Break.

GET A FIX ON   *to get a fix on something.* To pin something down; to determine the exact nature of something. Source: SAILING. To determine the position, or bearings, of your craft by the use of a compass. *See also* Get Your Bearings.

GET A FOOTHOLD   *to get a foothold in something.* To achieve a position in life, work, etc. Source: CLIMBING. SOED: 1625. To get a secure position for your foot in rock climbing. *See also* Get a Toehold.

GET A GRIP ON YOURSELF   *to get a grip on yourself.* To pull yourself together—i.e., to regain control of your senses, temper, and behavior in general. LTA: 1896. Source: WRESTLING. To gain control of yourself as you would gain control of your opponent in a wrestling match. *See also* Come to Grips with.

GET A HANDLE ON   *to get a handle on something.* To try to solve a slippery problem. DOC: 1970s. Source: FOOTBALL (or RUGBY). To try to grab hold of an erratically bouncing football, the only ball in sports that is not round. DOC.

GET A HEAD START   *to get/have a head start.* To get or have a lead at the beginning of a competition, such as a political "race." Source: FOOT RACING. To start a race a "head" ahead of your opponents. *See also* First out of the Blocks; Head Start.

GET A KICK OUT OF   *to get a kick out of something.* To get a thrill out of something. SOED: 1903. Source: FOOTBALL; SOCCER. To get the same feeling that a football or soccer ball has as it is propelled into the air. *See also* Kick an Idea around.

GET A NIBBLE   *to get a nibble.* To get an offer (e.g., of a job); or to get a response to your offer (e.g., of something for sale). Source: FISHING. SOED: 1658. To get a "strike" at your baited hook. *See also* Get a Bite.

GET A TOEHOLD   *to get a toehold.* To make a little progress; to "get a foot in the door." Source: CLIMBING. To find a hole for your toes while rock climbing. WRESTLING. To twist the foot (and toes) of your opponent. SOED. *See also* Get a Foothold; Toe the Line.

GET HOOKED ON   *to get hooked on something.* To become addicted to something: books, drugs, rock music, etc. Source: FISHING. For a fish to be caught on a fishing hook. *See also* Hook (v).

GET INTO THE SWING OF THINGS   *to get into the swing of things.* To adjust to the nature or rhythm of the activity at hand. Source: CHILDREN'S PLAY. To get on a child's swing and start swinging. (The ultimate source is the swing of the pendulum. DOC: mid-19th cent.)

GET LOST IN THE SHUFFLE   *to get lost in the shuffle*. For someone (or something) to be neglected because of the press of other business. Source: CARD GAMES. For a particular card to be lost track of in the deck when the cards are properly shuffled. (This is the purpose of shuffling). *See also* Fast Shuffle.

GET NOWHERE FAST   *to get nowhere fast*. To make no progress at all. Source: CAR RACING(?). For the power wheels of a racing car to spin uselessly in the mud or sand or snow. *See also* Spin Your Wheels. *Compare* Fast Starter.

GET OFF ON THE RIGHT FOOT   *to get off on the right foot*. To make a good start of something. Source: TRACK AND FIELD. To start a jump, such as the "long" jump or "triple" jump, on the proper foot, in light of your usual practice. (The original source is probably the military. CI.) *See also* Put Your Best Foot Forward. *Compare* Get Off on the Wrong Foot.

GET OFF ON THE WRONG FOOT   *to get off on the wrong foot*. To make a bad start of something. Source: TRACK AND FIELD. To start a jump on the "wrong" foot, in light of usual practice. *Compare* Get Off on the Right Foot.

GET OFF THE HOOK   *to get off the hook*. To get a reprieve. Source: FISHING. For a fish to get free of the hook on which it was temporarily caught. *See also* Let Someone off the Hook; Off the Hook.

GET OFF TO A FLYING START   *to get off to a flying start*. To make an impressive start of something. Source: FOOT RACING. To start a race by leaping ("flying") out of the starting blocks. CI. *See also* Get Off to a Good/Bad Start.

GET OFF TO A GOOD/BAD START   *to get off to a good/bad start*. To do well or poorly at a new activity; for a business or project to start out well or poorly. Source: RACING. For a racer to leave the starting line quickly and properly—or slowly and improperly. CI. *See also* Get Off to a Flying Start.

GET OFF YOUR HIGH HORSE   *to get off your high horse*. To stop being haughty or arrogant. Source: RIDING. It was once customary for persons of high rank to be mounted on tall ("high") horses—at tournaments, pageants, and other ceremonies. DOC; DPF; HOI. *Compare* Get on Your High Horse.

GET ON THE BANDWAGON   *to get on the bandwagon*. To offer support to a promising candidate. DA: 1931. Source: CIRCUS. DA: 1855. To join the circus parade, led by the wagon holding the band.

GET ON THE STICK   *to get on the stick*. To become more alert or productive. Source: ICE HOCKEY(?). To get the hockey stick on the puck and pass it or shoot it.

GET ON YOUR HIGH HORSE   *to get on your high horse.* To become haughty or arrogant. Source: RIDING. To be mounted on a tall ("high") horse—at a tournament, a pageant, or other ceremony—because of your high rank. CI; DOC; DPF; HOI. *Compare* Get off Your High Horse.

GET OUT OF HAND   *to get out of hand.* To get out of control. Source: RIDING. For the horse(s) to get out of the control of the reins in your hands—or the reins that have fallen out of your hands. WPO. *Compare* In Hand.

GET SENT TO THE SHOWERS   *to get sent to the showers.* To be withdrawn from action. Source: BASEBALL. For a player, usually the pitcher, to be removed from the lineup, as a result of which they can go take a shower, because baseball players, unlike the players of most other team sports, are not allowed to return to the game once they have been removed from the action. NDAS. *See also* Send Someone to the Showers.

GET SET   *to get set for something or get set to do something.* To get ready for something or get ready to do something. Source: FOOT RACING. From the command: "On your mark(s)! *Get set!* Go!" CI. *See also* From the Word Go.

GET SOMEONE DOWN   *That gets me down.* That depresses me. Source: WRESTLING(?). That is a putdown or takedown.

GET SOMEONE'S GOAT   *That gets my goat!* That bothers me. SOED: 1912. Source: HORSE RACING(?). The source is unknown, but the mythology is that the expression refers to the stealing of a racehorse's mascot, a goat, from the horse's stall before a big race. CI; DOC; HTB; WPO.

GET SOMETHING OFF THE GROUND   *to get/be unable to get something off the ground.* To get, or be unable to get, a business or project started. Source: FLYING. To take a plane off into the air—a takeoff. CI. *See also* Takeoff (n).

GET SQUARED AWAY   *to get squared away.* To get your affairs in order, your debts paid, etc. Source: SAILING. To set the sails at right angles to the ship or boat. LTA. *See also* Square Off.

GET STARTED   *to get started on something.* To begin a project or activity. Source: RACING. To begin a race. CI.

GET THE BALL ROLLING   *to get the ball rolling.* To get an activity started. Source: SOCCER. To start the soccer ball rolling toward the opponent's goal. SFS. *Compare* Keep the Ball Rolling.

GET THE DROP ON   *to get the drop on someone.* To do something before someone else has a chance to. Source: DUELING (Western style). HTB: 1869. To drop your hand to your holster, draw your revolver, and fire—before your adversary does. DPF.

GET THE JUMP ON   *to get the jump on someone.* To get a head start on someone. Source: FOOT RACING. To jump from the starting blocks ahead of another competitor in the race. *See also* Jump the Gun.

GET THE SHORT END OF THE STICK   *to get the short end of the stick.* To be treated unfairly. Source: DRAWING LOTS. To draw the shortest of the pieces into which a stick is broken for drawing lots. CI; HTB; WPO. *Also:* "get the *dirty* end of the stick," "get the *wrong* end of the stick."

GET THE UPPER HAND   *to get/have the upper hand.* To gain control over someone. Source: GAMBLING. 15th cent. To get the topmost handhold on a stick that is thrown to you by another person. When the stick is caught, the two contestants alternate handholds on it until the top of the stick is reached. The method is currently employed by sandlot baseball players, using a bat, to determine which team will take the field and which will get to bat. *Compare* Hand over Fist.

GET TO FIRST BASE   *to get to first base with someone.* ("He couldn't get to first base with her.") To be unable to make even the slightest impression on someone. DA: 1948. Source: BASEBALL. To be unable to get a hit or a walk or anything that will get you on first base. SFS.

GET UP AND FIGHT LIKE A MAN   *Get up and fight like a man!* "Don't take this lying down!" LTA: 1872. Source: BOXING. "Stop stalling!" The cry of the crowd at a 19th century boxing match, when a boxer could take advantage of the 30-second break following a knockdown by pretending to be knocked out. LTA.

GET UP FOR THE GAME   *to get up for the game.* To get psychologically prepared for a campaign (etc.). Source: SPORTS. To get "psyched up" for a game. FP.

GET UP OFF THE CANVAS   *to get up off the canvas.* To bounce back from adversity. Source: BOXING. To get up off the floor of the ring (the "canvas") after a knockdown. LOS.

GET YOUR AT-BATS   *to get your at-bats.* To get your chance to participate in an activity—either according to some prearranged rotation or just because of the law of averages. Source: BASEBALL. To appear as a batter according to the order of the written lineup; to accumulate "ABs" ("at-bats"). *See also* Get Your Turn at Bat.

GET YOUR BEARINGS   *to get your bearings.* To get oriented to a situation after having become disoriented. Source: SAILING; HUNTING; etc. To use a compass (etc.) to discover your exact position. CI. *See also* Bearing Down on; Get a Fix on. *Compare* Lose Your Bearings.

GET YOUR FEET WET   *to get your feet wet.* To get a taste of something new; to commence a new experience. Source: SWIMMING. To test the waters before wading or diving in.

GET YOUR HOOKS INTO   *to get your hooks into someone.* To get someone under your control. Source: FISHING(?). To hook a fish on your line. FALCONRY(?). For the hawk to get its talons into the prey.

GET YOUR SEA LEGS   *to get your sea legs.* To get used to the unfamiliar conditions of a new activity. Source: SAILING. SOED: 1712. To get used to the rolling motion of a sailing vessel. CI. *Compare* Get Your Second Wind.

GET YOUR SECOND WIND   *to get (or catch) your second wind.* To become more comfortable at a difficult task; to settle into the rhythm of a job. Source: FOOT RACING. DOC: early 19th cent. For a runner to feel suddenly fresh—easier to breathe, more strength, better rhythm, less pain—about halfway through a distance race. DPF. Long-distance swimmers also get this feeling, but it is not known if long-distance horses do. *Compare* Get Your Sea Legs; Have Legs. *Compare* Hit the Wall.

GET YOUR TURN AT BAT   *to get your turn at bat.* To get your chance to participate in an activity—either according to some prearranged plan or just because of the law of averages. Source: BASEBALL. LTA: 1870s. To appear as a batter according to the order of the written lineup. *See also* Get Your At-bats.

GIANT STEP   *See* Take a Giant Step.

GIMMICK   *a gimmick.* A gadget; an "angle"; a trick. Source: CARNIVAL. WNCD: 1926. An illegal device used by unscrupulous operators of certain carnival games, such as the wheel of fortune, to deter winning by slowing down the wheel. WPO. *See also* Scam.

GIPPER   *See* Win One for the Gipper.

GIVE A WIDE BERTH   *to give someone/something a wide berth.* To stay as far away from someone or something as possible. LTA: 1794. Source: SAILING. To give sufficient clearance to another vessel, especially when it is at anchor. CI; WPO.

GIVE IT A SHOT   *to give it a shot.* To give something a try. SOED: 1756. Source: SHOOTING. To take a shot at something with a bow or firearm and see what happens. *See also* Take a Potshot; Take a Shot at It.

GIVE IT THE GUN   *to give it the gun.* To cause a vehicle to accelerate rapidly. Source: FLYING. To cause an early model airplane to accelerate by pulling out its trigger-like throttle. WNWD. *Compare* Gun-shy.

GIVE IT TO SOMEONE WITH BOTH BARRELS   *to give it to someone with both barrels.* To attack someone verbally and vociferously. Source: HUNTING. To fire both barrels of a double-barreled shotgun at a quarry, such as a rabbit or pheasant. *See also* Double-barreled; Let Someone Have It with Both Barrels.

GIVE IT YOUR BEST SHOT   *Go ahead, give it your best shot!* Go ahead, do the best you can! Source: BOXING. Go ahead, throw your best punch! I can take anything you can dish out. Ultimately, the expression is from hunting and shooting: to take your best shot at a target or an animal. *See also* Take Your Best Shot.

GIVE SOMEONE FREE REIN   *to give someone free rein.* To allow someone complete freedom to think or act as they please. Source: RIDING. To relax the reins and allow the horse to go as fast as it wants to. CI. *See also* Free Agent; Give Someone Their Head.

GIVE SOMEONE SOME LEEWAY   *to give someone some leeway.* To allow someone freedom of movement, speech, etc. Source: SAILING. "Leeway" is the lateral movement of a sailing vessel, caused by the wind, as opposed to the forward movement, "headway." CI. *See also* Drift. *Compare* Make Headway.

GIVE SOMEONE SOME LINE   *to give someone some line.* To relax control over someone. Source: FISHING. To allow a fish to "run" with the bait or lure. *Also:* to "give someone some rope," perhaps in climbing.

GIVE SOMEONE THEIR HEAD   *to give someone their head.* To give someone free rein. Source: RIDING. To relax the reins and allow the horse to determine its own speed and direction. CI; DPF. *See also* Give Someone Free Rein.

GIVE THAT MAN A CIGAR   *Give that man a cigar!* Somebody finally came up with the right answer! Source: CARNIVAL. A cigar was once the prize given to the man who could ring the bell at the top of the pole by striking the platform at the base of the pole with a large mallet. *See also* Close, But No Cigar; Ring a Bell.

GLOVE   *See* Hang Up Your Gloves; Lay a Glove on; Put the Gloves on; Take Off the Gloves; With the Gloves off.

GLOVES ARE OFF   *The gloves are off.* The bargaining is about to get tough. Source: BOXING. The fight is about to get bloody, because the boxers have removed their gloves. CI. *See also* With the Gloves off. *Compare* Play Hardball.

GO   *See* From the Word Go; Have a Go at Something; No Go; One Down, Two to Go; On the Go; Touch and Go; Two Down, One to Go.

GOAL   *a goal in life.* The result that you hope to achieve. SOED: 1608. Source: SPORTS. WNCD: 1531. The target that you are aiming at; the finish line, the net, the hoop, etc.

GO ALONG FOR THE RIDE   *to go along for the ride.* To string along with something, even though you have no particular interest in the venture. Source: RIDING. To join a group of riders, even though you have no particular interest in their destination. CI.

GOAT   *See* Get Someone's Goat.

GO BELLY UP   *to go belly up.* To go out of business: to fail. Source: FISHING. For a fish to die, rise to the surface, and float upside down, with its belly up. *See also* Turn Turtle. *Compare* Go by the Boards.

GO BY THE BOARDS   *to go by the boards.* To go out of business: to fail. Source: SAILING. Mid-1800s. To fall overboard (i.e., over the "boards," on the side of the vessel). CI; DPF; HTB; WPO. *See also* Go Overboard; Swept away; Swept off Your Feet. *Compare* Go Belly Up.

GO DOWN FOR THE LONG COUNT   *to go down for the long count.* To die. Source: BOXING. To be knocked to the canvas unconscious, and to remain so beyond the count of ten: a "knockout." *See also* Down for the Count; Take the Long Count.

GO DOWN TO THE WIRE   *to go down to the wire.* To be settled only at the very last minute. Source: HORSE RACING. The "wire" is the finish line of a horse race. A race that "goes down to the wire" is not decided until this line is reached. The wire is elevated high above the horses to help the judges determine the first, second, and third place finishers and to enable the official photographers to line up their shots in case of a "photo finish." NDAS. *See also* Lead from Wire to Wire; Under the Wire.

GO FLAT OUT   *to go flat out.* To go all out. Sources: CAR RACING. To drive with the gas pedal "flat" against the floor of the race car: "with the pedal to the metal." OL. MOTORCYCLE RACING. To lie prone on the seat of a motorcycle, arms extended forward to the handle bars and legs stretched out straight behind. This position was used in 1948 and before. *See also* Flat-out (adj.).

GO FLY A KITE   *Go fly a kite!* Get lost! Source: KITE FLYING. Go elevate a fabric-covered frame (a "kite") into the air by pulling its string into the wind. CI: "meteorology." *See also* High as a Kite; Higher Than a Kite.

GO FOR ALL THE MARBLES   *to go for all the marbles.* To go all out to win. Source: MARBLES. To attempt to drive all of your opponents' marbles from the circle. *See also* Play for Keeps.

GO FOR BROKE   *to go for broke.* To give it all you've got. Source: GAM-BLING. DOC: 1880s. To bet all the money you have on one horse, one hand, one throw of the dice, etc. WPO.

GO FOR IT (1)   *to go for it.* To attempt something regardless of the conse-quences. Source: FOOTBALL. To attempt to make a first down on "fourth down and short yardage"—rather than punt the ball away or attempt a long field goal. LOS.

GO FOR IT (2)   *to go for it.* To go all out to achieve a goal. Source: OLYM-PIC GAMES. To go all out to win. Shortened form of "go for the gold" (q.v.).

GO FOR THE GOLD   *to go for the gold.* To go all out to win the highest honors. Source: OLYMPIC GAMES. To go all out to win a gold medal, sig-nifying a first place in the Modern Olympics. A shortened form is "go for it" (q.v.). Both expressions became popular in the 1984 Olympics. (The ultimate source may be archery: to go for the yellow or gold center of the target.)

GO FULL TILT   *to go full tilt.* To do something at top speed. Source: JOUSTING. For a competitor in a medieval tournament to ride at his opponent at full speed, with his lance lowered. *See also* At Full Tilt; Tilt at Windmills.

GO HEAD-TO-HEAD   *to go head-to-head with someone.* To argue vigor-ously with someone. Source: BOXING. To fight someone at close range. *See also* Go Toe-to-toe with; Head-to-head; Infighter.

GO INTO EXTRA INNINGS   *to go into extra innings.* To go beyond the allotted time limit. Source: BASEBALL. For a game to continue beyond the standard nine innings in order to break a tie. *Compare* Go into Overtime.

GO INTO OVERTIME   *to go into overtime.* To run late: e.g., for a meeting to go beyond the expected deadline. Source: BASKETBALL. For a game that finishes in a tie after regulation play to be extended into one or more additional five-minute periods. This expression is now used also in football and ice hockey, and it is sometimes applied to a baseball game that "goes into extra innings." *Compare* Go into Extra Innings.

GOLD   *See* Go for the Gold.

GOLDEN PARACHUTE   *a golden parachute.* Generous termination pay—"bailout pay"—for top executives, intended to "let them down gently." Source: FLYING. The purpose of a parachute is to let you down gently when you bail out of an airplane. *See also* Bail Out.

GOLF BALL-SIZE HAIL   Medium-size hail. Source: GOLF. Hail the size of golf balls (a little over an inch and a half in diameter). Earlier called "wal-nut-size hail," i.e., either an English walnut or an American walnut with the husk removed. *See also* Baseball-size Hail; Marble-size Hail; Softball-size Hail.

GOOD/BAD BREAK   *a good or bad break.* A stroke of good or bad luck. Source: POOL. A good or bad stroke of the cue ball at the rack of balls. If you have a "good" break (i.e., in which one of the racked balls goes into the pocket), you are allowed to continue shooting. If not, you're not. *See also* Get a Break.

GOOD BET   *X is a good bet to do something (e.g., get the job).* X is likely to get the job. Source: GAMBLING; BETTING. The odds favor X to win; X is the "odds-on favorite."

GOOD CATCH   *X is a good catch.* X would make a good mate. Source: FISHING. A "good catch" is the result of a successful fishing trip: a large number of large fish caught.

GOOD FOR OPENERS   *to be good for openers.* To be good enough to get an activity going. Source: POKER. A pair of jacks is usually good enough to allow a player to "open" the betting in a poker game. NDAS. *Also:* "How's *that* for openers?" *Compare* Good for Starters.

GOOD FOR STARTERS   *That's good for starters.* That's good enough to get things going. Source: POKER. That hand (containing a pair of jacks or better) qualifies you to start the betting. NDAS. *Compare* Good for Openers.

GOOD IN THE CLUTCH   *to be good in the clutch.* To be dependable in a crucial situation. Source: BASEBALL. To be reliable in a situation in which the game depends on you; i.e., you can be counted on to get a hit, make a play, throw a strike, steal a base, etc. The expression is also used in many other sports. *See also* In the Clutch. *Compare* Clutch-hitter.

GOOD SPORT   *a good sport.* Someone who goes along with the fun or allows themselves to be made fun of; a good loser. Source: SPORTS. Someone who plays by the spirit as well as the letter of the rules of the game. *See also* Make Sport. *Compare* Bad Sport.

GO OFF HALF-COCKED   *to go off half-cocked.* To speak or act prematurely—i.e., without proper consideration. LTA: 1833. Source: SHOOTING. For a musket to fire prematurely when the hammer is drawn back ("cocked") only half way and the weapon is thought to be safe. CI; DOC; DPF; HOI.

GO OFF THE DEEP END   *to go off the deep end.* To behave irresponsibly; to go crazy. LTA: 1918. Source: DIVING. To dive into the deep end of the pool, especially if you haven't done that before or you don't know how to swim. DOC; HTB; NDAS. *Compare* Go Overboard.

GOOSE EGG   *a goose egg.* Nothing. A big, fat zero. DA: 1949. Source: BASEBALL. LTA: 1866. No score: a zero on the scoreboard. The term derives from the resemblance of a zero to a goose egg. In cricket, a zero is called a *duck's* egg; in tennis it is a "generic" egg: French *l'oeuf* (English *love*), "the egg." *See also* Blank; Draw the Collar; Lay an Egg; Love Game; 0 for April.

GO OVERBOARD *to go overboard on something.* To expend all of your energy, money, affection, etc. on one thing. (Often negative: "Don't go overboard!") Source: SAILING. To fall into the water from the deck of a vessel. CI. *See also* Go by the Boards; Swept away; Swept off Your Feet. *Compare* Deep Six; Go off the Deep End.

GO SOMEONE ONE BETTER *to go someone one better.* To "top" someone's effort with one of your own. Source: BRIDGE. To bid one unit higher than your opponent; e.g., "four no-trump," following a bid of "three no-trump." CI. *See also* One-Upmanship.

GO THE DISTANCE *to go the distance.* To survive an extended test of your endurance. Source: BOXING. For a fighter to last for all of the scheduled rounds of a boxing match. LOS. The expression was probably borrowed by boxing from foot racing.

GO THE EXTRA MILE *to go the/that extra mile.* To perform above and beyond the call of duty. Source: FOOT RACING. For a long-distance runner to keep going for one more mile, e.g., in the marathon. *See also* One Hundred and Ten Percent.

GO THE ROUTE *to go the route.* To stick with a job until it's finished. Source: BASEBALL. DOC: early 1900s. To pitch a complete, nine-inning game. The expression could just as well have derived from "milkpersons" or "garbagepersons" or "paperpersons," but it seems to have originated with baseball writers.

GO TO BAT FOR *to go to bat for someone/something.* To support someone or something strongly. LTA: 1916. Source: BASEBALL. To come off the bench to bat for a scheduled hitter: to "pinch hit" for someone. SFS. *See also* Pinch Hit.

GO TOE-TO-TOE-WITH *to go toe-to-toe with someone.* To argue with someone at close range. Source: BOXING. For two boxers to fight at close range, with neither boxer retreating. *See also* Go Head-to-head; Toe-to-toe. *Compare* Put-down.

GO TO THE MAT FOR *to go to the mat for someone/over something.* To go all out to help a person or to defend a position. Source: WRESTLING. To be willing to risk a "fall" in a wrestling match.

GO UNDER *to go under.* To go out of business; to fail. WNCD: 1848. Source: SAILING; BOATING. For a ship or boat to capsize, sink, and "go under the water." *See also* Turn Turtle.

GO UP AGAINST *to go up against someone*. To face someone in a competition or debate. Source: BOXING. To be matched against another boxer in a fight. NDAS.

GO WITH THE FLOW *to go with the flow*. To let circumstances guide your behavior. Source: CANOEING. To let the current of the stream take the canoe wherever it will.

GRAB BAG *a grab bag*. A "mixed bag" of articles, purchased sight unseen. DA: 1879. Source: CARNIVAL. DA: 1855. An unseen prize that is drawn out of a box or "fished" out of an imaginary pond, behind a sheet or screen. Another name for the game is Fish.

GRAB THE BRASS RING *to grab the brass ring*. To win the prize. Source: CARNIVAL (Merry-go-round). To grab the brass ring that is placed just outside the reach of most riders of a merry-go-round, or "carousel" (q.v.). The reward is a free ride. WPO.

GRANDSTAND *to grandstand*. To show off. WNCD: 1927. Source: BASEBALL. NDAS: late 1800s. To make a play look more difficult than it really is—for the applause of the fans. *See also* Grandstand Play; Hot Dog; Hotdog; Play to the Grandstand.

GRANDSTAND PLAY *a grandstand play*. A move that is intended more to draw attention than to produce results. Source: BASEBALL. LTA: 1888. A fielding play that is either unnecessarily fancy or exaggerates the difficulty of its performance. DOC; FP; HOI. *See also* Grandstand; Play to the Grandstand.

GRASP AT STRAWS *to grasp at straws*. To try anything, however feeble, to survive. Source: SWIMMING. For a drowning person to reach out for anything that might help them stay afloat. CI; DOC.

GREEN *See* Rub of the Green.

GROUND *See* Get Something off the Ground; Hunting Ground; Keep Your Ear to the Ground; Make Up Ground; Run to the Ground.

GROUND RULES Rules of procedure established before an activity begins. Source: BASEBALL. DA: 1890. Local rules—for a particular ballpark—established before the game begins. LOS. *See also* Lay Down Some Ground Rules. *Compare* Play by House Rules.

GRUDGE MATCH *a grudge match*. A debate between two political candidates, usually arranged by the loser of the last one. Source: BOXING; WRESTLING. A rematch of two boxers or wrestlers who have fought before—usually requested by the loser of the last match.

GUARD *See* Drop Your Guard; Let down Your Guard; Off Guard; On Guard; On Your Guard.

GUESSING GAME   *a guessing game.* An interview that is characterized by many questions and few answers. Source: CHILDREN'S GAMES. A game such as Twenty Questions, which begins with "Is it animal?" (or vegetable or mineral). *See also* Hazard a Guess; Play Twenty Questions.

GUN-SHY   *to be gun-shy.* To be easily frightened or unnecessarily cautious because of past experiences. Source: HUNTING. SOED: 1884. For a hunting dog to be chronically afraid of the sound of a gun and therefore useless for hunting. *Compare* Give It the Gun; Jump the Gun.

GYMNASTICS   *See* Mental Gymnastics.

H

HACKER *a hacker*. A computer buff who likes to experiment with the system. Source: GOLF(?). An inept golfer, for whom every shot is an adventure: a "duffer" (q.v.).

HACKLES *See* Raise Someone's Hackles.

HAGGARD Worn-out, gaunt, wild-looking. SOED: 1697. Source: FAL-CONRY. M.Fren. *hagard*, "untamed hawk." SOED: 1567. A wild female hawk captured in adulthood for "hawking" but remaining untamed and unruly.

HAIL THE SIZE OF *hail the size of marbles, golf balls (or Ping-Pong balls), baseballs (or tennis balls), or softballs*. Small-size to very large-size hail. Source: SPORTS. Until the late 1970s, most radio and TV weatherpersons classified hail as pea-size, mothball-size, walnut-size (with or without the husk), and grapefruit-size. Surgeons used the same terms to describe the size of tumors. The switch to the missiles of sport by both groups of professionals is significant.

HALF-COCKED *See* Go off Half-cocked.

HALL OF FAMER *a hall of famer*. A superstar. Source: *Sports*. An athlete who has been elected to—or is certain to be elected to, on the basis of their current play—the Hall of Fame for that particular sport. The first sports Hall of Fame, for baseball, was established in Cooperstown, New York, in 1939.

HAND (n) *See* Bird in the Hand; Force Someone's Hand; Get Out of Hand; Get the Upper Hand; Hold a Pat Hand; Hot Hand; Overplay Your Hand; Play into Someone's Hand; Rotten Hand; Show Your Hand; Strengthen Your Hand; Throw In Your Hand; Tip Your Hand; Win Hands down.

HANDICAP (n) *to have a handicap*. To have a physical, mental, or emotional disability. LTA: 1870s. Source: HORSE RACING. WNCD: 1660. To have extra weight imposed on a horse because of the light weight of its jockey and saddle. OL. *Handicap* derives ultimately from a 14th-century gambling game called "hand in cap," which was played by two persons who deposited items in a cap and then had them redistributed by an "umpire." *See also* Handicap (v).

HANDICAP (v) *to handicap a contest.* To weigh the chances of winning of the participants in a contest (e.g., a political "race"). Source: HORSE RACING. SOED: 1856. To establish the odds of winning of the horses in an upcoming race. THT. "Weigh the chances" is a literal description of "evening the odds" by imposing extra weight on more highly favored horses. *See also* Handicap (n).

HAND OVER FIST *to make money hand over fist.* To make a lot of money in a short time. WNCD: 1825. Source: SAILING. To pull on a rope (e.g., to raise a sail) by putting one hand above the other. The original expression was "hand over hand." CI; DOC; HOI; LTA. This is not the same metaphor as "get the upper hand" (q.v.).

HAND SOMEONE A LINE *to hand someone a line.* To attempt to impress or fool someone with smooth talk. Source: FISHING(?). To tempt a fish by dangling a baited hook in front of it.

HANG A LEFT/RIGHT *to hang a left or right.* To turn left or turn right— while walking, driving, biking, etc. Source: SKIING; SURFING. To make a right or left turn while skiing or surfing. NDAS.

HANG BY YOUR FINGERTIPS *to be hanging by your fingertips/fingernails.* To be facing imminent disaster or ruin; to be barely hanging on. Source: CLIMBING. To have lost your foothold while rock climbing and be suspended only by your handhold (or fingerhold).

HANG FIRE *to hang fire.* To experience a delay. Source: SHOOTING. For a firearm, especially a muzzle-loader, not to fire as soon as expected when the trigger is pulled—or perhaps not fire at all. CI; DOC; DPF; NDAS. *See also* Flash in the Pan. *Compare* Fizzle Out; Sure-fire.

HANG IN THERE *Hang in there!* Hang on! Don't give up! DOC: 20th cent. Source: BOXING. Hang on to your opponent—"Clinch!"—in order to avoid more damage and gain time to recover. DOC.

HANG IT UP *to hang it up.* To retire. Source: SPORTS. To hang up your gloves, spikes, jock strap, etc. and retire from competition. *See also* Hang Up Your Gloves; Hang Up Your Spikes.

HANG LOOSE *Hang loose!* Relax! Source: SPORTS. DOC: 20th cent. (Advice to an athlete from a manager or coach or trainer.)

HANG TEN   *to hang ten.* To live on the edge. Source: SURFING. To ride a surfboard by crouching at the very front, with all ten toes hanging over the edge.

HANG UP YOUR GLOVES   *to hang up your gloves.* To retire. Source: BOXING. To retire from boxing. LOS. *See also* Hang It Up; Hang Up Your Spikes.

HANG UP YOUR SPIKES   *to hang up your spikes.* To retire. Source: BASEBALL. The expression probably originated in baseball, where metal spikes were first worn; but it has since been applied to track and field, golf, and football. *Also:* "hang up your cleats, skates, sneakers, goggles, jock strap, etc." *See also* Hang It Up; Hang Up Your Gloves.

HANKY-PANKY   Illegal or immoral activity or behavior: funny business, monkey business. SOED: 1841. Source: CARNIVAL. From *hanky-pank*, the "carny" name for a cheap game, such as the ring toss. NDAS.

HAPPY HUNTING GROUND   *the happy hunting ground(s).* The hereafter. DAE: 1840. Source: HUNTING. DA: 1837. The place where game is always plentiful and the hunters are always successful. (Amer. Indian.) *See also* Hunting Ground.

HARD-AND-FAST   *a hard-and-fast rule.* A rigid, unchangeable rule. SOED: 1867. Source: SAILING. Hard-and-fast aground—e.g., hung up on a sandbar. *See also* Hard Up.

HARDBALL TACTICS   *to use hardball tactics.* To take a get-tough approach. Source: BASEBALL. WNCD: 1944. To use the methods and equipment employed in *baseball*, as opposed to those used in *softball*. EOD. *Also:* "hardball politics." *See also* Play Hardball.

HARD CALL   *a hard call.* A difficult choice; a tough decision. Source: BASEBALL. A play that is so close that it is hard to call. GAMBLING. A race or fight that is hard to handicap because the contenders are so evenly matched. *See also* Call 'Em as You See 'Em; Too Close to Call. *Compare* Close Call.

HARD-NOSED   *to be hard-nosed.* To be tough and insensitive. WNCD: 1927. Source: BOXING. For your nose to be toughened by countless blows to the face. *Also:* "a hardnose."

HARD ON THE HEELS OF   *to be hard on the heels of someone.* To be close to apprehending someone (e.g., a wanted criminal) or overtaking someone (e.g., a business competitor). Source: RACING; HUNTING. To be close behind a competitor in a race or close behind a quarry in a hunt.

HARD TO CALL   *to be hard to call.* To be difficult to predict. Source: HORSE RACING. A race is "hard to call" if two or more horses are handicapped at the same low odds and any one of them could be the winner. Used also in other sports, such as boxing. *See also* Too Close to Call; Tough Call.

HARD TO PIN DOWN   *to be hard to pin down*. To be hard to locate or get straight information from. Source: WRESTLING. To be hard to catch and "pin" (with the shoulders pressed to the mat for a count of *3*). *See also* Pin Down.

HARD UP   *to be hard up*. To be almost broke. LTA: 1820s. Source: SAIL-ING. To have "run aground." CI. For the rudder to be as far "over" as it can go. LTA. *See also* Hard-and-fast.

HARK BACK   *to hark back to something*. To recall a subject mentioned earlier. WNCD: 1834. Source: FOX HUNTING. SOED: 1610. For the hunts-man to call back the hounds to an earlier track when they have lost the scent of the fox. DPF. *See also* On a Cold Trail.

HAT TRICK   *a hat trick*. Three successes in a row—e.g., three Oscars awarded to the same actor. Immediate Source: ICE HOCKEY. Three goals scored in the same game by the same player. (Originally three *unanswered* goals: a "pure" hat trick.) LOS. Ultimate Source: CRICKET. WNCD: 1882. The knocking down of a wicket, or the putting out of three batsmen, by the bowler, on three successive balls, the prize being a new hat (a "bowler"?) to the bowler. CI; DPF; WPO. Also used in soccer and horse racing.

HAVE A CARD UP YOUR SLEEVE   *to have a card up your sleeve*. To have something in reserve, e.g., an alternative plan of action or a secret weapon. Source: CARD GAMES. To have an extra card concealed in your sleeve or cuff for use at an opportune time. CI. *See also* Ace up Your Sleeve; Card; Have Something up Your Sleeve.

HAVE A CHIP ON YOUR SHOULDER   *to have—or carry—a chip on your shoulder*. To be looking for a fight. LTA: 1934. Source: CHILDREN'S GAMES. WPO: 1830. To put a chip of wood on your shoulder and dare another child to knock it off. CI; DOC; DPF; HOI. *See also* Cocky; Knock It Off.

HAVE A FIELD DAY   *to have a field day*. To have a wonderful, uninhibited time. Immediate Source: CHILDREN'S GAMES. For children to be excused from classes for a day to participate in various sports and games on an athletic field. OL. Ultimate Source: MILITARY. SOED: 1747. A military review or exercise. CI; DOC; DPF.

HAVE A GLASS JAW   *to have a glass jaw*. To be unable to take criticism or abuse. Source: BOXING. LTA: 1914. To be unable to take a sharp blow to the jaw without its breaking.

HAVE A GO AT SOMETHING   *to have a go at something*. To give some-thing a try. Source: FOOT RACING. To be prepared to race at the word "Go!"

CI. BOXING. To engage in a boxing match: a "go." LTA: 1890. *See also* From the Word Go; On the Go.

HAVE A GOOD LINEUP *to have a good lineup.* To have a quality roster of persons scheduled for an activity or event. Source: BASEBALL. DA: 1896. To have a quality roster of players scheduled for the game or season. The names of the starting players on a team in order of their appearance at the plate (the "lineup") are presented to the home plate umpire before the start of the game.

HAVE A LARK *to have a lark.* To have a lot of fun. Source: SPORTS. DPF: ca. 1800. To have a contest (O.E. *lac*) or other form of sport or play. *See also* For a Lark.

HAVE ALL YOUR DUCKS IN A ROW *to have/get all your ducks in a row.* To have or get all of your affairs in order. Source: BOWLING. To have or get all of your duckpins ("ducks") set up for the next game. Duckpins is a variation of bowling, with ten smaller pins and a smaller ball with no finger holes. DPF.

HAVE A LOT OF CLOUT *to have/carry a lot of clout.* To have a lot of power or influence. Source: BASEBALL. To be able to hit a baseball a long way.

HAVE A LOT OF MOXIE *to have a lot of moxie.* To have a lot of guts; to have nerves of ice. Source: BASEBALL. This expression derives from the cry of vendors of a popular soft drink, Moxie, in eastern ballparks in the late 1800s. LOS; NDAS; WPO. Moxie was still available as late as the 1920s. DA.

HAVE A LOT ON THE BALL *to have a lot on the ball.* To have a lot of talent or brains. LTA: 1912. Source: BASEBALL. DOC: Mid 1930s. For a pitcher to be able to throw the baseball with a lot of speed (or spit). DOC. CI indicates soccer. *See also* Have Something on the Ball; Lot; On the Ball.

HAVE A LOT RIDING ON *to have a lot riding on something.* To have a lot of money invested in a single venture. Source: GAMBLING; BETTING. To have a lot of money bet on a certain horse or race.

HAVE AN OFF DAY *to have an off day.* To not be performing as well as usual. Source: BASEBALL. To be playing as if no game were scheduled for that day—and therefore no statistics are kept.

HAVE A POINT *to have a point.* To make a good observation. Source: CRAPS. To have made the first throw of the dice without shooting a 2, 3, or 12 ("losers") or a 7 or 11 ("winners")—i.e., to have thrown a 4, 5, 6, 8, or 10 (the "point"). *See also* Beside the Point.

HAVE A RINGSIDE SEAT *to have a ringside seat.* To be close to the action. Source: BOXING. To have a seat in the front row—"at ringside" (q.v.)— at a boxing match. CI. *Compare* In at the Death; In at the Kill.

HAVE A SCORE TO SETTLE   *to have a score to settle.* To have a long-standing wrong to right. Source: SPORTS(?). To have a difficult loss to avenge.

HAVE A STAKE IN   *to have a stake in something.* To have an investment or interest in something. Source: GAMBLING. SOED: 1540. To have a wager on a horse or a hand of poker. CI.

HAVE LEGS   *to have legs.* For a theatrical production to have a long "run." Source: FOOT RACING. For a runner to have the stamina and endurance to complete a long run. NDAS. *Compare* Get Your Second Wind.

HAVE ONLY ONE OAR IN THE WATER   *to have only one oar in the water.* To be mentally deficient. Source: BOATING. To be using only one of the two oars in a rowboat, causing the boat to go around in circles. *See also* Row with Only One Oar.

HAVE OTHER FISH TO FRY   *to have other fish to fry.* To have other—more important—things to do. Source: FISHING. HTB: Mid-17th cent. To have other fish to catch and prepare. DPF. *See also* More Fish in the Ocean.

HAVE SOMEONE IN THE BULLPEN   *to have someone in the bullpen.* To have someone in reserve. Source: BASEBALL. LTA: 1910. To have a pitcher warming up in the "bullpen," usually along the left or right field line, where Bull Durham chewing tobacco was once advertised. WPO. The overflow crowd was sometimes also "herded" there. NDAS.

HAVE SOMEONE IN YOUR CORNER   *to have someone in your corner.* To have support, possibly divine, for your cause. Source: BOXING. To have a trainer or "second" or "corner person" in your corner of the ring between rounds of a fight.

HAVE SOMEONE ON THE ROPES   *to have someone on the ropes.* To have your opponent in serious trouble. DOC: Early 1800s. Source: BOXING. To have your opponent pinned against, and possibly holding onto, the ropes of the ring, defenseless. FP; SFS. *See Also* On the Ropes; Rope Someone in.

HAVE SOMETHING IN YOUR SIGHTS   *to have something in your sights.* To have a clear-cut goal. Source: SHOOTING. To have the sights of your firearm aimed at a target. CI. *See also* Have Your Sights Set on Something; Set Your Sights on.

HAVE SOMETHING ON THE BALL   *to have something on the ball.* To have a special kind of talent. DA: 1912. Source: BASEBALL. For a pitcher to have an extra amount of speed or spin (or spit) on the baseball. *See also* Have a Lot on the Ball; On the Ball.

HAVE SOMETHING UP YOUR SLEEVE   *to have something up your sleeve.* To have a hidden plan: a secret weapon. Source: CARD GAMES. To have a card hidden in your cuff or sleeve for use at an opportune time. CI. *See also* Ace up Your Sleeve; Have a Card up Your Sleeve.

HAVE THE BOOK ON SOMEONE   *to have the book on someone.* To know all about someone's background and expected behavior. Source: BASEBALL. To have extensive "scouting reports" on an opposing player. *Compare* Make Book On.

HAVE THE INSIDE TRACK   *to have the inside track.* To have a special advantage over your opponents. Source: HORSE RACING. To be racing—or scheduled to race—closest to the inside rail, the shortest route around a racetrack.

HAVE THE WIND TAKEN OUT OF YOUR SAILS   *to have the wind taken out of your sails.* To be given a serious setback in your plans or ambitions. Source: SAILING. To be deprived of the wind by another craft sailing on your windward side.

HAVE TWO STRIKES AGAINST YOU   *to have two strikes against you.* To be at a considerable disadvantage from the outset. LTA: 1940s. Source: BASEBALL. For a batter to have two "strikes" called against them, out of an allowable three, by the home plate umpire—and to have only one more chance to get a hit in that time at bat. FP. *Compare* Strike Out.

HAVE YOUR SIGHTS SET ON SOMETHING   *to have your sights set on something.* To have a goal clearly in mind. Source: SHOOTING. To have the sights of your firearm aimed at a target. CI. *See also* Have Something in Your Sights; Set Your Sights on.

HAYMAKER   *to deliver/land a haymaker.* To deliver a severe blow to someone's aspirations. Source: BOXING. LTA: 1912. To deliver a powerful blow to your opponent's head or body.

HAZARD A GUESS   *to hazard a guess.* To offer an estimate; to venture an opinion. Source: CRAPS. All senses of "hazard" derive from the French *hasard,* a dice game, ultimately from the Arabic *az-zahr,* "the die." WNCD: 14th cent. The game of *hasard* was brought to New Orleans in the early 19th century and renamed after the term for the lowest throw of the dice: *craps,* snakeeyes. DPF; HF; LTA. *See also* Guessing Game.

HEAD (n)   *See* Can't Make Heads or Tails; Dive in Head First; Give Someone Their Head; Go Head-to-head; In over Your Head; Keep Your Head above Water; Make Headway; Play over Your Head.

HEAD IS SPINNING   *My head is spinning.* "I'm dizzy" (either literally or because of an overabundance of incoming information). SOED: 1819. Source: CHILDREN'S TOYS. My head is spinning like a child's "top." *Also:* "My head is swimming," 1702. *See also* Topsy-turvy. *Compare* Spin Your Wheels.

HEADLINE *a headline.* A title for a newspaper article. WNCD: 1824. Source: SAILING. SOED: 1626. A rope extending from the bow of a ship to the center of the forward sail: a "bowline." *Compare* Mainstay.

HEADLOCK *to have a headlock on someone; to have someone in a head-lock.* To have someone in a helpless position. Source: WRESTLING. WNCD: 1905. To have your arm "locked" around your opponent's "head."

HEAD OVER HEELS *to be/fall head over heels in love with someone/something.* To be or become totally enamored of someone or something. DOC: 1771. Source: GYMNASTICS; ACROBATICS. WNCD: 1770. This is not a technical term in gymnastics or acrobatics (or tumbling), but it aptly describes the position of a gymnast during a somersault, which, once started, cannot be stopped. CI; DOC. The expression first came into English in the 14th century as *"heels over head,"* then reversed to *"head over heels"* in the 18th century. DOC.

HEADS I WIN, TAILS YOU LOSE You can't win, and I can't lose. Source: COINS (Flipping Coins). If the upside of the flipped coin shows heads, I win; if it shows tails I still win (and you still lose). *See also* Can't Make Heads or Tails; Upside Down.

HEAD START *a head start.* A time advantage over the competition. Source: RACING. WNCD: 1886. A start of a race in which a racer leaps ahead of the other racers by a head's length or has a handicap of a small distance. *See also* Get a Head Start.

HEAD-TO-HEAD *a head-to-head confrontation.* A confrontation that is both direct and personal. WNCD: 1728. Source: BOXING. A match in which the boxers fight head-to-head with each other, at close range. *See also* Go Head to Head.

HEAVY GOING *to be heavy going.* For conditions to be unsuitable for making much progress. Source: HORSE RACING. For the track to be wet or muddy, making it difficult for the horses to generate much speed. CI.

HEAVYWEIGHT *a heavyweight.* A leader in the field of business or politics. LTA: 1879. Source: BOXING. LTA: 1850s. A boxer in the weight class called "heavyweight"—over 175 pounds, although a lighter boxer can always attempt to fight in this class. The term is also used in WRESTLING and WEIGHT LIFTING.

HEDGE YOUR BETS *to hedge your bets.* To act defensively in order to protect you own interests or investments; to support both sides of an issue or campaign. DAE: 1879. Source: GAMBLING; BETTING. SOED: 1813. To make "cross bets"—counterbalancing bets—in order to avoid losing a large amount of money. CI; DPF. *See also* Play the Field.

HEELS (n)   *See* Close on the Heels; Dig In Your Heels; Hard on the Heels Of; Head over Heels; Swing from the Heels.

HIDE AND SEEK   *See* Play Hide and Seek.

HIGH AND DRY   *to be left high and dry.* To be stranded. Source: SAILING. WNCD: 1882. For a boat to be left on the beach by the ebbing tide. CI. *Compare* Left in the Lurch.

HIGH AS A KITE   *to be high as a kite.* To be intoxicated with alcohol, drugs, or excitement. Source: KITE FLYING. To be as high in the air as a child's kite. CI. The toy is named after the soaring of a falcon, or "kite." SOED. *See also* Go Fly a Kite; Higher Than a Kite. *Compare* Loaded to the Gills.

HIGHER THAN A KITE   *to be higher than a kite.* To be drunk as a skunk; to be all keyed up with emotion. Source: KITE FLYING. DAE: 1867. To be higher in the sky than a child's kite. *See also* Go Fly a Kite; High as a Kite. *Compare* Loaded to the Gills.

HIGH JINKS   Drunken pranks. WNCD: 1825. Source: DICE GAMES. SOED: 1700. Performances and recitations given at drinking parties as a result of having lost a throw of the dice and desiring to avoid a fine as penalty. HTB.

HIGHLY TOUTED   *to be highly touted.* To be highly recommended or praised. Source: HORSE RACING. To be highly rated ("touted") by the handicappers of a horserace. *See also* Smart Money; Tout.

HIGH ROLLER   *a high roller.* A big spender. WNCD: 1881. Source: CRAPS. NDAS: Late 1800s. A crapshooter who bets heavily on each roll of the dice.

HIGH-STAKES   *high-stakes lobbying, etc.* High-pressure lobbying for large-scale profits. Source: POKER. In "high-stakes" poker, the maximum amount that can be bet at any one time is either very large or unlimited. *See also* Play for High Stakes.

HIGH STRUNG (p.a.)   *to be high strung.* To be tense and nervous. WNCD: 1748. Source: TENNIS. To have the same tension as the strings of a tightly strung tennis racket. The expression probably derives from tennis rackets—or longbows or crossbows—rather than stringed musical instruments, which must always maintain the *same* tension.

HIGHTAIL IT   *to hightail it (for) home.* To get home as fast as possible. WNCD: 1925. Source: HUNTING; RIDING. For the whitetail deer to raise its tail and head for safety when approached by a hunter; for a horse to elevate its tail when galloping or frolicking. NDAS.

HIKE   *See* Take a Hike.

HIT (n) *a hit.* A success. ("The play was a hit.") Source: FENCING. Shakespeare, *Hamlet,* 1601. A touch of the point of your foil or rapier on the body of your opponent. The word is also used in shooting, cricket, baseball, softball, football, etc. *See also* Make a Hit; No Runs, No Hits, No Errors; Pinch Hit; Smash Hit.

HIT-AND-RUN (adj.) *a hit-and-run driver.* A driver who hits a pedestrian, or cyclist, etc. and then drives away from the scene of the accident. Source: BASEBALL. WNCD: 1899. A "hit-and-run" play is a prearranged play in which the runner on first base knows that the batter will swing at the next pitch, enabling the runner to get a head start for second base. CI.

HIT A SNAG *to hit a snag.* To encounter an unexpected problem. DA: 1829. Source: BOATING. DA: 1804. For a boat to run into, or get hung up on, an underwater obstacle, such as a sunken log.

HIT BELOW THE BELT *to hit below the belt.* To violate the rules of fair play. LTA: 1928. Source: BOXING. To strike a blow—a "low blow"—below the belt of your opponent's trunks. SFS. The term and the metaphor originated when the Marquess of Queensberry rules were established in 1867. DOC; HTB; WPO. *See also* Low Blow.

HIT HOME *to hit home.* ("That really hits home.") For something to have deep personal relevance. Source: HUNTING. For an arrow or bullet to strike the animal that it was aimed at. *See also* Home Free.

HIT IT OFF *to hit it off with someone.* To make a favorable impression on someone. Source: CRICKET(?). To knock all of the bails off the wicket.

HIT ON *to hit on someone.* To make a verbal "pass" at someone. Source: BOXING(?). To throw a series of punches at your opponent.

HIT-OR-MISS (adj.) *a hit-or-miss situation.* A win or lose situation, with no in-between. WNCD: 1654. Source: HUNTING. A situation in which you either kill the quarry or lose it altogether. DOC. *Also:* "a hit-or-miss attempt."

HIT OR MISS (adv.) *to do something hit or miss.* To do something haphazardly. DOC: 16th cent. Source: HUNTING. To shoot haphazardly at a quarry. DOC.

HIT THE BULL'S-EYE *to hit the bull's-eye.* To be precisely correct. Source: ARCHERY. To hit the center of an archery target, which consists of a yellow circle surrounded by a red ring—and presumably resembles the eye of an angry bull. CI: "darts." *See also* Hit the Spot. *Compare* Come to the Point.

HIT THE DECK *to hit the deck.* To drop to the floor; to get out of bed. Immediate Source: BOXING. To drop to the canvas as a result of a knockdown blow. Ultimate Source: SAILING. To drop to the deck of the ship or boat from your bunk; to fall flat on the deck in order to avoid being hit by the boom. *Compare* Hit the Ground Running.

HIT THE GROUND RUNNING   *to hit the ground running.* To start attacking a problem immediately. Source: RODEO(?). To have your legs already moving when you leave your horse to "bulldog" a steer or tie up a roped calf. It is possible that this expression, which was one of President Reagan's favorites, simply refers to sailors leaving their bunks in an emergency at sea. *Compare* Hit the Deck.

HIT THE JACKPOT   *to hit the jackpot.* To become suddenly affluent. DAE: 1903. Source: POKER. DAE: 1887. To win all of the stakes in the "pot," which grows until a player has a pair of jacks or better and can open the betting. CI; DPF; SOE; WPO. The expression is also used for winning the payoff on a slot machine and for winning the top prize in a lottery.

HIT THE SPOT   *to hit the spot.* ("This beer really hits the spot.") For something to please the palate. Source: SHOOTING. To hit the "bull's-eye" (q.v.) or center of the target. DOC. *Compare* Come to the Point.

HIT THE WALL   *to hit the wall.* To encounter a serious obstacle. Source: FOOT RACING. For a long-distance runner to experience severe fatigue and pain about three-quarters of the way through the race. Car racing may be the ultimate source. *Compare* Get Your Second Wind.

HIT YOUR STRIDE   *to hit your stride.* To achieve your normal level of performance or productivity. Source: FOOT RACING. To reach your normal racing speed and rhythm. CI.

HOBBY   *a hobby.* An avocation or pastime. SOED: 1816. Source: CHILDREN'S TOYS. A "hobby-horse": a stick with an imitation horse's head on the end, which the child "rides." DPF; HF; WPO. From the 16th-century "Morris Dances," in which one of the characters was costumed as a "hobby-horse"—i.e., a "hobby," or small horse. *See also* Ride a Hobby-horse.

HOCKEY PUCK   *a hockey puck.* A stupid or inept person. Source: ICE HOCKEY (via comedian Don Rickles). To be as intelligent as the flat, round, hard-rubber object that is "bandied about" (q.v.) on the ice by hockey players.

HOCUS-POCUS   Magic, as opposed to science. Source: JUGGLING. SOED: 1647. From a medieval juggler's fake Latin incantation while performing his magic. NDAS.

HOG ON ICE   *as independent as a hog on ice.* As independent as a hog trying to move, or even stand up, on a frozen pond—i.e., not independent at all. DAE: 1894. Source: CURLING. As "independent" as a curling stone, of the 16th-century Scottish variety, that never reached its mark but was allowed to remain on the ice as a hazard to the other curlers. HOI. WPO: a hog that has been butchered and put "on ice." *Compare* There's the Rub.

HOLD A PAT HAND *to hold a pat hand.* To be satisfied with what you have. Source: POKER. SOED: 1889. To be satisfied with the hand that you have been dealt—in "five-card draw"—choosing not to draw any replacement cards. DOC; SPD. *See also* Sit Tight; Stand Pat.

HOLD A RAFFLE *to hold a raffle.* To sell chances on winning a substantial prize, such as a car. Source: DICE GAMES. "Raffle" was a 14th-century betting game in which each player, in turn, threw three dice, the winner being the one with the highest total. THT. The name derives from that of an earlier game in France. WNWD. *See also* Raffle Something Off.

HOLD AT BAY *to hold something at bay.* To hold something—e.g., famine, flood, disease—in check. Source: HUNTING. DOC: 1530. For hunting dogs to corner a quarry and let the hunter know, by their "baying" (O.Fren. *abai*), where they are. *See also* Hold in Check; In Full Cry.

HOLD IN CHECK *to hold something/someone in check.* To restrain or control something or someone. Source: CHESS. To put your opponent's king in danger—"in check." *See also* Check (n); Check (v); Hold at Bay.

HOLDING ALL THE CARDS *to be holding all the cards.* To be in complete control. Source: CARD GAMES. To be holding a hand that is unbeatable.

HOLDOUT *a holdout.* Someone who refuses to participate in a deal. Source: POKER. A card that is "held out" (concealed) from play by one of the players, for use at a later time. The term also applies to professional athletes who "hold out" for more money before signing their contracts.

HOLD THE LINE *to hold the line on something.* To resist an increase in something: taxes, wages, inflation, etc. Source: FOOTBALL. To "hold that line!"—i.e., to defend against a gain by the offensive team across the line of scrimmage. FP; SPD. The term is probably originally from the military: to hold a line of defense.

HOLD THE TRUMP CARD *to hold the trump card.* To have the upper hand. Source: CARD GAMES. To have in your hand a card of the suit ("trump," the suit of the winning bid) that outranks all others for that particular trick. *See also* Card. *Compare* Trumped-up.

HOLD UP YOUR END *to hold up your end of the bargain (etc.).* To perform as promised. Source: CRICKET. To protect your wicket. CI. Brit.: *"keep up your end."*

HOLD YOUR HORSES *Hold your horses!* Take it easy! HTB: 1844. Source: HORSE RACING. A command to drivers in harness races to keep their horses from jumping the gun. HTB.

HOLE   *See* Ace in the Hole; In the Hole; Nineteenth Hole; Round Peg in a Square Hole; Show Your Hole Card; Square Peg in a Round Hole.

HOME FREE   *to be home free.* To have approached your goal without expectation of further difficulty. Source: CHILDREN'S GAMES. To reach "home" (a tree or other object) "free" (i.e., without being caught—as in the games of Hide and Seek, Kick the Can, Icebox, etc.). "Ollie Ollie Ox in Free" signals the cessation of these games. *See also* Free-for-all; Hit Home; Pick Up Your Marbles and Go Home.

HOMESTRETCH   *to be coming down the homestretch.* To be approaching a successful end to an activity. Source: HORSE RACING. For a horse to have rounded the final turn and be coming down the straightaway toward the finish line. *See also* In the Homestretch.

HOODWINK   *to hoodwink someone.* To trick someone: to pull the wool over their eyes. Source: FALCONRY. WNCD: 1562. To blindfold a falcon, or hawk, with a hood while it is being transported or prepared for flight. Falconry is also known as hawking. *See also* Hoodwinked; Snooker.

HOODWINKED   *to be hoodwinked.* To be tricked or outsmarted. Source: FALCONRY (Hawking). For the falcon to be blindfolded with a hood while it is being transported or prepared for flight. *See also* Hoodwink.

HOOK (n)   *See* Get off the Hook; Get Your Hooks into; Let Someone off the Hook; Off the Hook; On Your Own Hook; Set the Hook; Set Your Hooks for.

HOOK (v)   *to hook something or someone.* To land ("hook") a good job; to find ("hook") a good mate. Source: FISHING. To catch a fish on a hook. *See also* Get Hooked on; Hook Up with.

HOOK, LINE, AND SINKER   *to swallow something hook, line, and sinker.* To be incredibly gullible; to believe a preposterous story. DA: 1838. Source: FISHING. For the fish to take off with all of your gear: the fishing hook, the fishing line, and the lead sinker—and probably the cork bobber, too. CI; DOC; HOI. *Compare* Lock, Stock, and Barrel; Whole Shooting Match.

HOOK UP   *to hook something up.* To prepare an electrical or electronic appliance for use by attaching its wires in the proper places. Source: FISHING. To attach a fishing hook to a fishing line. WNWD.

HOOK UP WITH   *To hook up with someone.* To join up with someone: e.g., to "hook up with"—i.e., get a job with—IBM (etc.). WNCD: 1925. Source: FISHING. To cross lines, or hooks, with another angler. *See also* Hook (v). *Compare* Run Afoul of.

HOPSCOTCH   *to hopscotch around Europe (etc.).* To jump from one place to another, spending little time in any one. Source: HOPSCOTCH. To play "hopscotch," the children's game in which a player must throw a stone into one of the designated numbered squares drawn ("scotched") on the ground and then hop in the squares to retrieve it—and then hop "back to square one" (q.v.). *See also* Pinball.

HOP, SKIP, AND A JUMP   *a hop, skip (or step), and a jump from here.* Not very far from here. WNCD: 1760. Source: TRACK AND FIELD. WNCD: 1719. A field event consisting of a hop, a skip (or step), and a jump, in that order. Originally called "Hop, Skip, and Jump"; then "Hop, Step, and Jump"; now "Triple Jump." *See also* Skip.

HORSE (n)   *See* Back the Wrong Horse; Don't Look a Gift Horse in the Mouth; Fall off a Horse; Get off Your High Horse; Get on Your High Horse; Hold Your Horses; Ride a Hobby-horse; Stalking Horse; Straight from the Horse's Mouth.

HORSE OF A DIFFERENT/ANOTHER COLOR   *That's a horse of a different (another) color.* That's an entirely different matter. DOC: 1798. Source: HORSE RACING. That's an entirely different horse—not the one I thought I was betting on. DOC; HOI; WPO. Racehorses are identified by the "colors" ("silks") worn by their jockeys, as well as by their numbers. Knights in medievals tournaments were also identified by their "colors." *See also* Bring in a Ringer; Whole New/'Nother Ball Game. *Compare* Dark Horse.

HORSE RACE   *to develop into a horse race.* For a campaign to develop into an exciting contest between two individuals. Source: HORSE RACING. DAE: 1721. For a race to develop into an exciting contest between two horses.

HORSES FOR COURSES   *There are horses for courses.* Some people are more suited to certain tasks than others are. ("Different strokes for different folks.") Source: HORSE RACING. Some horses are more suited to certain tracks ("courses"), and to certain racing conditions, than others are. CI. *See also* Course.

HORSESHOES   *See* Close Counts in Horseshoes.

HOT   *When you're hot, you're hot.* ("And when you're not, you're not.") When you're lucky, you can't do anything wrong. Source: SPORTS; GAMES. When you're on a hot streak or holding a hot hand you "can't lose for winning."

HOT DOG (n)   *a hot dog.* A show-off. Source: BASEBALL. A player who shows off for the fans, the "hot-dog eaters." LOS. Hot dogs were first sold at the Polo Grounds, home of the New York Giants, in the early 1900s. HTB. *See also* Grandstand; Hotdog (v).

HOTDOG (v)   *to hotdog.* To show off. WNCD: 1962. Source: BASEBALL. To show off for the fans, the "hot-dog eaters." Also used in skiing, surfing, and other sports. *See also* Grandstand; Hot Dog (n).

HOT HAND   *to have/hold a hot hand.* To be enjoying a string of successes. Source: POKER. To be holding an exceptionally good hand of cards or having a succession of such hands. Also used in basketball and other sports.

HOT ON THE TRAIL   *to be hot on the trail of someone/something.* To be close to apprehending someone or finding something. Source: HUNTING. For the hounds to have a strong, fresh scent and be about to run the fox to the ground. *See also* Run to the Ground.

HOT-RODDER   *a hot-rodder.* A young, reckless driver. Source: CAR RACING. A drag racer. The sport of drag racing was organized in California in the early 1930s.

HOT STREAK   *a hot streak.* A streak of good luck or unusual success. Source: BASEBALL. A baseball player who is on a "hot streak" can get a hit every time they go to the plate—that is, until the streak ends. A batter who hits in streaks is a streak-hitter.

HOT TO TROT   *to be hot to trot.* To be ready and willing to engage in sex. Source: HORSE RACING; FOX HUNTING. For a racehorse (such as a "trotter") or a "hunter" (a fox-trotter) to be impatient for the action to start.

HOUND (v)   *to hound someone.* To pester someone; to follow someone persistently. WNCD: 1528. Source: FOX HUNTING. For a hound to pursue a fox, or other game, incessantly. *Compare* Rock Hound.

HOUSE OF CARDS   *a house of cards.* A flimsy or unstable establishment. WNCD: 1903. Source: CHILDREN'S GAMES. A miniature house built out of playing cards, without glue, tape, clips, etc. It doesn't last long. *See also* Build Sand Castles.

HOW ABOUT THAT, SPORTS FANS   *How about that, sports fans!* Isn't that something! Source: SPORTS. An exclamation of radio and TV announcers of sports events. NDAS. *See also* Fan.

HOW THE LAND LIES   *to see how the land lies.* To discover what the conditions are before making a move. Source: SAILING. To get your bearings from landmarks on the coast. CI.

HOYLE   *See* Not According to Hoyle.

HUBBUB   *a hubbub.* An uproar from a noisy crowd. SOED: 1779. Source: DICE GAMES. DAE: 1634. A game similar to craps that was played by the American Indians and accompanied by shouts resembling "Hubbub!" WNWD: from the Gaelic *ubub,* an invective.

HUDDLE (n)   *to call for a huddle.* To have a brief consultation, or caucus. Source: FOOTBALL. LTA: 1929. For the entire team, offensive or defensive, to come together on the field to learn what the strategy will be for the next play. SFS.

HUDDLE (v) *to huddle.* For a small group of people to consult together. Source: FOOTBALL. For either of the two teams on the field, offensive or defensive, to come together briefly to discuss the next play. NDAS. *See Also* Huddle (n).

HUNT DOWN *to hunt someone down.* To search for someone until you find them. Source: HUNTING. SOED: 1684. To track down a quarry. *See also* In the Hunt.

HUNTING GROUND *a hunting ground.* A battlefield; a war zone. Source: HUNTING. DAE: 1721. An area traditionally used for hunting by the American Indians. *See also* Happy Hunting Ground.

HURDLE (n) *to put, place, erect, etc. hurdles in someone's way or path.* To attempt to block, or frustrate, someone's efforts. Source: TRACK AND FIELD. To put hurdles on a racetrack. An even higher hurdle, with a pond in the landing area, is used in a "steeplechase" race. *See also* Hurdle (v).

HURDLE (v) *to hurdle an obstacle.* To overcome an obstacle. Source: TRACK AND FIELD. WNCD: 1896. To leap over the frames of metal or wood that are positioned at regular intervals on the track for a hurdle race. *See also* Hurdle (n).

HUSTLE *to hustle someone.* To swindle someone; to shake someone down. Source: GAMBLING. To shake up coins or lots in a container. From the Dutch *husselen,* "to shake." WNWD. The term is also used in golf and pool to denote the practice of "hustlers"—skillful but unscrupulous players who bet a novice that they can make certain difficult shots or scores. LOS. *See also* Sandbag.

I

ICE *See* Break the Ice; Cut No Ice; Hog on Ice; Skate on Thin Ice; Tread on Thin Ice.

IN *to be in.* ("Are you 'in'?" "I'm 'in.' ") To be included in a business deal (etc.). Source: POKER. To be "in" the game—i.e., having "anted up" and ready for the "deal." *See also* Count Me in; Cut Me in; Deal Me in. *Compare* Out.

IN A LATHER *to be in a lather.* To be angry or upset. Source: HORSE RACING; RIDING. For a horse to have worked up a foamy sweat from a heavy workout. CI.

IN A SLUMP *to be in a slump.* To be performing poorly or unsuccessfully. Source: BASEBALL. For a baseball player, or the entire team, to be experiencing a succession of hitless or winless games.

IN AT THE DEATH *to be in at the death.* To be present at the closing of a business or other institution. DOC: 1800. Source: FOX HUNTING. To be present at the killing of the fox. CI. *See also* Have a Ringside Seat; In at the Kill.

IN AT THE KILL *to be in at the kill.* To be present at the termination or dissolution of something. Source: FOX HUNTING. To be in attendance at the killing of the fox. CI; DOC. *See also* Have a Ringside Seat; In at the Death; Kill Two Birds with One Stone.

IN CHECK *See* Hold in Check.

IN DEEP WATER *to be in deep water.* To be in serious difficulty or trouble. Source: SWIMMING. To be in water that is deeper than you are tall, and you can't swim. CI. *See also* In over Your Head; Out of Your Depth.

INFIGHTER *an infighter.* A person who prefers to engage in direct confrontation with an opponent. LTA: 1848. Source: BOXING. LTA: 1816. A boxer who excels at fighting at close quarters. LOS. *See also* Go Head-to-head.

INFIGHTING   Bitter, personal battling within a group or organization. Source: BOXING. SOED: 1812. Close-range boxing, especially featuring short blows to the body.

IN FULL CRY   In enthusiastic pursuit. Source: FOX HUNTING. At the climax of the hunt, when the fox is cornered and the hounds are at their loudest. CI; DOC. *See also* Hold at Bay.

IN FULL SWING   *to be in full swing.* ("The party was in full swing when we got there.") For something to be at the peak of its activity. SOED: 1570. Source: DUELING. For a sword to be swung in a full arc. CI.

IN HAND   *to have everything in hand.* To have everything under control. Source: RIDING. To hold, "in hand," the reins of a horse that responds easily and promptly. CI. *Compare* Get out of Hand.

IN HOCK   *to be in hock to someone.* To be in debt to someone. Source: POKER. To be in debt to the "bank" or "house" because of a series of losses. NDAS. "Hock" is from the Dutch *hok,* "prison."

IN HOT PURSUIT   *to be in hot pursuit of someone.* To be close on the heels of someone, e.g., a wanted criminal. Source: FOX HUNTING. For the hounds to be close on the heels of the fox. SOED.

IN JEOPARDY   *to be in jeopardy.* To be in danger. Source: CHESS. THT: 16th cent. To have a 50–50 chance of winning or losing. In the TV gameshow *JEOPARDY!,* a contestant is "in jeopardy" if they give a wrong "question"; i.e., they lose the amount that they would have won.

IN ONE FELL SWOOP   *to accomplish something in/at one fell swoop.* To accomplish something in a single, swift action. Source: FALCONRY. Shakespeare, *Macbeth,* 1606. For a hawk to seize its prey in a single deadly ("fell") sweep ("swoop"). CI.

IN OVER YOUR HEAD   *to be/get in over your head.* To have overextended yourself—financially, professionally, socially, etc.—and to be unable to do anything about it. Source: SWIMMING. To be or get in water that is deeper than you are tall, and you can't swim. DOC. *See also* Above Your Head; In Deep Water; Out of Your Depth.

INSIDE STRAIGHT   *See* Draw to an Inside Straight; Fill an Inside Straight; Like Drawing to an Inside Straight; Like Trying to Fill an Inside Straight.

IN SOMEONE'S WAKE   *to be in someone's wake.* To follow someone who is more prominent or important. Source: SAILING; BOATING. A vessel that sails "in the wake" of another vessel finds the journey more difficult, because the "wake" (the churned-up water) is rougher to negotiate. CI. *See also* In the Wake of. *Compare* Eat Someone's Dust.

IN SPADES *to do something in spades.* To do something perfectly, decisively, or with class. Source: BRIDGE. To take a hand of bridge with "spades," the highest valued suit, as "trump."

INSTANT REPLAY *an instant replay.* A reoccurrence of an earlier event; a case of *deja vu.* Source: FOOTBALL. WNCD: 1966. A replaying—often again and again—of the television tape of the play that just took place. LOS. *See also* Run That by Me Again.

IN THE BAG *to be in the bag.* For a goal to be reached or reachable. Source: HUNTING. For game to be killed and placed in a "game bag." CI; DOC. *See also* Bird in the Hand.

IN THE BALLPARK *to be in the ballpark.* To be fairly close or fairly accurate as an estimate of cost, weight, size, age, etc. Source: BASEBALL. To be somewhere within the confines of the "park" in which the game of baseball is played. OL; SFS. *Also:* "not even in the ballpark," i.e., not even close. *See also* Ballpark; Ballpark Figure.

IN THE CATBIRD SEAT *to be (sitting) in the catbird seat.* To be sitting pretty: everything going your way. Source: BASEBALL. For a batter to have a count of three balls and no strikes. The pitcher *has* to throw a strike or else you walk. Attributed to Red Barber, radio sportscaster for the Brooklyn Dodgers. DOC; WPO. Made famous in literature by James Thurber. NDAS.

IN THE CHIPS *to be in the chips.* To be rich. Source: POKER. To have won an abundance of chips in a poker game.

IN THE CLUTCH In a critical situation. Source: BASEBALL. In a situation when the outcome of the game depends on you. Used also in many other sports. *See also* Choke; Clutch; Good in the Clutch.

IN THE HOLE *to be in the hole.* To be in debt. DA: 1908. Source: POKER. To have all of your money in the "pot" (or "hole"). In gambling casinos, the hole is an actual slot in the table for the deposit of the house's "cut" from each hand. HTB. DA: To be behind in a baseball game, 1889. *See also* Ace in the Hole.

IN THE HOMESTRETCH *to be in the homestretch.* To be in the final stage of a project, with the end in sight. DA: 1866. Source: HORSE RACING. DA: 1841. For the horses to have rounded the final turn and be in the straightaway leading to the finish line. *See also* Down the Stretch; Home Free.

IN THE HUNT *to be very much in the hunt.* To be very much in the running for a job, contract, political office, etc. Source: FOX HUNTING. To be deeply involved in the "chase." *See also* Hunt Down.

IN THE LEAD *to be in the lead.* To be the front-runner in a competition, e.g., a political "race." Source: RACING. To lead all of the other competitors in a race. *See also* Lead from Start to Finish.

IN THE LINEUP *to be in the lineup.* To be scheduled to participate. Source: BASEBALL. To be scheduled to start or play in a game. To be in the "starting" lineup is to be listed on the card that is presented by the manager to the home plate umpire at the beginning of the game. "Substitutes" are later penciled in to replace "starters."

IN THE LONG RUN Eventually. Source: FOOT RACING. In a long-distance race, such as the cross-country or marathon, the winner is not always the runner who gets the fastest start. CI; DOC; DPF. *See also* Race Is Not to the Swift.

IN THE MONEY *to be in the money.* To be suddenly affluent. Source: HORSE RACING. For a horse to finish in one of the top three positions in a race: first ("win"), second ("place"), and third ("show"). Only these three finishes "pay off" (q.v.), unless the bettor "backs the field" (q.v.). CI. *Also:* "out of the money."

IN THE NICK OF TIME *to happen in the nick of time.* To happen just before a deadline or disaster. SOED: 1643. Source: SOCCER. To score just before the end of the game. Soccer was at one time scored by notching a stick once for each goal, the last of which was "the nick in time." WPO. *Compare* Under the Wire.

IN THERE PITCHING *to still be in there pitching.* To still be active and vocal. Source: BASEBALL. To still be throwing the ball to the catcher in hopes that the batter won't hit it. SFS.

IN THERE PUNCHING *to still be in there punching.* ("How are you doing?" "Still in there punching.") To still be alive, active, and kicking. Source: BOXING. To still be throwing punches at your opponents. *See also* Punching Bag.

IN THE RUNNING *to be in the running for something.* To be under consideration for a job; to be a candidate for office. Source: HORSE RACING. To be in contention to win a race. DPF.

IN THE SWIM *to be in the swim.* To be in the right crowd, in style, up to date, *au courant.* SOED: 1869. Source: FISHING. To have dropped your hook among a school (or "swim") of fish—the right place to be fishing. DPF.

IN THE WAKE OF *for something to be in the wake of something else.* For something to happen immediately following something else, and perhaps result from that earlier occurrence. Source: BOATING; SAILING. For the water to be churned up behind ("in the wake of") a moving vessel. CI. *See also* In Someone's Wake.

IN THE WRONG LEAGUE *to be in the wrong league.* To be outmatched, outclassed. Source: BASEBALL. To be in the "major" leagues but belonging in the "minors."

IN TOW   *to have someone in tow.* To be accompanied by a date. Source: SAILING. To be towing another vessel. Also a sign on cars in traffic: In Tow.

IN TWO SHAKES OF A LAMB'S TAIL   *to be ready in two shakes of a lamb's tail.* To be ready in no time. WPO: 1840. Source: DICE GAMES. To be ready in the time it takes to shake up dice in a tumbler. WPO. *See also* Tinhorn.

INVESTIGATE   *to investigate something.* To search for evidence about something. WNCD: 1510. Source: HUNTING. To search for traces ("tracks," "vestiges") of a quarry. THT. *See also* Vestige.

IRON MAN   *an iron man.* A person of great toughness and endurance. WCND: 1914. Source: BASEBALL. A player, especially a catcher or pitcher, who has great toughness and endurance: a "man of iron" (though not of steel). Catchers of this sort sometimes acquire the nickname "Scrap Iron."

IT AIN'T OVER TILL IT'S OVER   "Don't count your chickens before they hatch." A modern proverb. Source: BASEBALL. The game isn't over until the last out. As long as there's one out to go, anything can happen. Attributed to Yogi Berra. *See also* Bird in the Hand.

ITCHY TRIGGER FINGER   *to have an itchy trigger finger.* To be quick to take offense and retaliate. Source: SHOOTING. To be too anxious to shoot your firearm—prematurely. *See also* Trigger-happy.

I'VE GOT YOU COVERED   *I've got you covered!* Stick 'em up! Source: CRAPS. I'll match your bet.

IVY LEAGUE   *the Ivy League.* The eight oldest colleges of the northeastern United States. WNCD: 1939. Source: FOOTBALL. The "Ivy League" schools were so called because of the nickname given to their football league by a sportswriter. HTB.

J

JACK-IN-THE-BOX *X is a little jack-in-the-box.* X is the kind of child who pops up everywhere. Source: CHILDREN'S TOYS. WNCD: 1702. X is like a box from which a clown ("Jack") pops up when the top is lifted. DPF. In the 16th century a "jack-in-the-box" was a box of junk ("jack") that was substituted for a box of money in a swindle by this name. HF. *Compare* Buy a Pig in a Poke.

JACKPOT *See* Hit the Jackpot.

JACKRABBIT START *a jackrabbit start.* The sudden acceleration of a car or truck or cycle from a stoplight when the light turns green. Source: HUNTING. The sudden leap of a jackrabbit from its cover when it senses the presence of a dog or hunter. DAE.

JEOPARDY *See* In Jeopardy.

JOCK *a jock.* An athlete: male only (LTA: 1960s); male or female (LTA: 1970s). Source: SPORTS. WNCD: 1922. Short for "Jockey," the brand name of a line of athletic supporters ("jock straps"). The ultimate source is the jockey in the sport of horse racing. LTA: 1825. *See also* Disc Jockey.

JOCKEY FOR POSITION *to jockey for position.* To maneuver into a more favorable position or status. Source: HORSE RACING. For a jockey to maneuver his or her horse into a more favorable position for winning a race. CI.

JUDGMENT CALL *a judgment call.* A decision that is based on the judgment of one individual. Source: BASEBALL. The decision of an umpire that is based on his or her best judgment in that particular case. *See also* Call 'Em as You See 'Em; Close Call; Make the Right Call; Too Close to Call.

JUGGLE *to juggle two or more things at once.* To carry on two or more tasks—e.g., hold two or more jobs—at once. Source: JUGGLING. WNCD:

14th cent. To keep two or more objects in motion in the air at the same time. *See also* Bicycle (v); Juggle the Books; Up in the Air.

JUGGLE THE BOOKS   *to juggle the books.* To make a set of financial accounts appear to "balance" when they really don't. Source: JUGGLING. WNCD: 14th cent. To make two or more objects appear to be constantly in the air when they really aren't. *See also* Juggle; Up in the Air.

JUKE   *to juke someone.* To outmaneuver or trick someone. NDAS. Immediate Source: FOOTBALL. WNCD: 1967. To fake someone out of position: to "deke" someone. Ultimate Source: HUNTING. SOED: 1450. For an animal to duck, or dodge a bullet. Originally *jouk. See also* Deke; Duck (v).

JUMPING-OFF POINT   *a jumping-off point (or place).* A starting point or place. DAE: 1834. Source: TRACK AND FIELD; DIVING. A place for beginning a leap—a high jump, long jump, etc.—or a dive. *See also* Pride of Place.

JUMP IN WITH BOTH FEET   *to jump in with both feet.* To join in an activity enthusiastically. Source: DIVING. To jump in the water "feet first," without bothering to execute a "correct" dive.

JUMP THE GUN   *to jump the gun.* To act prematurely. Source: FOOT RACING. To commit a "false start"—i.e., to leave the starting line before the gun fires. CI; HOI. Used also in rowing, speed skating, and swimming. *See also* False Start; Get the Jump On. *Compare* Gun-shy.

JUMP THROUGH HOOPS   *to make someone jump through hoops.* To force someone to perform meaningless tasks, possibly as a test of their character. Source: CIRCUS. To make an animal, such as a dog or large cat, jump through a suspended hoop, which is sometimes set on fire. CI. *Compare* Put Someone through Their Paces.

JUMP TO A CONCLUSION   *to jump to a conclusion.* To leap from insufficient evidence to an unwarranted conclusion. Source: TRACK AND FIELD. To perform any of the many jumping events at a track meet: the high jump, long jump, triple jump, etc.

JUNKET   *to go on a junket.* To take a pleasure trip at taxpayers' expense. DA: 1886. Source: FISHING. SOED: M.E. To carry your "catch" of fish in a basket (Fren. *jonquette*). THT.

K

KAYO *to kayo something*. To defeat a plan or proposal. Source: BOXING. WNCD: 1920. To "kayo" your opponent; i.e., to knock your opponent down for the count of ten (a "knockout" or "K.O.") or to win the fight because your opponent is unable to continue (a "technical knockout" or "T.K.O."). LOS.

KEEL OVER *to keel over*. To fall down unconscious: to faint. DAE: 1832. Source: SAILING. SOED: 1828. For a sailboat to roll over, with the "keel" up. *Compare* Stay on an Even Keel.

KEEP A WEATHER EYE OPEN *to keep a weather eye open*. To be ever vigilant. Source: SAILING. To keep an eye on the weather. CI.

KEEPER *That's a keeper*. That's a good specimen—of manhood or womanhood. Source: FISHING. That's a legal-size fish—legal for "keeping."

KEEP IT UP *Keep it up*. Keep up the good work. Source: BADMINTON (Shuttlecock). Keep the "bird" or "shuttlecock" up in the air—the object of the games. CI. Badminton is played with a stringed racquet, shuttlecock with a paddle. This difference corresponds to the one between racquetball and paddleball.

KEEP PACE WITH *to keep pace with someone*. To keep up with someone's rate of activity or production. Source: RACING. To keep up with another runner in a race—matching them stride for stride. CI. In a harness race for "pacers," each horse must maintain the unusual left-side–right-side gait, or "pace," throughout the race. *See also* Change of Pace; Off the Pace; Pacemaker; Pacesetter; Put Someone through Their Paces; Set the Pace.

KEEP THE BALL ROLLING *to keep the ball rolling*. To keep up the momentum; to keep a conversation going. Source: ICE HOCKEY (Bandy). To keep the ball—not yet a puck—rolling, from player to player, toward the goal, in Bandy, the precursor of modern hockey. Bandy was a 16th-century Irish game, but this expression dates from the 1840s. HOI. Modern field hockey, which is also played with a ball, but on grass, probably most resembles Irish Bandy. CI, DOC, and SFS name soccer as the probable source of this term. *See also* Bandy about; Bandy-legged; Bandy Words. *Compare* Get the Ball Rolling.

KEEP TRACK OF   *to keep track of something/someone.* To pay attention to something, such as the time, or to keep in touch with a friend. Source: HUNT-ING. To follow the track of an animal. *Compare* Lose Track of.

KEEP YOUR EAR TO THE GROUND   *to keep your ear to the ground.* To stay alert and attentive. Source: HUNTING. For hunters (Native Americans) to use this technique for tracking large animals such as bison. CI.

KEEP YOUR EYE ON THE BALL   *to keep your eye on the ball.* To concentrate on the action at hand; to pay attention to what you're doing. DAE: 1907. Source: SPORTS. To keep your attention on the ball (etc.) rather than on the opposing players or the crowd or the goal. We suspect that the term originated in tennis; HTB suspects football; LTA suspects baseball.

KEEP YOUR HEAD ABOVE WATER   *to keep your head above water.* To barely survive, especially financially. DOC: 1742. Source: SWIMMING. To be barely avoiding drowning—by treading water or standing on your toes. DOC. *See also* Up to Your Ears; Up to Your Eyeballs; Up to Your Neck.

KETTLE OF FISH   *That's a pretty kettle of fish you've gotten us into.* That's a fine mess you've gotten us into. SOED: 1742. Source: FISHING. That's a fine mess of fish you've caught—enough to fill a kettle. Now, who's going to clean them? DOC; HOI; SOED; WPO.

KIBITZ   *to kibitz.* To offer unwanted advice. Source: CARD GAMES. For an onlooker at a card game to offer unwanted advice. *See also* Kibitzer.

KIBITZER   *a kibitzer.* Someone who offers unwanted advice. Source: CARD GAMES. WNCD: 1925. An onlooker at a card game who offers unwanted advice. WPO.

KICK AN IDEA AROUND   *to kick an idea around.* For a group of people to brainstorm an idea. LTA: 1947. Source: SOCCER. For a team of soccer players to kick the ball back and forth during a game or while warming up for one. SFS. *See also* Get a Kick out of.

KICK IN   *to kick in.* To contribute to a fund-raiser. WNCD: 1908. Source: SOCCER(?). To kick the ball into the goal. POKER(?). To "ante" into the "pot."

KICKOFF (adj.)   *a kickoff banquet (etc.).* A banquet or other celebration to mark the beginning of a fund-raiser or political campaign. Source: FOOT-BALL. DA: 1887. A kickoff is the kicking of the ball off the "tee" to the opposing team at the start of a game or half or after a score. SOED: rugby, 1857. *See also* Kick Off (v).

KICK OFF (v) *to kick off a campaign (etc.).* To inaugurate a campaign (etc.). Source: FOOTBALL. WNCD: 1857. To kick the football to the opposing team at the start of a game or half or after a score. *See also* Kickoff (adj.).

KILL TWO BIRDS WITH ONE STONE *to kill two birds with one stone.* To achieve two goals. with a single try. DOC: 1656. Source: HUNTING. To kill two birds with one stone from a sling or slingshot. DOC. *See also* Bird in the Hand; In at the Kill; Make a Killing.

KIND *See* Four of a Kind; Three of a Kind; Two of a Kind.

KINGPIN *a kingpin.* The key person in an organization. DAE: 1884. Often used pejoratively: a kingpin of the drug trade. Source: BOWLING. WNCD: 1801. The "headpin" or "centerpin" of a rack of bowling pins. DPF; LOS. *Compare* Mainstay.

KISS (n) *a kiss.* A light touch. Source: BILLIARDS. SOED: 1836. A light touch of one ball by another. DPF. Also used in bowling. *Compare* Carom (n).

KISS (v) *to kiss something.* To touch something lightly—e.g., for one car to "kiss" another. Source: BILLIARDS. SOED: 1579. For one ball to touch another ball lightly. DPF. Also used in bowling. *Compare* Carom (v).

KITE *See* Go Fly a Kite; High as a Kite; Higher Than a Kite.

KITTY *the kitty.* The till; the piggy bank. Source: POKER. WNCD: 1887. The money set aside from the "pot" for refreshments (in a friendly game); the percentage of the stakes set aside for the "house" (in a gambling casino). HTB.

KNOCK-DOWN-DRAG-OUT *a knock-down-drag-out fight.* A free-for-all; a brawl. WNCD: 1887. Source: BOXING. LTA: 1827. A rough-and-tumble fight in which one "knocked-down" boxer is "dragged-out" and replaced by another.

KNOCK 'EM DEAD *to knock 'em dead.* To score a stunning success. Source: BOXING. To knock an opponent unconscious: a "knockout" (q.v.) or "kayo" (q.v.). *See also* Dead as a Mackerel.

KNOCK INTO A COCKED HAT *to knock someone into a cocked hat.* To defeat someone soundly. Source: BOWLING. LTA: 1833. To knock down all of the pins except the corner pins of the triangle. DPF. The remaining corner pins resemble a Revolutionary War hat. HOI. There once was a variation of bowling that employed only the three corner pins. DA: 1858.

KNOCK IT OFF   *Knock it off!* Cut it out! Stop it! Source: CHILDREN'S GAMES. Knock that chip off your shoulder! *See also* Have a Chip on Your Shoulder.

KNOCK ON WOOD   *to knock on wood.* To rap your knuckles on the nearest piece of wood, so as to encourage the continuance of your good fortune. A superstition. Source: CARD GAMES(?). To rap your knuckles on the table to signal "Pass!" (in Knock Poker) or "Deal me another card" (in Blackjack). CHILDREN'S GAMES(?) To render yourself "safe" in a game of Wood Tag. HTB; WPO.

KNOCKOUT   *a knockout.* ("He's/she's a "knockout!"") He's a remarkably handsome man; she's a remarkably beautiful woman. ("He/she "knocks me out."") LTA: 1894. Source: BOXING. WNCD: 1887. A rendering senseless, at least for the count of ten, of your opponent. *Also:* "K.O." and "kayo." The *K* of K.O. is used by baseball fans in the bleachers to record the number of strikeouts issued by their favorite pitcher—on *K* cards. *See also* Don't Count Me Out; Down and Out; Knock Someone Cold; Win by a Knockout.

KNOCKOUT BLOW   *a knockout blow.* A stunning defeat of an opponent or an opponent's proposal. Source: BOXING. SOED: 1894. A blow that knocks an opponent unconscious or at least unable to rise before the count of ten. LOS. *Also:* a "knockout punch." LTA: 1890s.

KNOCKOUT DROPS   *knockout drops.* A spiked drink—a Mickey Finn, or Mickey. WNCD: 1895. Source: BOXING. A drink so powerful that it "knocks you out." WNCD: 1887.

KNOCK OUT OF THE BOX   *to knock someone out of the box.* To defeat an opponent, at least temporarily. Source: BASEBALL. For the team at bat to get so many hits and runs that the pitcher is removed. DPF; LOS; NDAS. *See also* Fast out of the Box; Out of the Box.

KNOCK SOMEONE COLD   *to knock someone cold.* To make a strong impression on someone, e.g., an audience. DA: 1942. Source: BOXING. LTA: 1896. To knock someone out, i.e., unconscious. CI. *See also* Knockout.

KNOCK SOMEONE FOR A LOOP   *to knock someone for a loop.* To shock or defeat someone. LTA: 1918. Source: BOXING. To knock someone into the shape of a knot, or "loop." *See also* Put Someone away.

KNOCK THE SPOTS OFF   *to knock the spots off someone/something.* To defeat a person or a proposal. DAE: 1861. Source: SHOOTING. To hit the spots—one-spot, two-spot, etc.—on a playing card used as a target. DOC. BOXING. LTA: 1850. To knock the freckles off your opponent. HTB; WPO.

KNOCK THE STUFFINGS OUT OF   *to knock the stuffings out of someone.* To defeat someone badly. Source: CHILDREN'S PLAY. For a child, in anger, to punch their stuffed toy until its cloth or sawdust stuffing falls out. CI. LTA: BOXING, 1883.

KNOCK YOURSELF OUT   *Don't knock yourself out!* Don't work too hard! Source: BOXING. Don't fight so hard that you cause your own defeat. (Advice from the "corner" person.)

KNOW THE ROPES   *to know the ropes.* (Often negative: "X doesn't know the ropes.") To know the ins and outs of a procedure. Source: SAILING. LTA: 1840. To know the functions of all of the ropes on a sailing vessel. CI. *See also* Rope Someone in.

KNOW THE SCORE   *to know the score.* (Often negative: "X doesn't know the score.") To be sophisticated and knowledgeable about something. Source: SPORTS. To know where you, or your team, stand at any given time during a game. CI. *Joke:* "I know the score of the game before it starts." "Oh, what is it?" "Nothing to nothing." *See also* But Who's Counting.

KNOW YOUR OATS   *to know your oats.* To know how to recognize talent. Source: HORSE RACING. To know how to pick a winning horse.

KNUCKLE DOWN   *to knuckle down.* To get down to business. WNCD: 1864. Source: MARBLES. SOED: 1740. To turn your shooting hand over so that the knuckles of your fingers are down and the "shooter" is in position to be snapped off your first finger by your thumb. DOC; HOI; WPO. *See also* Knuckle under.

KNUCKLE UNDER   *to knuckle under.* To give up or give in. WNCD: 1869. Source: MARBLES. SOED: 1740. To yield to an opponent's demand to shoot with the knuckles of your shooting hand resting on the ground. DOC; HOI. *See also* Knuckle down.

L

LAID LOW *to be laid low by the flu (etc.).* To be put out of action by influenza or some other illness. Source: BOXING. To be knocked flat on your back by a blow from your opponent. CI.

LAME DUCK *a lame duck.* A person who is near the end of their term of office and has no possibility of reappointment or reelection. DAE: 1863. Source: HUNTING. WNCD: 1761. The allusion is to a duck that has been shot, but not killed, by a hunter and has limited mobility and only a short time to live. DOC. *Compare* Sitting Duck.

LAND (v) *to land a job (etc.).* To get a job. Source: FISHING. SOED: 1613. To land a fish—i.e., bring a fish to land.

LAND ON YOUR FEET *to always land on your feet.* To always survive a potential disaster. Source: GYMNASTICS; ACROBATICS. To always complete a gymnastic routine by coming to a two-point landing. *Also:* for a cat to always land on its four feet, regardless of how it is held when dropped.

LARGE *See* By and Large; Loom Large.

LAURELS *See* Rest on Your Laurels.

LAY A GLOVE ON *They didn't lay a glove on you!* They didn't do you the least bit of harm. Source: BOXING. Your opponent didn't land a single blow on you. (Words of encouragement to a losing boxer.) LOS; SPD.

LAY AN EGG *to lay an egg.* To fail miserably. Source: CRICKET. To fail to score. The egg is a duck's egg, so called because of its resemblance to a zero *(O).* DOC; HOI; WPO. Called a goose egg in American baseball and love in tennis. *See also* Blank; Draw the Collar; Goose Egg; Love Game.

LAY DOWN SOME GROUND RULES *to lay down some ground rules.* To predetermine the parameters of an activity. Source: BASEBALL. To determine the local rules that will apply in a particular ballpark for a particular game. LOS. *See also* Ground Rules.

LAY IT ON THE LINE *to lay it on the line.* To speak frankly or bluntly. DOC: 1929. Source: GAMBLING. To lay your bet on the "sideline" in a crap game or on the counter of a betting window at a racetrack. CI; DOC. *See also* Lay Something on the Line; Put Your Money on the Line.

LAY ODDS *I'll lay you odds that something will happen.* I firmly believe that something will happen. Source: GAMBLING. I'd be willing to bet—and give you an advantage ("odds") if you accept the bet—that something that I consider a sure thing is going to happen. All senses of "odds" derive from betting. *See also* Odds.

LAY OF THE LAND *the lay of the land.* The conditions that prevail in a given situation. Source: SAILING. The characteristics of a coastline that provide information about location and landing. CI.

LAYOUT *the layout.* The arrangement of something—e.g., furniture in a room, rooms in a house, buildings on a lot, etc. DAE: 1869. Source: CARD GAMES. DAE: 1851. The arrangement of cards on the table, as for a game of solitaire.

LAY SOMETHING ON THE LINE *to lay something on the line.* To risk your job or your reputation. Source: GAMBLING. To lay your bet on the counter of a betting window at a racetrack. CI; DOC. *See also* Lay It on the Line; Put Your Money on the Line.

LAY YOUR CARDS ON THE TABLE *to lay your cards on the table.* To come clean, confess, tell it like it is. Source: CARD GAMES. To reveal all of the cards in your hand at the conclusion of the game, as in poker and gin rummy. DOC. *See also* Put Your Cards on the Table. *Compare* Stonewall.

LEAD FROM START TO FINISH *to lead from start to finish.* To be ahead in a contest all the way, from beginning to end. Source: RACING. DOC: 1868. To lead in a race from the starting line (or gate or pole) to the finish line. *Also:* "to trail from start to finish." *See also* In the Lead; Spot Someone a Lead; Take the Lead.

LEAD FROM WIRE TO WIRE *to lead from wire to wire.* To be ahead throughout an entire contest or campaign. Source: HORSE RACING. To lead a race from the first pass "under the wire" to the final pass (in races that begin in a "starting gate"). *See also* Go down to the Wire; Under the Wire.

LEADING LIGHT *a leading light.* The foremost person in a field. Source: SAILING. A light, as from a lighthouse or buoy, that "leads" vessels toward a safe harbor, or at least away from danger. CI.

LEAD WITH YOUR CHIN   *to lead with your chin*. To invite trouble. Source: BOXING. To stick out your chin and dare your opponent to hit it. (Not recommended.)

LEAGUE   *See* Big-League; Bush League; In the Wrong League; Major-League; Minor-League; Minor-Leaguer; Not in the Same League with; Out of Your League.

LEAPFROG   *to leapfrog (over) something*. To hurdle something. Source: CHILDREN'S GAMES (Leapfrog). Shakespeare, *Henry V,* 1599. To approach a bent-over person from behind, place your hands on their back, and "leap" over them in a straddle fashion. HF. HF believes that the bent-over person is the "leapfrog." *See also* Pinball.

LEAVE IN THE LURCH   *to leave someone in the lurch*. To abandon (desert, jilt) someone. SOED: 1584. Source: CARD GAMES. To double the score on a losing opponent. The expression is now used in cribbage but was originally applied to the 16th-century French game of *lourche,* which resembled backgammon. CI; DOC; HOI. *See also* Left in the Lurch.

LEFT AT THE POST   *to be left at the post*. To be left behind, probably for your own fault. Source: HORSE RACING. To be left at the "starting post" (now "starting gate"), probably because your horse wouldn't move. *Compare* Left in the Lurch.

LEFT HOLDING THE BAG   *to be left holding the bag*. To be left to take the blame. Source: CHILDREN'S GAMES (Snipe Hunt). To be left in the woods, at night, holding a bag, waiting for a nonexistent "snipe" to come along. A prank. HTB; NDAS. *Compare* Come away Empty-handed.

LEFT IN THE LURCH   *to be left in the lurch (waiting at the church)*. To be abandoned, deserted, jilted, or at any rate left helpless. Source: CARD GAMES. To have only half the score of your winning opponent; i.e., to be far behind at the end of the game. From the 16th-century French game of *lourche,* which resembled backgammon. The expression is still used in the game of cribbage. DOC; HOI. *See also* Leave in the Lurch. *Compare* High and Dry; Left at the Post.

LEG   *See* Get Your Sea Legs; Have Legs; One Leg at a Time; On the First/Last Leg of a Journey.

LEG UP   *to have (get, give someone) a leg up*. To get some help or have an advantage; to help someone else. DOC: 1837. Source: RIDING. To get an assist in mounting your horse. CI; DOC; DPF.

LET DOWN YOUR GUARD   *to let down your guard*. To relax your defenses. Source: BOXING; FENCING. To lower your gloves or foil. SOED. *See also* Drop Your Guard; Off Guard.

LET IT RIDE   *to let it ride.* To let it go; to leave it alone. Source: ROU-LETTE. To allow the winnings from one bet to become the stakes for the next. The use of the term "ride" alludes to the ball traveling around the wheel. *See also* Parlay.

LET SLIP THE DOGS OF WAR   *Let slip the dogs of war!* Shakespeare, *Julius Caesar,* 1599. Let the war begin! Source: DOG RACING. Release the greyhounds from the gates. DOC. This is a double allusion (to ARCHERY). It also refers to the release of the "dogs," or "catches," on the crossbows, allowing the strings to propel the bolts. *See also* Dogfight (n); War Games. *Compare* Screw Your Courage to the Sticking Point.

LET SOMEONE HAVE IT WITH BOTH BARRELS   *to let someone have it with both barrels.* To attack someone verbally and vociferously. Source: HUNTING. To fire both barrels of a shotgun—"over-and-under" or "side-by-side"—at a quarry such as a rabbit or a pheasant. *See also* Double-barreled; Give It to Someone with Both Barrels.

LET SOMEONE OFF THE HOOK   *to let someone off the hook.* To relieve someone from responsibility or blame. Source: FISHING. To release a fish from the hook and return it to the water. *See also* Get off the Hook; Off the Hook.

LET'S PLAY BALL   *Let's play ball!* Let's get started! Source: BASEBALL. From the umpire's cry of "Play ball!" at the start of a game. *See also* Play Ball.

LETTER   *to letter in something.* To specialize in something extracurricular in college—e.g., "girl/boy watching." Source: FOOTBALL. LTA: 1914. To receive a cloth letter, such as *U,* as a symbol of having made the football team. The tradition started at the University of Chicago. LTA. *See also* Earn a Letter.

LET THE CAT OUT OF THE BAG   *to let the cat out of the bag.* To accidentally reveal a secret. LTA: 1760. Source: CON GAMES. To let the pig out of the poke—i.e., to accidentally open the sack that supposedly contains a pig for sale at the market but that in reality contains a cat. DOC; DPF. *See also* Buy a Pig in a Poke.

LET THE GAMES BEGIN   *Let the games begin!* Let the party begin! Source: OLYMPIC GAMES. This exhortation is spoken by the president of the International Olympic Committee at the end of the opening ceremony of a Modern Olympiad, the revival of the ancient Greek Olympics in 1896.

LEVEL THE PLAYING FIELD   *to level the playing field.* To create fairer conditions for a competition: to even the odds. Source: FOOTBALL; SOC-CER. To mark off or lay out the field of play so that neither team has to start out running uphill.

LIE LOW   *to lie low.* To hide out; to keep a low profile. Source: HUNTING. DOC: 1880. To keep out of sight when pursuing a quarry.

LIFE IN THE FAST LANE   Life under extreme pressure and stress. Source: CAR RACING(?). The "fast" lane on an oval race track is the inside lane on the curve and the outside lane on the straightaway. The expression may just as well have come from highway driving, where the slower traffic, especially on hills, is instructed to stay in a certain lane or lanes.

LIFESAVER   *a lifesaver.* A friend in need. Source: SWIMMING. DAE: 1887. A lifeguard. SAILING. SOED: 1804. A life preserver. Lifesavers is the trademark of a candy shaped like a life preserver.

LIGHTWEIGHT   *a lightweight.* A person of little influence or importance. LTA: 1882. Source: BOXING. A boxer in the 127–135 pound class. LOS.

LIKE A FISH OUT OF WATER   *to be like a fish out of water.* To be totally out of place, out of your element. DOC: Early 1600s. Source: FISHING. To be like a fish that has been caught and is flopping around on land. DOC; HTB. *Compare* Round Peg in a Square Hole.

LIKE CATCHING A GREASED PIG   *Doing that is like catching (trying to catch) a greased pig.* Doing that is practically impossible. Source: CHILDREN'S GAMES. Doing that is like trying to catch a pig that has been covered with grease at a country fair. DPF.

LIKE DRAWING TO AN INSIDE STRAIGHT   *That's like drawing to an inside straight.* That's like trying to do something that is highly unlikely to succeed. Source: POKER. That's like trying to draw the single card that would complete the series consisting of *AB—DE* (e.g., 5,6—8,9, looking for a 7) in draw poker. *See also* Draw to an Inside Straight; Fill an Inside Straight; Like Trying to Fill an Inside Straight.

LIKE RATS LEAVING A SINKING SHIP   *to be like rats leaving a sinking ship.* To be starting to panic, as when a large number of employees begin to leave a failing business. Source: SAILING. It was once believed that rats know when a ship is going to sink and abandon it in haste before it does so. *See also* Rat Race; Ship of State.

LIKE SHOOTING FISH IN A BARREL   *like (as easy as) shooting fish in a barrel.* Too easy—no challenge. LTA: 1939. Source: SHOOTING. Freshly caught fish are sometimes put in a barrel of water to keep them alive until they're needed for eating. Shooting them under these conditions would be much too easy. This is probably not a real game, because you might also shoot holes in the barrel.

LIKE THE CUT OF SOMEONE'S JIB   *to like—or dislike—the cut of someone's jib.* To like—or dislike—someone's physical appearance. LTA: 1825.

Source: SAILING. The "jib" is a large, triangular, easily identifiable "fore-sail." HTB; WPO.

LIKE TRYING TO FILL AN INSIDE STRAIGHT *to be like trying to fill an inside straight.* To be practically impossible. Source: POKER. To be like trying to fill the hole in the center of a sequence of five cards: e.g., 5,6—8,9. *See also* Draw to an Inside Straight; Fill an Inside Straight; Like Drawing to an Inside Straight.

LOADED DICE *See* Play with Loaded Dice.

LOADED FOR BEAR *to be loaded for bear.* To be prepared for anything. Source: HUNTING. HTB: Mid-1800s. To have your rifle loaded for killing bear, even though you're hunting for something smaller.

LOADED QUESTION *a loaded question.* A question that, if answered, would force the answerer to reveal something that they would prefer not to: "Have you stopped beating your wife yet?" Source: CRAPS. "Loaded" is used here in the same sense as in "loaded dice," which are weighted in such a way that their score is predictable. CI. *See also* Play with Loaded Dice. *Compare* Dice Are Loaded against You.

LOADED TO THE GILLS *to be loaded to the gills.* To be falling-down drunk. SOED: 1890. Source: FISHING. To have drunk as much alcohol as a fish drinks water. WPO. *See also* Drink Like a Fish. *Compare* High as a Kite; Higher Than a Kite.

LOAD THE DICE *to load the dice against someone.* To put someone at a disadvantage in a competition. Source: DICE GAMES. To weight the dice so that they will almost always turn up in your favor. SOE. *See also* Dice Are Loaded against You; Play with Loaded Dice.

LOB *to lob something.* To throw something, such as a hand grenade, high and far, keeping the arm straight. Source: TENNIS. SOED: 1847. To hit a tennis ball high into the air and to the rear of your opponent's court. Also used in Cricket: "to make a slow, underhand throw." SOED.

LOCK, STOCK, AND BARREL *to be cleaned out lock, stock, and barrel.* To be cleaned out completely, e.g., by a robbery or fire. WNCD: 1842. Source: SHOOTING. To lose an entire firearm: the "lock" (the firing device), the "stock" (the wooden shoulder rest), and the "barrel." CI; DOC. Originally *"stock, lock* and barrel." *Compare* Hook, Line, and Sinker; Whole Shooting Match.

LOG *See* As Easy as Falling off a Log.

LOGGERHEADS *See* At Loggerheads.

LONG IN THE TOOTH *to be long in the tooth.* To be old. WPO: 1852. Source: HORSE RACING. For a horse to be judged old on the basis of its receding gums. CI. *See also* Don't Look a Gift Horse in the Mouth.

LONG ODDS *to have long odds.* To have little chance of success. Source: GAMBLING; BETTING. The greater the ratio between the first number and the second—e.g. 50 to 1—the less chance there is (1 in 50) of winning, according to the handicappers. DPF. *See also* Odds; Overcome Long Odds.

LONG SHOT *a long shot.* A risky investment. Immediate Source: GAMBLING; BETTING. A bet, e.g., on a horse, that has little chance of paying off. FP. Ultimate Source: SHOOTING. A long-distance shot with little chance of hitting the target. DOC. *See also* Not by a Long Shot.

LONG SUIT *your long suit.* Your strength, forte, specialty. DOC: 1903. Source: CARD GAMES. WNCD: 1876. The large number of cards in your hand of the same ''suit'' (spades, clubs, hearts, diamonds), which can lead to a high bid and many points. DOC. *See also* Strong Suit.

LOOK WHAT THE CAT DRAGGED IN *Well, look what the cat dragged in!* Look who just walked in! Source: HUNTING. Look at what the family cat hunted, caught, killed, and brought home to show us.

LOOM LARGE *to loom large.* To become increasingly important or threatening. Source: SAILING. For a shadowy figure, such as a rock, an iceberg, or another vessel, to come suddenly into view in the fog or darkness. CI.

LOOSE *See* Hang Loose; Play Fast and Loose; Tie Up Some Loose Ends.

LOSE *See* Can't Win for Losing; Heads I Win, Tails You Lose; Play a Losing Game; Win a Few, Lose a Few; Win, Lose, or Draw; Win or Lose.

LOSE TRACK OF *to lose track of something or someone.* To lose contact or be out of touch with something or someone. DA: 1871. Source: HUNTING. To lose the trail of a hunted animal. CI. *Compare* Keep Track of.

LOSE YOUR BEARINGS *to lose your bearings.* To become lost or disoriented. Source: SAILING. To lose track of your position relative to other objects or the compass. CI; LTA. The compass is also used in hunting, hiking, etc. *See also* Bearing Down on. *Compare* Get Your Bearings.

LOSE YOUR GRIP *to lose your grip.* (''You're losing your grip.'') To lose your command or control over something. DAE: 1876. Source: WRESTLING. To lose the strength in your grip. CI.

LOSE YOUR MARBLES *to lose (all) your marbles.* To become mentally incompetent. Source: MARBLES. To have (all) your marbles shot from the circle by your opponent.

LOSE YOUR TOUCH   *to lose your touch.* ("You're losing your touch.") To become less skillful at something. Source: SPORTS. To lose your sense of how hard to hit the ball—in "finesse" games such as billiards, pool, and golf.

LOT   *a lot of trouble, money, pain, etc.* More than your share of trouble (etc.). Source: DRAWING LOTS. WNCD: 12th cent. All senses of "lot" derive from the drawing of "lots": i.e., extracting tokens of different value from a container. The practice is ancient. *See also* Cast in Your Lot; Have a Lot on the Ball.

LOTTERY   *See* Win the Lottery.

LOVE GAME   *a love game.* ("It was a love game.") No contest. Source: TENNIS. A game won by the score of 45 to 0. The *0* is "love": from the French *l'oeuf,* "the egg." In cricket, a zero is called a duck's egg; in baseball it is a goose egg. WPO. *See also* Blank; Draw the Collar; Goose Egg; Lay an Egg; Shutout.

LOW BLOW   *a low blow.* An unfair action or remark. WNCD: 1952. Source: BOXING. An illegal blow below the belt. SFS. *See also* Hit below the Belt.

LOWER THE BOOM   *to lower the boom.* To get tough. Immediate Source: BOXING. To throw a knockout punch. NDAS. Ultimate Source: SAILING. To lower the pole that anchors the bottom of a sail. WPO.

LUCK   *See* Out of Luck; Press Your Luck; Stroke of Good Luck; Try Your Luck at Something.

LUCK OF THE DRAW   *the luck of the draw.* Fate; fortune. Source: DRAWING LOTS. The luck associated with drawing lots from a container that may hold only one lucky number (color, length, shape, size, etc.). POKER. The expression is also used in "draw" poker, where up to three of the five cards may be discarded and new ones "drawn." *See also* Down on Your Luck.

LURCH   *See* Leave in the Lurch; Left in the Lurch.

LURE (n)   *a lure.* A strong attraction or temptation. WNCD: 14th cent. Immediate Source: FISHING. An artificial bait designed to attract fish. Ultimate Source: FALCONRY. A bait, on the end of a string, used to recall the hawk.

LURE (v)   *to lure someone somewhere.* To lead someone into a trap. Source: FALCONRY. WNCD: 14th cent. To recall the hawk by twirling a lure.

M

MAIN EVENT *the main event.* The main attraction. Source: BOXING. LTA: 1920s. The principal match of a series of boxing matches on one "card." LOS.

MAINSTAY *the mainstay of an organization or operation.* The primary supporter of a group or venture. SOED: 1787. Source: SAILING. SOED: 1485. The rope from the bow of a vessel to the mainmast, serving as the primary support of the latter. LTA. *Compare* Headline; Kingpin.

MAINSTREAM *in the mainstream.* In accord with the majority viewpoint, behavior, culture, etc. WNCD: 1831. Source: BOATING. In the center of the river or stream, where the current is swiftest and the most progress can be made by a boat going downstream. WNWD. *Also:* "to mainstream."

MAJOR-LEAGUE *a major-league effort or performance.* A first-class effort or performance. Source: BASEBALL. LTA: 1882. An effort or performance that is characteristic of the major leagues—the "big" leagues of baseball (the American League and the National League)—as opposed to one characteristic of the "minor" leagues (the "farm" clubs). LOS. *See also* Not in the Same League with.

MAKE A BID FOR SOMETHING *to make a bid for something.* To become a candidate for office, a job, etc. Source: BRIDGE. To make a declaration of the number of "tricks" in a particular suit (or "no trump") that you hope to take in the next hand. *See also* Bid. *Compare* Enter the Lists; Throw Your Hat in the Ring.

MAKE A CLEAN BREAK *to make a clean break.* To separate yourself completely from another person, an addiction, a job, etc. Source: BOXING. To separate yourself physically from your opponent—either voluntarily or by orders of the referee.

MAKE A COMEBACK   *to make a (remarkable) comeback.* To make a remarkable recovery. Source: BOXING. To make a remarkable recovery from a knockdown or from an undistinguished series of earlier rounds. SFS.

MAKE A HIT   *to make a hit with someone.* To get along well with a new acquaintance; to make a good impression on someone. Source: BASEBALL. DAE: 1875. To strike the ball safely with the bat. *See also* Hit (n).

MAKE A KILLING   *to make a killing.* To make a lot of money on an investment—e.g., in the stock market. Source: HORSE RACING. To win a lot of money at the racetrack. CI. *See also* Kill Two Birds with One Stone.

MAKE A MISCUE   *to make a miscue.* To make a mistake. Source: BILLIARDS. SOED: 1873. To fail to strike the cue ball solidly with the cue stick—usually not because there is insufficient chalk on the cue tip, though that is what often gets the blame. *See also* Miscue.

MAKE A PASS AT   *to make a pass at someone.* To make a physical or verbal sexual advance toward someone. Source: FENCING. To make a thrust at your opponent with a rapier or foil. CI. *See also* Thrust. *Compare* Pass (v).

MAKE A PLAY FOR   *to make a play for someone.* To attempt to gain the affections of someone. Source: CHESS. To execute a prearranged strategy—a "gambit" (q.v.). CI.

MAKE A POINT   *to make a point of something.* To make it a habit to do something—e.g., to be on time. Source: SHOOTING(?). To hit the target—the "mark" or "point." CRAPS(?). To throw the same combination as the one thrown previously—the "point": 3, 5, 6, 8, 9, or 10. *See also* Beside the Point; Come to the Point.

MAKE A RUN AT   *to make a run at something.* To try for a position, run for an office, etc. Source: POOL(?). To pocket a string of balls without missing or "scratching." FOOTBALL(?). To carry the ball toward the opponent's goal line. *Compare* Run-in.

MAKE A SPLASH   *to make a (big) splash.* To draw a lot of attention to yourself. Source: DIVING. To belly flop into the water, causing a big splash and drawing attention to yourself.

MAKE BOOK ON   *to make book on something.* To regard something as a sure thing. Source: GAMBLING. For a bookmaker (or "bookie") to take bets on something. WPO. *Compare* Have the Book on Someone.

MAKE GREAT STRIDES   *to make great strides.* To make considerable progress. Source: RACING. For a person, horse, dog, etc. to stretch out its legs, lengthen its pace, and make great progress. CI. *See also* Take Something in Stride.

MAKE HEADWAY *to make headway.* To make progress. Source: SAIL-ING. To make *forward* progress. CI. *Compare* Give Someone Some Leeway.

MAKE NO BONES ABOUT IT Without any doubt. ("The Democrats are going to win, make no bones about it.") Source: CRAPS. Without any urging of the dice (the "bones") to turn up favorably. DOC; DPF; WPO. CI indicates that the bones are soupbones. *See also* Make No Bones about Something; Make No Bones about Wanting to Do Something.

MAKE NO BONES ABOUT SOMETHING *to make no bones about something.* To offer no objection to something; to do something without delay. ("She made no bones about accepting the presidency.") Source: CRAPS. To have no need to urge the dice to turn up in your favor. DOC; DPF. The earliest dice, perhaps 3,000 B.C., were made of bone. *See also* Make No Bones about It; Make No Bones about Wanting to Do Something.

MAKE NO BONES ABOUT WANTING TO DO SOMETHING *to make no bones about wanting to do something.* To withhold no feelings about want-ing to do something. ("She made no bones about wanting to be president.") Source: CRAPS. To feel no need to urge the dice to turn up in your favor. *See also* Make No Bones about It; Make No Bones about Something.

MAKE SOMEONE EAT YOUR DUST *to make someone eat your dust.* To pull ahead of someone in a competition or campaign. Source: RACING. To pull into the lead in a race and make the other competitors run in the dust kicked up by your horse's hooves or your car's tires.

MAKE SPORT *to make sport of someone.* To make fun of someone. Source: SPORTS. To treat someone as if they were live game taken in the sport of hunting and then "badgered." *See also* Badger; Bad Sport; Good Sport; Spoil-sport.

MAKE THE CUT *to make the cut.* To survive the elimination process and become a member of a group. Source: SPORTS. To survive the tryouts and be named a member of a team (baseball, football, etc.); to score well enough on the first two days to be allowed to play on the last two (GOLF). LOS.

MAKE THE RIGHT CALL *to make the right call.* To make the right de-cision. Source: BASEBALL. For the umpire to make the right judgment: "safe or out," "fair or foul," "ball or strike," etc. *See also* Call 'Em as You See 'Em; Judgment Call.

MAKE THE TEAM *to make the team.* To be selected as a member of a select group or organization. Source: SPORTS. To become a member of a team in football, baseball, basketball, etc. *See also* Team Player.

MAKE TRACKS *to make tracks for someplace.* To set out for someplace in a hurry. DA: 1827. Source: HUNTING. For an animal to flee from a hunter, leaving only its tracks behind. DOC. *Compare* Cover Up Your Tracks.

MAKE UP FOR LOST TIME *to make up for lost time.* To work harder in order to get back on the prearranged schedule. Source: FOOT RACING(?). To run harder in order to compensate for a hesitation or delay.

MAKE UP GROUND *to make up ground.* To gain on your opponent or your objective. Source: FOOT RACING. To gain on a runner who is ahead of you.

MAKE WAVES *to make waves.* (Often neg.: "Don't make waves!") To cause or start trouble. Source: BOATING. To operate a boat in such a way that it creates waves and interferes with other boaters and swimmers.

MAKE YOUR MARK *to make your mark.* To become successful and famous. DAE: 1854. Source: SHOOTING(?). To hit the target, the "mark." Graffiti is just as likely a source: "Kilroy was here."

MAKE YOUR MOVE *to make your move.* ("When are you going to make your move?") To take deliberate action. Source: CHESS; CHECKERS. To move your chesspiece or checker. *See also* Move.

MAKE YOUR POINT *to make your point.* ("Okay, you've made your point!") To argue or debate an issue. Source: CRAPS(?). To throw the same combination as the one previously thrown—the "point": 4, 5, 6, 8, 9, or 10. SHOOTING(?). To hit the target, or the center of the target.

MALL *a mall; a shopping mall.* A large shopping center, originally outdoors (e.g., a street with many shops, closed off to vehicular traffic) but now also enclosed. Source: PALL-MALL. WNCD: 1644. The game of pall-mall was introduced from the European continent to London in the mid-17th century, in St. James's Park. The "mall" was a mallet, and the "pall" was a wooden ball. The object of the game was to hit the ball through a ring suspended at the end of the "alley," which was renamed Pall-Mall. DPF; THT; WPO. The name of the game is sometimes pronounced "pell-mell" (q.v.).

MANO A MANO One on one (Span. "hand to hand"): in direct competition. Source: BULLFIGHTING. The pitting of one bullfighter against only one other (three bulls apiece), rather than the usual three bullfighters competing against each other (with two bulls apiece). *Compare* One-on-one.

MARATHON *a marathon meeting (etc.).* An extremely long, seemingly endless meeting—e.g., a "marathon bargaining session." Source: FOOT RACING. A footrace of 26 miles and 385 yards (set in 1924), much or all of it outside a stadium. OLYMPIC GAMES. The marathon was instituted in the first Modern Olympics in 1896 and was not part of the ancient Olympics. The name comes from the Battle of Marathon (490 B.C.), the victory of which (Greeks over Persians) was announced by a runner (from Marathon to Athens, about 20 miles), who then purportedly fell dead. DPF. This word is the basis for the formation of such words as "telethon," "sellathon," "phonathon," etc.

MARBLES *See* Go for All the Marbles; Lose Your Marbles; Marble-size Hail; Not Have All Your Marbles; Pick Up Your Marbles and Go Home.

MARBLE-SIZE HAIL Small-size hail—larger than pea-size but smaller than walnut-size, in the old terminology. Formerly called mothball-size hail. Source: MARBLES. Hail the size of marbles, which vary from approximately a half inch to three quarters of an inch (a "shooter") in diameter. *See also* Baseball-size Hail; Golf Ball-size Hail; Softball-size Hail.

MARK (n) *See* Easy Mark; Fall Short of the Mark/Target; Make Your Mark; Miss Your Mark; Not up to the Mark; Off the Mark; Quick off the Mark; Wide of the Mark.

MARKER *See* Call in a Marker.

MATCHUP *a good matchup.* A good pairing of opponents who are of equal ability. Source: BOXING. WNCD: 1964. A good pairing of boxers of equal ability, weight, height, reach, etc. *See also* Evenly Matched.

MEAL TICKET *your meal ticket.* Your primary source of income or support. WNCD: 1899. Source: BASEBALL. The ticket that was once given to ballplayers for one free meal at a restaurant. LOS. *See also* Franchise.

MEET YOUR MATCH *to meet your match.* To be confronted with a situation that is more than you can handle. Source: BOXING. To be pitted against a better boxer than you are. *Also:* "to finally meet your match."

MENTAL GYMNASTICS Exercise of the mind. Source: GYMNASTICS. SOED: 1710. Gymnastics is exercise of the body, as in a "gymnasium," where Greek athletes once exercised naked *(gymnos).*

MERRY-GO-ROUND *See* On a Merry-go-round.

MILE *See* Go the Extra Mile; Miss by a Country Mile; Miss Is as Good as a Mile.

MIND LIKE A STEEL TRAP *to have a mind like a steel trap.* To have a mind that misses nothing and retains everything. (Often said facetiously.) Source: TRAPPING. To have a mind like a steel-jawed trap that seizes and holds any medium- to large-size animal that "springs" it.

MINOR-LEAGUE *a minor-league effort or performance.* A mediocre effort or performance. DA: 1948. Source: BASEBALL. DA: 1889. An effort or performance characteristic of the "minor," rather than the "major," leagues of baseball. *See also* Bush (adj.); Bush League; Minor-leaguer; Not in the Same League with; Sent down to the Minors.

MINOR-LEAGUER *a minor-leaguer.* A person of minor importance. DA: 1906. Source: BASEBALL. LTA: 1882. A player from a "minor" league, an organization of "farm" clubs and independent teams, classified as *AAA* ("Triple A''—the highest), *AA* (''Double A''), and *A* (''Single A''—the lowest, sometimes called the ''bush'' league). The classifications were originally *A, B, C,* and *D.* LOS.

MISCUE *a miscue.* A mistake. Source: BILLIARDS. SOED: 1873. A failure to strike the cue ball solidly with the cue stick: ''miss'' plus ''cue.'' *See also* Make a Miscue.

MISMATCH *a mismatch.* A confrontation between two unequal opponents. Source: BOXING. A pairing of boxers of unequal ability, weight, height, reach, etc.

MISS BY A COUNTRY MILE *to miss by a country mile.* To guess completely wrong. Source: SHOOTING. To miss a target by as far as you can see. *Compare* Never Miss a Trick.

MISS IS AS GOOD AS A MILE *A miss is as good as a mile.* A proverb. Failure is failure, any way you look at it. DOC: 1821. Source: SHOOTING. Missing a target is missing a target—whether by a little bit or a lot (a ''mile''). DOC.

MISS THE POINT *to miss the point.* To misunderstand. Source: SHOOTING. To fail to hit the center of the target (the ''point'').

MISS YOUR MARK *to miss your mark.* To fail to achieve your goal. Source: SHOOTING. To fail to hit the target, or the center of the target.

MIXED BAG *a mixed bag.* A mixture of good and bad. WNCD: 1926. Source: HUNTING. A mixed bag of game, representing different species. CI.

MIX IT UP *to mix it up.* To intensify an argument. Source: BOXING. LTA: 1905. To intensify the action of a boxing match. LOS.

MOMENT OF TRUTH *the moment of truth.* The critical test of character or ability. WNCD: 1691. Source: BULLFIGHTING. The moment at which the matador thrusts home the final sword to kill the bull. CI; DOC.

MONDAY-MORNING QUARTERBACK *a Monday-morning quarterback.* A second-guesser. WNCD: 1941. Source: FOOTBALL. An unqualified critic who second-guesses the strategy of the weekend football game on the following Monday. DOC; LOS; SFS; WPO. *See also* Armchair Quaterback; Quarterback.

MONEY *See* Even Money; Finish out of the Money; In the Money; Play with House Money; Put Your Money on the Line; Put Your Money Where Your Mouth Is; Right on the Money; Run for the Money; Smart Money.

MORE FISH IN THE OCEAN *There are plenty more fish in the ocean.* There are other, more promising opportunities that will arise. Source: FISHING. That fish got away, but there will be plenty of chances to catch another one. CI. *Also:* "You're not the only fish in the ocean." *See also* Have Other Fish to Fry.

MORE THAN ONE WAY TO SKIN A CAT *There's more than one way to skin a cat.* A proverb. There's more than one way to do just about everything. DOC: 1830s. Source: GYMNASTICS. There's more than one way to execute the movement called "Skin a Cat"—i.e., to hang from a bar, pass your body between your arms, and wind up facing in the same direction. In fact, there are only *two* ways to do that—forward or backward.

MOUNT A FULL-COURT PRESS *to mount a full-court press.* To make an all-out effort for or against something. Source: BASKETBALL. For the team on defense to guard the offensive players over the entire ("full") floor ("court"), not just in front of their own basket. EOD; OL; SPD.

MOUSE *See* Play Cat and Mouse; When the Cat's away, the Mice Will Play.

MOUTH *See* Don't Look a Gift House in the Mouth; Put Your Money Where Your Mouth Is; Shoot Off Your Mouth; Straight from the Horse's Mouth.

MOVE *to make a good/bad move.* ("That was the best/worst move I ever made.") To make a smart or dumb decision. Source: CHESS; CHECKERS. WNCD: 1656. To make a smart or dumb move of your chesspiece or checker, one that could contribute to winning or losing the game. *See also* All the Right Moves; Make Your Move; Your Move.

MOXIE *See* Have a Lot of Moxie.

MUDDY THE WATER *to muddy the water(s).* To confuse the issue. DOC: 1837. Source: FISHING. To stir up the water of the stream in which others are trying to "fly-fish." DOC.

MUDSLINGING Hurling disparaging remarks at someone. WNCD: 1890. Source: CHILDREN'S PLAY(?). Throwing mud at your playmates.

MUFF *to muff something.* To bungle something—e.g., your lines in a play. WNCD: 1827. Source: CRICKET. To mishandle a ball as if your glove were a "muffin." WNWD indicates BASEBALL.

MUSICAL CHAIRS *See* Play Musical Chairs.

MY BALL *It's my ball.* I can do anything I want to: I own the tools. Source: BASEBALL; FOOTBALL. It's *my* ball, so you'd better give me my way or I'll leave, and take *my* ball with me. *Compare* Your Ball Game.

N

NAME OF THE GAME   *That's the name of the game.* That's what its all about. WNCD: 1966. Source: SPORTS; GAMES. That's the object of the game—to put the puck in the net, the football in the end zone, the home run in the stands, etc. DOC; FP; SPD. *Joke:* "What's the name of the game?" "Gin." "That's right: Gin!"

NATURAL   *a natural.* A born winner. DA: 1925. Source: CRAPS. A winning combination of 7 or 11 on the first throw of the dice. DA. In blackjack or "21" it is an ace and a 10.

NECK AND NECK   *to be neck and neck.* To be tied for the lead. WNCD: 1799. Source: HORSE RACING. To be tied for the lead in a horse race. CI. *See also* Up to Your Neck.

NET (v)   *to net a criminal.* To catch a criminal. SOED: 1801. Source: FISHING. To net a fish—to catch a fish in a net. *See also* Throw a Net over.

NETWORK   *a network.* An organization of units (as in radio and TV "networks") or of individuals (as in "spy network" or "old-boy network"). Source: FISHING. WNCD: 1560. A net, or series of nets, for catching fish without catching water.

NEVER GIVE A SUCKER AN EVEN BREAK   Never pass up an opportunity to take advantage of someone. Attributed to W. C. Fields. WPO: 1923. Source: POOL. Never give a novice a chance to win. *See also* Sucker. *Compare* Nice Guys Finish Last.

NEVER MISS A TRICK   *for someone to never miss a trick.* For someone to be very resourceful at capitalizing on every opportunity. Source: BRIDGE. For someone to take every trick in a hand of bridge—and to do it habitually. CI. *See also* Every Trick in the Book. *Compare* Miss by a Country Mile.

NEW DEAL   *the New Deal.* Franklin Delano Roosevelt's economic recovery program in the 1930s. WNCD. Source: POKER. The dispensing ("dealing") of cards at the start of a new hand or game. EOD; SOE; SPD; WPO. *Also:* Theodore Roosevelt's "Square Deal," Harry S. Truman's "Fair Deal." The phrase originated in Mark Twain's *Connecticut Yankee* in 1899. *See also* Fair Deal; Raw Deal.

NIBBLE *See* Get a Nibble.

NICE GUYS FINISH LAST Success is based on accomplishments, not personality. A modern maxim. Source: BASEBALL. Winning is the name of the game. Attributed to Leo Durocher. FP: 1940s. *Compare* Finish out of the Money; Never Give a Sucker an Even Break.

NINETEENTH HOLE *the nineteenth hole.* The bar. Source: GOLF. The "watering hole" after a round of eighteen holes of golf.

NIP AND TUCK *to be nip and tuck.* To be too close to call—e.g., an election. WNCD: 1832. Source: HORSE RACING. DAE: 1836. For the leading horses to be running neck and neck. FENCING. For the two opponents to be nipping ("nicking") each other with their swords ("tucks"). WPO.

NO CONTEST *It was no contest.* It was a piece of cake. Source: SPORTS. It was a lopsided victory. *See also* Win in a Walkover.

NO DICE *No dice!* Nothing doing! Source: CRAPS. Your last throw of the dice is disallowed.

NO GO *That's a no go.* That's unacceptable. DAE: 1835. Source: FOOT RACING. That's a false start—first "Go!" then "No go!" (or one pistol shot following another). The expression was adopted by NASA and popularized by them. *See also* False Start; From the Word Go; On the Go.

NO GREAT SHAKES *He's no great shakes as a politician (etc.).* He's not a very good politician (etc.). DOC: 1819. Source: DICE GAMES. His chances of success are no better than a shake of the dice in a tumbler. CI; DOC; DPF; HTB. *See also* Tinhorn.

NO HOLDS BARRED No restrictions or limitations. WNCD: 1942. Source: WRESTLING. Freestyle wrestling, in which no holds are forbidden, as opposed to Greco-Roman style, which is more rigidly regulated. CI. *Compare* Rough-and-tumble.

NO PAIN, NO GAIN No struggle, no progress. Source: SPORTS (esp. Football). A coach's rationalization for the necessity of grueling workouts and all-out efforts. Also used in bodybuilding.

NO RUNS, NO HITS, NO ERRORS No results; no luck. Source: BASEBALL. Nothing accomplished by a team in a particular inning (or game), as recorded in the "line score" on the scoreboard and in the newspapers. *See also* Hit (n).

NOSEDIVE (n)   *See* Take a Nosedive.

NOSE SOMEONE OUT   *to nose someone out.* To defeat someone by the narrowest of margins. Source: HORSE RACING. For a horse to win a race by the length of its nose. FP.

NO-SHOW   *a no-show.* Someone who doesn't appear as scheduled—e.g., for a plane, a meeting, etc. WNCD: 1941. Source: HORSE RACING. A horse that doesn't finish in at least third place in a race. SPORTS. A season-ticket holder who doesn't appear for a particular game. WNCD. *Compare* Show.

NO SKIN OFF MY NOSE   *That's no skin off my nose.* That doesn't affect or concern me in the least. DOC: 1920s. Source: BOXING. That blow didn't affect me in the least. It didn't even take any skin off my nose. DOC.

NOT ACCORDING TO HOYLE   *That's not according to Hoyle.* That's not according to the rules; that's not fair. Source: CARD GAMES. That's not according to the rules set down in 1742 by Edmond Hoyle, the leading authority on card games, in *A Short Treatise on the Game of Whist,* and in later rule books written by him and by other codifiers who used the name Hoyle. DOC; DPF; HOI. *See also* Every Trick in the Book. *Compare* Not Cricket.

NOT ALL FUN AND GAMES   *It's not all fun and games.* It's not as easy as it looks; it's not a glamorous occupation. Source: GAMES. It's not just amusement or play. *See also* Fun and Games.

NOT BY A LONG SHOT   *"You don't think X is going to win?" "No, not by a long shot."* X doesn't have a chance. Source: SHOOTING. A "long shot" is one which, because of the distance, is not very likely to hit the target. DOC. *See also* Long Shot.

NOT CRICKET   *That's not cricket.* That's not according to the rules; that's not fair. Source: CRICKET. SOED: 1902. That's not according to the rules of cricket. DOC. The game of cricket goes back to at least 1600. *Compare* Dirty Pool; Not According to Hoyle.

NOT FIT TO HOLD A CANDLE TO   *X can't hold a candle to Y.* X is vastly inferior to Y. Source: DICE GAMES. Mid-16th cent. X is not a fit enough dice player to hold a candle for the rest of the players to see by. CI indicates the source is "work," not "games."

NOT HAVE ALL YOUR MARBLES   *to not have all your marbles.* To be mentally deficient. Source: MARBLES. To have had all of your marbles shot from the circle by your opponent—or simply to have misplaced some of them.

NOT HAVE BOTH OARS IN THE WATER   *to not have both oars in the water.* To be mentally deficient. Source: BOATING. To be going around in circles. It is impossible to maneuver a rowboat with only one oar. *See also* Not Rowing with Both Oars.

NOT IN THE CARDS *It's not in the cards.* It's not destined or fated to happen. Source: CARD GAMES. This expression probably derives from telling fortunes with Tarot cards, which were themselves used in the 14th century for playing a game called Tarot.

NOT IN THE SAME LEAGUE WITH   *X is not in the same league with Y.* X is not as talented as Y. Source: BASEBALL. X belongs in the "minor" leagues rather than the "majors." *See also* Major-league; Minor-leaguer.

NOT MANY CARDS LEFT TO PLAY   *There aren't many cards left to play.* There aren't many options left to choose from. Source: CARD GAMES. There aren't many cards left in my hand. (This is a *good* sign in some card games.)

NOT OUT OF THE WOODS YET   *We're not out of the woods yet.* We shouldn't get our hopes too high: our problems are not completely solved yet. Source: HUNTING; HIKING. We're no longer lost, but we're still in the woods.

NOT PLAYING WITH A FULL DECK   *X isn't playing with a full deck.* X must be mentally deficient. Source: CARD GAMES. X is playing solitaire with a short deck. (There's no way X can win.) *Compare* Not Rowing with Both Oars.

NOT ROWING WITH BOTH OARS   *X isn't rowing with both oars.* X must be mentally deficient. Source: BOATING; ROWING. X is rowing with only one oar, causing the boat to go around in circles. *See also* Not Have Both Oars in the Water; Row with Only One Oar. *Compare* Not Playing with a Full Deck.

NOT UP TO SCRATCH   *This work is not up to scratch.* This work is not up to the expected standards of quality. LTA: 1839. Source: BOXING. A boxer who was "not up to scratch" in the early 19th century was not up to the line, scratched in the dirt, at which boxers started the match and to which they were to return after a knockdown (i.e., at the end of a round). CI; DOC; DPF; SFS. The starting line for all sorts of races, including horse races, was once scratched in the dirt also. LTA: 1821. *See also* Not up to the Mark; Set-to. *Compare* Start from Scratch.

NOT UP TO THE MARK   Not up to the required standard. Source: BOXING. Not back to the line ("mark"), scratched in the dirt in the center of the "ring" of spectators, after a knockdown. *See also* Not up to Scratch.

NOT WORTH THE GAMBLE   *It's not worth the gamble.* It's not worth the risk. Source: GAMBLING. The wager is not likely to pay off, i.e., return more than the original bet, if that. *See also* Gamble Away.

NO-WIN SITUATION   *a no-win situation.* A situation from which neither side can benefit or in which a judgment is not acceptable to either side. Source:

GAMES. A situation in which neither opponent can win the game: a "stale-mate" (q.v.).

NUMBER ONE   *We're number one!* We're the best!. WNCD: 1839. Source: SPORTS. We're the champions! (or are going to *be* the champions). NDAS. This exclamation is often accompanied, in the United States, by raising the first finger in the air—and in Europe by giving a "thumbs up" sign, the European version of "one." *Compare* A-number-one.

NUMBERS GAME   *to play the numbers game.* To use numbers or figures misleadingly, especially in advertising and politics. Source: GAMBLING; BETTING. To conduct an illegal lottery, the "numbers racket," which takes small bets on series of numbers that appear in certain sections of that day's newspaper. SPD. *See also* Your Number Is up.

O

OAR *See* Have Only One Oar in the Water; Not Have Both Oars in the Water; Not Rowing with Both Oars; Rest on Your Oars; Row with Only One Oar.

ODDBALL *an oddball.* A weird or eccentric person. WNCD: 1945. Source: POOL. A pool ball with an odd number: 1, 3, 5, 7, 9, 11, 13, 15.

ODD MAN OUT *the odd man out.* The person who is left out of something—e.g., the losing candidate in a run-off election. DOC: 1889. Source: COINS. The one eliminated from further participation in a game of matching coins. If two of three players toss "heads," the one who tosses "tails" is the "odd man out." This is now a convenient way of determining who will be left off a team, but originally it was simply a coin-toss game in which the *winner* was the one out of three who did not match the other two. CI; DOC.

ODDS *The odds are that . . .* The chances are that . . . Source: GAMBLING; BETTING. SOED: 1589. The "odds"—the chances of winning, as established by the odds makers—predict that . . . *See also* Against All Odds; Beat the Odds; By All Odds; Lay Odds; Long Odds; Overcome Long Odds.

ODDS ARE AGAINST *The odds are against something.* The chances of something succeeding are not favorable. Source: GAMBLING; BETTING. The chances of winning—the "odds"—have been determined by the odds makers (or handicappers) to be slim: e.g., 50 to 1 against.

ODDS MAKERS *according to the odds makers.* According to the political analysts. Source: GAMBLING; BETTING. According to the handicappers, who establish "odds" (chances of winning) in horse races and other sporting events.

ODDS-ON FAVORITE *an odds-on favorite.* A very heavy favorite. WNCD: 1890. Source: GAMBLING; BETTING. A contestant whom the handicappers have established as having the best chance of winning: "The odds are on X to win." The expression may have originated in betting on horse races. *Also:* an "odds-on bet."

-OFF   *a bake-off, cook-off, etc.* A competition to determine the best performer in a particular activity. Source: SPORTS. From "play-off." LTA: 1933. A play-off is a tournament to determine either an overall winner or a winner that will proceed to the championship tournament (as in the American and National League play-offs). *See also* Battle Royal; Play-off.

OFF AND RUNNING   *They're off and running.* The competition has begun. DOC: 1967. Source: HORSE RACING. "They're off and running," or at least "They're off," is the announcement by the person who "calls" the race (over the public address system or on radio and TV) that the race has begun—i.e., the horses have left the "starting gate" and are running down the "stretch." DOC.

OFF AT THE CRACK OF THE BAT   *to be off at the crack of the bat.* To get started in a hurry. Source: BASEBALL. For a fielder to start fielding a ball at the instant it is hit; for a batter to start for first base—or a runner to start for a succeeding base—at the instant the ball is hit.

OFF-BASE (adj.)   *an off-base action or remark.* An inappropriate action or remark. Source: BASEBALL. The action of being caught off base, e.g., by the pitcher, and "tagged out" by an infielder. *See also* Caught off Base; Off Base (p.a.).

OFF BASE (p.a.)   *to be (way) off base.* To miss the point; to be out of line. LTA: 1912. Source: BASEBALL. To be caught off the base and tagged out. SFS. *See also* Caught off Base; Off-base (adj.).

OFF-COLOR   *an off-color joke (etc.).* A dirty, or "blue," joke. WPO: 1900. Source: ARCHERY(?). The "bull's-eye" of an archery target consists of a yellow center (the "pupil") surrounded by a red ring (the "iris"). The next ring is blue, so a hit in that ring misses the bull's-eye and can be said to be "off-color" or "blue." WPO indicates that "off-color" refers to the blue light of a nightclub or strip joint.

OFF GUARD   *to take someone off guard.* To surprise or shock someone. Source: FENCING. To touch your opponent with your weapon when they are not *en garde,* i.e., when they are not prepared for the attack. *See also* Catch Someone Off Guard; Drop Your Guard; Let Down Your Guard.

OFFSIDES   *to be offsides.* To do or say something inappropriate or out of line. Source: FOOTBALL. To be beyond the line of scrimmage when the ball is snapped. Also used in rugby and ice hockey. LTA.

OFF STRIDE   *to catch someone off stride.* To catch someone off balance; to take someone by surprise. Source: FOOT RACING. To overtake someone in a race who has lost their rhythm or pace.

OFF TARGET   *to be off target.* To miss the point or be out of line. Source: SHOOTING. To miss the target completely. *See also* Target (v).

OFF THE HOOK   *to be/get off the hook.* To be relieved of an obligation or problem; to get out of some difficulty or trouble. Source: FISHING. For a fish to get free of the hook that it was temporarily caught on. CI. *See also* Get off the Hook; Let Someone off the Hook.

OFF THE MARK   *to be off the mark.* To be wrong. Source: SHOOTING. For a shot to miss the target or the center of the target. *Compare* Quick off the Mark.

OFF THE PACE   *to be off the pace.* To be falling behind the competition. A euphemism. Source: RACING. For a horse or a runner to be falling behind the leaders in a race. *See also* Change of Pace; Keep Pace with; Pacemaker; Pacesetter; Put Someone through Their Paces; Set the Pace.

OFF THE TOP   *to take your money off the top.* To take your "cut" of the money before it has been split up or any deductions have been made. Source: GAMBLING. To take your "cut" of the winnings before they have been reduced or divided.

OFF-THE-WALL (adj.)   *an off-the-wall remark; off-the-wall behavior.* A bizarre or eccentric remark or action. WNCD: 1971. Source: RACQUETBALL (Paddleball). An action or remark as unpredictable as a ball coming off the wall in a game of racquetball (or handball or squash). DOC; NDAS. *See also* Off the Wall (p.a.).

OFF THE WALL (p.a.)   *to be off the wall.* To be weird, eccentric, bizarre. Source: RACQUETBALL (Paddleball). To be as unpredictable as a ball coming "off the wall" in a game of racquetball. DOC. The expression dates only from the mid-1970s, but the older sports of handball and squash could just as well have given birth to it. *See also* Off-the-wall (adj.).

OFF TO THE RACES   *We're off to the races.* We're on our way. Source: HORSE RACING. We're off to the racetrack.

OFF YOUR GAME   *a little off your game.* Not at your usual level of performance. Source: SPORTS. Not playing as well as usual.

0 FOR APRIL   *to be 0 for April.* To be unsuccessful for an entire month or longer. Source: BASEBALL. To be without a hit or a run or a win for an entire month or longer. The "0" is pronounced "oh" and represents a zero or "goose egg" (q.v.). The Baltimore Orioles almost went "0 for April" in 1988, losing their first twenty-one games before beating the Chicago White Sox on April 29. They lost again on the next day and finished the month at "One for April."

OLD COLLEGE TRY *to give it the old college try.* To go all out, sparing no effort and having no fear of injury. Source: FOOTBALL. To throw caution to the wind when carrying the ball, catching the ball, or tackling an opposing player. FP.

OLD PRO *an old pro.* An experienced performer—a "veteran." Source: SPORTS (probably Baseball). SOED: *pro,* 1848. An experienced ball player in the professional ranks. *See also* Pro.

OLYMPIC-CLASS *an olympic-class performer (drinker, lover, typist, etc.).* A performer who is among the best in the world. Source: OLYMPIC GAMES. An athlete who is among the best in the world—equal to the participants in the Olympic Games. *Compare* World-class.

ON A COLD TRAIL *to be on a cold trail.* To be searching for something that disappeared a long time ago and left behind little evidence of its whereabouts. Source: HUNTING. For a dog to be on the trail of an animal that passed by some time ago and left little or no scent. *See also* Hark Back; On the Wrong Track.

ON A MERRY-GO-ROUND *to be on a merry-go-round.* To be on a nonstop cycle of activity. Source: CARNIVAL. SOED: 1856. To be on a carousel—a continuously revolving platform with rising and falling "horses" or other "animals." *Compare* Rat Race.

ON A ROLL *to be on a roll; to be really rolling now.* To be enjoying a stretch of good luck or a series of successes. Source: CRAPS. To have a series of successful rolls of the dice—e.g., a 7 or 11 on the first throw, or repeated throws of the "point" (4, 5, 6, 8, 9, 10). NDAS. *See also* On a Winning Streak; Roll of the Dice.

ON A WINNING STREAK *to be on a winning streak.* To be enjoying a series of successes. Source: SPORTS; GAMES; GAMBLING. SOED: 1882. To be enjoying a series of victories or winnings. CI. *See also* On a Roll.

ON BOARD *Glad to have you on board (or aboard).* Glad to have you as a member of our organization. Source: SAILING. Welcome on board (i.e., on the deck of) the ship or boat. *See also* All Aboard; Welcome Aboard.

ON CENTER COURT *to be on center court.* To be the center of attention. Source: TENNIS. To play a match on the main ("center") court of a complex of courts, as at Wimbledon. LOS. Brit.: "centre court."

ON DECK *to be on deck.* To be due to appear next. DAE: 1889. Immediate Source: BASEBALL. LTA: late 1860s. To be in the "on-deck circle"—i.e., due to appear next at bat. LOS. *Also:* "in the hole." Ultimate Source: SAILING. To be *on* the decks rather than *below* them. *Compare* Up.

ONE DOWN, TWO TO GO   One task accomplished, two remaining. Source: BASEBALL. One batter "out" in the inning, two more to "retire." Each batter gets three strikes in an inning, and each team get three outs. LOS.

ONE FELL SWOOP   *See* In One Fell Swoop.

ONE-HORSE RACE   *a one-horse race.* A campaign in which one of the candidates is the clear front-runner. Source: HORSE RACING. A race in which one of the horses is the clear favorite.

ONE HUNDRED AND TEN PERCENT   *to give 110, 120, 130, etc. percent.* To perform beyond your normal limits. Source: SPORTS (esp. BASEBALL). To perform beyond your physical capabilities. *See also* Above Your Head; Play over Your Head.

ONE LEG AT A TIME   *They put their pants on the same way you do: one leg at a time.* They're only human, just like you. Source: FOOTBALL. Your opponents are no better than you are: they put their pants (jock straps, etc.) on one leg at a time. (A coach psyching up his players just before a tough game.) Of course, if you sit on a bench, you can put your pants on *two* legs at a time.

ONE-ON-ONE   Head-to-head: in direct confrontation. Source: BASKETBALL. WNCD: 1967. "One-on-one" is an abbreviated form of basketball, with only one player on a side, and utilizing only one basket and half the court. "How 'bout a little one-on-one?" *Compare* Mano a Mano.

ONE-SHOT DEAL   *a one-shot deal.* A one-time occurrence—e.g., of a pay raise. WNCD: 1927. Source: SHOOTING. A shooting match in which each contestant is allowed only one shot. HUNTING. The killing of a quarry with only one shot.

ONE SIDED   *to be one sided.* To be biased or partial. SOED: 1833. Source: SPORTS. WNCD: 1813. For one of the competitors in a sports event to have a clear advantage over the other. CI. *See also* Choose Up Sides; Side with.

ONE-TWO PUNCH   *to give someone the old one-two punch.* To launch a two-pronged attack on someone. Source: BOXING. WNCD: 1811. To throw a combination of blows, one from each hand. LOS.

ONE-UPMANSHIP   The practice of topping an opponent, verbally or socially. WNCD: 1952. Source: GOLF. "One up" is the match play score of a golfer who has won one more "hole" than their opponent. "One-upmanship" is formed on the pattern of gamesmanship and sportsmanship. *See also* Go Someone One Better; One up on; White Elephant.

ONE UP ON   *to be one up on someone.* To be at an advantage over someone else. WNCD: 1919. Source: GOLF. To have won one more "hole" than your opponent in a match play tournament. CI. *See also* One-upmanship.

ON GUARD *to be on guard.* To be prepared for any attack. Source: FENC-ING; BOXING. To be *en garde;* to be prepared to defend yourself at all times. CI. *See also* Catch Someone Off Guard; On Your Guard.

ONLY GAME IN TOWN *the only game in town.* The only thing worth doing, the only place worth going to, etc. Source: POKER; CRAPS. The only poker game or crap game available, however crooked. *Joke:* "Why do you keep playing in that crooked game?" "It's the only game in town."

ON SOMEONE'S TAIL *to be on someone's tail.* To be in hot pursuit of someone (e.g., a wanted criminal). Source: FOX HUNTING. For the hounds to have picked up the fox's scent and perhaps even sighted its tail. *See also* Put a Tail on; Tail (v).

ON TARGET *to be right on target.* To be precisely correct. Source: SHOOTING. For a shot to hit the target precisely where it was aimed. *See also* Target (v).

ON THE BALL *to be on the ball.* To be bright, alert, sharp. DOC: 1935. Source: BASEBALL. DOC: 1912. For a pitcher to have a lot of speed or spin (or spit) on the baseball. CI: SOCCER. DAE: POLO, 1897. *See also* Have a Lot on the Ball; Have Something on the Ball.

ON THE BUBBLE *to be on the bubble.* To be on the spot, in a precarious position—e.g., in danger of being laid off. Source: CAR RACING. To occupy the last qualifying position for a race, from which you can be "bumped" by a faster nonqualifier, as in the Indianapolis 500. The expression is also used in golf to describe those in danger of not making the "cut" if the players still on the course play too well. The ultimate source of the metaphor is either "bubble blowing" (on a bubble that is about to burst) or the carpenter's "bubble" (on a bubble that can go either way). *See also* Burst Someone's Bubble.

ON THE EDGE *to be living on the edge.* To be living dangerously, on the brink of disaster. Source: SKIING(?). To be skiing down a dangerously steep hill, requiring constant turns, keeping the skier "on the edge" of their skis at all times.

ON THE FIRST/LAST LEG OF A JOURNEY On the first/last part of a journey. Source: SAILING. SOED: 1867. On the first/last "tack" of a sailing trip. *See also* Take a Different Tack.

ON THE FLIP SIDE *on the flip side, . . .* On the other hand, . . . Source: COINS. On the "down" side of a flipped coin—the side that doesn't "count." *See also* Flip Side.

ON THE FLY *to grab something on the fly.* To grab a quick lunch (etc.) without interrupting your busy schedule. Source: BASEBALL. DAE: 1868. To catch a "fly ball" on the run, before it hits the ground.

ON THE GO   *to be always on the go.* To be busy all the time. Source: FOOT RACING. To do everything as if you just heard the word "Go!" CI. *See also* From the Word Go; Have a Go at; No Go.

ON THE LINE   *See* Lay It on the Line; Lay Something on the Line; Put Your Money on the Line.

ON THE NOSE   *right on the nose.* Exactly right. Source: HORSE RACING. To place a bet "on the nose" is to bet that that horse will win—i.e., that its nose will cross the finish line first.

ON THE REBOUND   *to marry someone on the rebound.* To marry someone after being rejected by someone else. Source: BASKETBALL(?). A "rebound" is the bouncing off the backboard (now glass, not wooden "boards") of a ball that was shot but did not go through the hoop. The expression could have originated in any of the "ball" sports, including the oldest of them all, HAND-BALL. CI.

ON THE RIGHT TRACK   *to be on the right track.* To be headed in the right direction. Source: HUNTING. To be following the right trail ("track") of a quarry. *See also* On the Track of.

ON THE ROCKS   *to be on the rocks.* For your marriage or business or psyche to be in big trouble. Source: SAILING. HTB: ca. 1750. For a sailing vessel to be hung on the rocks. CI. Also applied to alcoholic drinks: over ice, as opposed to "straight up" or "straight" or "up" or "neat." *See also* Rock Hound; Washed Up (p.a.).

ON THE ROPES   *to be on the ropes.* To be in serious trouble. LTA: 1924. Source: BOXING. LTA: 1850s. To be pinned against, or hanging on, the ropes of the ring, defenseless. DOC; SFS. *See also* Have Someone on the Ropes.

ON THE SIDE   *to make some extra money on the side.* To make some extra money by taking on an additional job. Source: CRAPS(?). To make some extra money by taking on "side" bets at the crap game.

ON THE SPOT   *to be on the spot.* To be in trouble. LTA: 1928. Source: POOL(?). For a ball to be "spotted—placed on the white dot at the end of the table opposite from where the rack is made—after a "scratch." The ball cannot be struck directly by the cue ball in this position. DOC and WPO suggest that the phrase derives from the practice of showing an ace of spades to a criminal before the execution.

ON THE TRACK OF   *to be on the track of someone/something.* To be on the trail of a criminal or a solution to a problem. Source: HUNTING. To be on the trail of an animal. CI. *See also* On the Right Track; On the Wrong Track.

ON THE WINNING SIDE   *to be on the winning side.* To be a member of the winning "team." Source: SPORTS. To be a member of a winning sports team. FP.

ON THE WRONG TRACK   *to be on the wrong track.* To be headed in the wrong direction, looking in the wrong place, following the wrong lead, etc. Source: HUNTING. To be following the wrong trail of an animal. *See also* On a Cold Trail; On the Track Of.

ON YOUR GAME   *to be on your game.* To be performing at the best of your ability. Source: SPORTS; GAMES. To be preforming at the best of your ability in a sport or game. NDAS.

ON YOUR GUARD   *to be on your guard.* To be prepared for any eventuality. Source: FENCING; BOXING. To be *en garde:* prepared to defend yourself at all times. CI. *See also* Catch Someone Off Guard; On Guard.

ON YOUR OWN HOOK   *to do something on your own hook.* To do something all by yourself or on your own initiative. Source: FISHING. To catch a fish all by yourself or with your own tackle. WPO.

ON YOUR TOES   *to be/stay on your toes.* To be alert and prepared. Source: BOXING. To be prepared to move away—"on your toes"—from your opponent's attack. LOS. *See also* Toe the Line.

OPEN AND ABOVEBOARD   *to be open and aboveboard.* To be overt and honest. DOC: 17th cent. Source: CARD GAMES. To hold your hand of cards in plain view ("open"), above the table (the "board"), to avoid the impression of cheating (or substituting cards below the table). DOC; DPF; SOED; THT. *See also* Aboveboard. *Compare* Under the Table.

OPENING GAMBIT   *an opening gambit.* A bold initiative. Source: CHESS. A "gambit"—i.e., an opening move in which a piece is sacrificed for an advantageous position. Not all opening moves are "gambits." OL. *See also* Debut; Gambit.

OPEN SEASON   *for it to be open season on something.* For something to be the target of critics: "It seems to be open season on sitcoms." Source: HUNTING. WNCD: 1890. For it to be the legal time of the year to hunt and take certain game. WPO. *See also* Fair Game. *Compare* Out of Season.

OTHER SIDE OF THE COIN   *the other side of the coin.* The other side of the issue. Source: COINS. The bottom side of a flipped coin.

OUT (1)   *to be out.* To be sound asleep or unconscious. Source: BOXING. To be knocked unconscious: a "knockout." LOS. *See also* Down and out; Down But Not out; Out Like a Light.

OUT (2) *to be out.* To have withdrawn from an activity. Source: POKER. To have withdrawn from a poker game. *See also* Count Me out; Deal Me out; Dealt out. *Compare* In.

OUTBLUFF *to outbluff someone.* To outmaneuver someone. Source: POKER. To pretend, by "raising," to have a better hand than another player who is doing the same thing—and to cause them to "fold." FP. *See also* Bluff (v); Bluffing.

OUTFOX *to outfox someone.* To outsmart someone. WNCD: 1924. Source: FOX HUNTING. For the hounds or hunters to outsmart the fox in a fox hunt.

OUT IN LEFT FIELD *to be out in left field.* To be disoriented or deranged. Source: BASEBALL. To be in the part of the outfield where the sun and the wind play tricks with the ball, and the walls and fans contribute to the "terror." Left field is that part of the outfield that is in the left field of vision from home plate. *See also* Come out of Left Field.

OUT LIKE A LIGHT *to be out like a light.* To be sound asleep or unconscious, like a light that has been turned off. Source: BOXING. To be knocked unconscious: a "knockout." LOS. *See also* Out (1); Punch Someone's Lights Out.

OUT-OF-BOUNDS *to be out-of-bounds.* For your actions or words to be improper or out of line. Source: BASEBALL. WNCD: 1857. For the batted ball to fly outside the marked boundaries of the playing field. Also used in football, basketball, soccer, golf, etc.

OUT OF LUCK *to be out of luck.* To be unlucky. "You're out of luck. I just sold the last pair." Source: GAMBLING. For your luck to have "run out" in a game of chance.

OUT OF SEASON *to be out of season.* To be off limits. Source: HUNTING; FISHING. To be outside the legal time period for taking game. *Compare* Open Season.

OUT OF THE BLOCKS *to get out of the (starting) blocks fast.* To get off to a fast start. Source: FOOT RACING. To get away fast from the starting line, where both feet are braced against wooden or metal "blocks." Starting blocks are not usually used in long-distance races, such as the mile and the marathon. *See also* First out of the Blocks.

OUT OF THE BOX *first time out of the box.* Your first attempt at doing something. Source: BASEBALL(?). Your first time (into and) out of the batter's box. The phrase is also used in other sports, such as golf. The metaphor may actually be based on a "hat box" rather than a "batter's box." *See also* Fast out of the Box; Knock out of the Box.

OUT OF THE RUNNING   *to be out of the running.* To be out of contention for a position. Source: HORSE RACING. For a horse to be out of contention to win a race. DPF.

OUT OF THE STARTING GATE   *to be first out of the starting gate.* To take an early lead in a political "race." Source: HORSE RACING. For a horse to leave the starting gate immediately upon its opening.

OUT OF YOUR DEPTH   *to be out of your depth.* To be in a situation that you are not prepared to handle. Source: SWIMMING. To be in water that is deeper than your ability to swim. CI. *See also* In Deep Water; In over Your Head.

OUT OF YOUR LEAGUE   *to be out of your league.* To be outmatched or outclassed. Source: BASEBALL. To be in the "major" leagues but to really belong in the "minors." The "major" (or "big") leagues are the American and the National, each of which is divided into "divisions": East and West.

OUT ON A LIMB   *to be/go out on a limb.* To be in a precarious position; to get into a precarious position for someone. DOC: 1897. Source: HUNTING. For a treed animal to have climbed out onto the end of a limb and therefore become an easy mark for a hunter. CI; DOC. *Compare* Up a Tree.

OUT ON YOUR FEET   *to be out on your feet.* To be totally fatigued. Source: BOXING. To be knocked out while still standing: a "technical knockout" or "T.K.O." LOS.

OUTSIDE CHANCE   *to have an outside chance of succeeding.* To have very little likelihood of succeeding. Source: GAMBLING; BETTING. To have "odds against" that are almost beyond ("outside") the realm of probability (e.g., 50 to 1).

OVER A BARREL   *to be—or have someone—over a barrel.* To be at someone's mercy; to have someone else at your mercy. DOC: 1939. Source: SWIMMING. To be draped—or have someone else draped—over a barrel, lying on its side, for the purpose of letting the water drain out after a near-drowning. DOC; HTB.

OVERBOARD   *See* Go Overboard.

OVERCOME LONG ODDS   *to overcome long odds.* To survive an ordeal, conquer an illness, etc. Source: HORSE RACING. To win a race in spite of heavy odds against: e.g., 50 to 1. *See also* Long Odds; Odds.

OVERHAUL   *to overhaul something.* To repair something, e.g., a motor or an engine. Source: SAILING. SOED: 1705. To turn a boat upside down ("haul it over"), so that the "keel" is over the "hull." LTA. *See also* Turn Turtle.

OVERPLAY YOUR HAND   *to overplay your hand.* To take excessive action. Source: BRIDGE. To lose a "trick" because of overbidding or poor strategy.

OVERTRAINED   *to be overtrained.* To be overprepared. Source: BOXING. SOED: 1856.To have trained so hard for a match that you can't perform at your peak when the time comes.

P

PACEMAKER   *a pacemaker.* A leader or innovator; a device to regulate the heartbeat. Source: RACING. WNCD: 1884. A "pacesetter": one who moves quickly to the front of the pack and establishes the speed of the race. The role is temporary and sacrificial. *See also* Change of Pace; Keep Pace with; Off the Pace; Pacesetter; Put Someone through Their Paces; Running Mate; Set the Pace.

PACESETTER   *a pacesetter.* A leader in a field (such as fashion); an innovator. Source: RACING. WNCD: 1895. A racer who moves to the front at the outset and determines the speed of the race. The role is often temporary and sacrificial. *See also* Keep Pace with; Off the Pace; Pacemaker; Running Mate; Set the Pace.

PACK A WALLOP   *to pack a wallop.* For a drink to have a high alcoholic content. DOC: 1922. Source: BOXING. For a boxer to have "clout": to be capable of throwing a punch with great force. DOC.

PADDLE YOUR OWN CANOE   *to paddle your own canoe.* To be independent or self-sufficient. DAE: 1840. Source: CANOEING. To operate your canoe alone, heading in any direction, and at any speed you please. CI; DOC; DPF; HOI.

PALM SOMETHING OFF   *to palm something off on someone.* To cheat someone by selling them an inferior product. SOED: 1679. Source: CON GAMES. SOED: 1673. To conceal something, such as a card or a "pea," in the palm of your hand for use at a more appropriate time: "sleight of hand." CI; DPF. *See also* Shell Game.

PALOOKA   *a big palooka.* A brawny, but not very brainy, man: a "goon" or "ape." Source: SPORTS; BOXING. WNCD: 1925. A brawny, but not very brainy (and probably over-the-hill), boxer—like Joe Palooka, the hero of an old comic strip. LOS.

PARACHUTE   *See* Golden Parachute.

PAR FOR THE COURSE   *That's par for the course.* That's typical—typically bad. DOC: 1961. Source: GOLF. That's normal (''par'') for this course. ''Par'' is the score that an accomplished golfer would be expected to make on a particular hole or course. CI; DOC. *See also* Course; Under Par; Up to Par.

PARLAY   *to parlay something into something else.* To turn something small, such as a store, into something large, such as a chain of stores. DA: 1949. Source: GAMBLING; BETTING. To bet your winnings, along with your original wager, on a following chance. Originally used in Faro: *paralee,* 1828. *See also* Let it Ride.

PARRY   *to parry a question (etc.).* To turn aside a question or accusation. SOED: 1718. Source: FENCING. SOED: 1672. To use your sword to deflect the thrust of your opponent's sword. *Compare* Thrust.

PASS (v)   *to ''pass'' on something.* To decline an invitation for something. Source: BRIDGE. To decline to bid (''I pass'') when it's your turn to do so. OL. *Compare* Make a Pass at.

PASS THE BUCK   *to pass the buck.* To put the responsibility or blame on someone else. Source: POKER. DOC: 1872. For the dealer to place a buckhorn knife (the ''buck'') in front of the player to their left—either to remind that player that they are the next dealer or to forfeit the deal to that person. CI; DOC; DPF; HOI; SOE. *See also* Buck; Buck Passer; Buck Sheet; Buck Stops Here. *Compare* Punt.

PASS THE TORCH   *to pass the torch.* To pass the reins of leadership to your successor. Source: OLYMPIC GAMES. To pass the torch, lit in Athens, Greece (the site of the original Olympics, founded in 776 B.C.), to the next runner, on its way to the site of the next Modern Olympiad or next Winter Games. This tradition was established at the Berlin Games of 1936. DPF; SPD. The ''baton'' in ancient Greek relay races was also a ''torch.'' *See also* Carry a/the Torch; Torch Is Passed.

PAWN (n)   *a pawn in the game of life (etc.).* A person who is ''pushed around,'' or ''used,'' by someone else. SOED: mid-19th cent. Source: CHESS. WNCD: 14th cent. A chesspiece of the lowest rank and greatest number. The pawn ''belongs'' to a king or queen.

PAYOFF (n)   *the payoff.* The reward for, or result of, doing something. Source: GAMBLING; BETTING. The winnings from successful gambling and betting.

PAY OFF (v)   *to pay off.* To yield a profit. Source: GAMBLING; BETTING. For a wager to return more than the original amount bet; for a ''one-armed bandit'' (a slot machine) to reward a winner in coins.

PELL-MELL *to run pell-mell.* For a crowd of people to run headlong, in a confused fashion. WNCD: 1596. Source: PALL-MALL. For the players of pall-mall to run recklessly down the alley to hit the ball. "Pell-mell" is a variant pronunciation of "pall-mall." DPF; THT. *See also* Mall.

PENNY ANTE Trivial, inconsequential, "chicken feed." WNCD: 1868. Source: POKER. WNCD: 1855. Low-stakes poker, in which only pennies are required as the "ante" (the initial contribution to the "pot" before the dealing starts). *See also* Ante Up.

PERFECT TEN *a perfect ten.* A model of perfection. Source: SPORTS. The perfect score in gymnastics and diving, where the scale is from one to ten. The perfect score in ice skating is six.

PHOTO FINISH *a photo finish.* An extremely close finish, e.g., in an election. Source: HORSE RACING. WNCD: 1936. A finish in a horse race that is so close that the winner can be determined only by the photograph that is taken of it. The "wire" plays a prominent role in this photo. *See also* Dead Heat; Under the Wire.

PICK UP YOUR MARBLES AND GO HOME *to pick up your marbles and go home.* To withdraw from an activity, especially in anger. Source: MARBLES. To withdraw from a game of marbles, in anger, by picking up your marbles and leaving. If you owned all the marbles, the game ends. *See also* Home Free.

PIECE OF THE ACTION *to want or get a piece of the action.* To want or get a share in a deal. Source: GAMBLING; BETTING. To get in on the "side betting" at a crap game or the ringside betting at a boxing match. NDAS.

PIG *See* Buy a Pig in a Poke; Like Catching a Greased Pig.

PIGEON *a pigeon (ready to be plucked).* An easy mark; a sucker; a dupe. SOED: 1593. Source: HUNTING. Pigeons are easy marks for hunters who use nets or snares. DPF; NDAS. *See also* Clay Pigeon; Stool Pigeon.

PIGGYBACK *to ride piggyback.* For a child to ride on the back or shoulders of an adult. Source: CHILDREN'S GAMES. WCND: 1565. For a child to ride on the back of a pig, which is more their size than a horse. WPO. The metaphor is also used to describe the transporting of one vehicle on another—e.g., a semitrailer on a railroad flatcar.

PILLAR TO POST *See* From Pillar to Post.

PILOT *a pilot.* A television show, submitted to the network for their consideration, and often aired whether the rest of the series is contracted or not. Source: SAILING. SOED: 1530. A "steersman" of a ship or boat who guides the vessel through treacherous waters or tricky maneuvers.

PILOT LIGHT *a pilot light.* A tiny gas jet, always lit, which ignites the main jets when they are activated. Source: SAILING. A light on a ship or boat which leads the way and remains on constantly.

PINBALL *to pinball around.* To bounce around randomly from one place to another. Source: PINBALL. For the steel ball, propelled onto an inclined plane studded with steel pins, to roll down, bouncing off the pins until it comes to rest at the bottom (or is hit back up by paddles or flippers). *See also* Hopscotch; Leapfrog; Pinballed.

PINBALLED *to be pinballed.* To be bounced around. Source: PINBALL. To be bounced around like the steel ball in a pinball game. *See also* Pinball.

PINCH HIT *to pinch hit for someone.* To go to bat for someone; to substitute for someone. Source: BASEBALL. WNCD: 1915. To bat for a player who was previously in the lineup. "Pinch *bat*" would be a more accurate term. *See also* Hit (n).

PIN DOWN *to pin someone down.* To force someone to divulge facts or answer questions truthfully. SOED: 1710. Source: WRESTLING. To press your opponent's shoulders to the mat for a count of *3*—i.e., to "pin" them. *See also* Hard to Pin down.

PING-PONG DIPLOMACY Using sports and games to improve relations between countries. Source: TABLE TENNIS. SOED: 1900. (An echoic word. WPO.) Ping-Pong is the trademark of a brand of table-tennis equipment that has become almost synonymous with the name of the game itself. The allusion is to the 1971 trip to China of the U.S. table-tennis team, which contributed to the reopening of diplomatic relations between the two countries. *See also* Ping-Ponged.

PING-PONGED *to be Ping-Ponged.* To be bounced around; to be given the runaround. Source: TABLE TENNIS. To be bounced back and forth like a Ping-Pong ball. NDAS. *See also* Ping-Pong Diplomacy.

PINNED IN A CORNER *to be pinned in a corner.* To be rendered helpless. Source: BOXING. To be forced into one of the four corners of a boxing "ring" by your opponent. The term must have originated after boxing moved from a "ring" of spectators to the "squared circle" of today's boxing arena.

PIN SOMETHING ON SOMEONE *to pin something on someone.* To assign blame to someone for something. Source: CHILDREN'S GAMES. To "pin the tail on the donkey," a game in which one of the players is blindfolded, handed a paper "tail" with a pin through it, spun around, and told to pin the tail appropriately on a paper donkey on the wall. *Compare* Put a Tail on.

PIT AGAINST   *to pit someone against someone else.* To match X against Y in a competition or campaign. SOED: 1754. Source: COCKFIGHTING. To put gamecock X into a "pit" with gamecock Y. *See also* Pitted against.

PIT BULL TERRIER   *a pit bull terrier.* A mixed breed of dog by this name. Source: HUNTING; DOG FIGHTING. The terrier was originally bred and trained to burrow (Fren. *terrier*) for small animals; now the mixed breed called pit bull is sometimes bred and trained as an attack dog and sometimes as a fighting dog (in the "pits.").

PITFALL   *a pitfall.* A drawback or danger. SOED: 1586. Source: HUNTING. WNCD: 14th cent. A concealed pit for capturing large animals (which "fall" into the "pit"). *Compare* Death Trap.

PIT STOP   *to make a pit stop.* To interrupt a trip in order to use the bathroom. Source: CAR RACING. WNCD: 1932. To leave the main track, during a race, in order to stop in the service area (the "pits") for fuel, a tire change, etc. The "pit" area at the Indianapolis 500 used to be called "Gasoline Alley," which was adopted as the name of a comic strip. The *pit* in "pit stop" derives from the *pit* of "cockpit," where the action takes place in a cockfight. *See also* Cockpit.

PITTED AGAINST   *to be pitted against someone.* To be matched against someone in a competition or campaign. SOED: 1754. Source: COCKFIGHTING. To be matched against another gamecock in a cockfight. WPO. *See also* Pit against.

PLAY (n)   *See* Child's Play; Come into Play; Grandstand Play; Make a Play for; Power Play; Squeeze Play.

PLAY (v)   *See* Not Many Cards Left to Play; Not Playing with a Full Deck; Roll Over and Play Dead; Two Can Play This Game; When the Cat's away, the Mice Will Play.

PLAY A HUNCH   *to play a hunch.* To act on intuition. Source: GAMBLING; BETTING. To bet according to "feeling" rather than to odds or track record. The expression derives from the medieval belief that touching a hunchback's hump would bring good luck. WPO.

PLAY ALONG WITH   *to play along with someone/something.* To "humor" or indulge someone; to go along with a gag or scheme. Source: SPORTS; GAMES. To play at a sport or game with others. CI.

PLAY A LOSING GAME   *to be playing a losing game.* To be in a no-win situation. Source: GAMES. To be playing a game, e.g., a "con" game, that you have no chance of winning. CI. *See also* Cards Are Stacked against You; Play with Loaded Dice.

PLAY A WAITING GAME   *to play a waiting game.* To wait until you get what you want. Source: GAMES. For a player to be rested early in the game so that they will be fresh in the later stages. SOED. *Compare* Play for Time.

PLAY BALL   *to play ball.* To go along with something; to cooperate with someone. LTA: 1901. Source: BASEBALL. DA: 1867. To play baseball. From the umpire's cry of "Play ball!" which starts the game. HTB; LOS. *See also* Let's Play Ball.

PLAY BOTH ENDS AGAINST THE MIDDLE   *to play both ends against the middle.* To play off your opponents against each other in order to improve your own position. Source: POKER. The metaphor is obscure, but it may refer to "drawing to an outside straight," where the attempt is to draw consecutively higher or lower cards than the ones you already hold: e.g., a "5" and a "9" to go with the series "6, 7, 8." *See also* Draw to an Inside Straight. *Compare* Fill an Inside Straight.

PLAY BY HOUSE RULES.   *to play by house rules.* To observe the rules of the establishment. Source: GAMBLING. To play by the local rules of the gambling establishment (the "house") rather than, or in addition to, the general rules of the game being played. *Compare* Ground Rules.

PLAY-BY-PLAY   *a play-by-play account or description.* A detailed account or description of an event. Source: BASEBALL. WNCD: 1931. A radio or TV announcer's report of every "play" executed in a baseball game. LOS. Now used for many other sports. *See also* Blow-by-blow.

PLAY CAT AND MOUSE   *to play cat and mouse with someone.* To "toy" with someone; to "string" someone along. HTB: 1913. Source: ANIMAL GAMES. For a cat to "toy" with a live mouse that it has caught. HTB. *See also* Cat and Mouse Game.

PLAY CATCH-UP   *to play catch-up.* To attempt to draw even with the competition. Source: SPORTS. To attempt to come from behind and win a game or series. NDAS. *See also* Catch Up.

PLAY CHICKEN   *to play chicken.* For two persons to threaten or taunt each other, each waiting for the other to back down. Source: GAMES ("Chicken"). For two persons to drive their cars (etc.) at each other, each waiting for the other to swerve away from a head-on collision, i.e., to "chicken out." WNWD.

PLAY DOCTOR   *to play doctor.* For adults to engage in sexual exploration. Source: CHILDREN'S GAMES. For children to assume the roles of doctor, nurse, and patient.

PLAY FAIR   *to play fair.* To act honestly and equitably toward others. Source: SPORTS; GAMES. To play according to the spirit as well as the letter of the rules of the sport or game. CI. *See also* Spirit of Fair Play.

PLAY FAST AND LOOSE *to play fast and loose with someone.* To betray someone's trust. SOED: 1557. Source: CON GAMES. To play the 14th century game of "Fast and Loose" (literally: "tied and untied") at an English country fair, where a "sharper" tricked a "rube" into betting that a stick that he had put through the loops in a belt would secure the belt. It didn't. CI; DOC; DPF; HOI; HTB; SOE. *See also* Shell Game.

PLAY FOR HIGH STAKES *to be playing for high stakes.* To be involved in a high-risk venture. Source: POKER. To be playing in a game where the bets are high. *See also* High-stakes.

PLAY FOR KEEPS *to play for keeps.* To compete as if nothing else mattered but winning: to play hardball. Source: MARBLES. To play a version of marbles in which the winner gets to keep all the marbles that have been shot from the circle: winner take all. NDAS. *See also* Go for All the Marbles.

PLAY FOR TIME *to be playing for time.* To be attempting to postpone disaster. Source: CRICKET. To be attempting to prolong a tie game until time runs out. CI; DPF. *Compare* Play a Waiting Game.

PLAY GAMES *to play games with someone.* To "toy" with someone; to not take someone seriously. Source: GAMES. To play a game with someone.

PLAY HARDBALL *to play hardball.* To get tough. Source: BASEBALL. To play baseball, as opposed to softball. FP; SPD. *See also* Gloves Are off; Hardball Tactics.

PLAY HIDE AND SEEK *to play hide and seek.* To avoid a pursuer, such as a reporter or a policeman. Source: CHILDREN'S GAMES (Hide and Seek). SOED: 1672. For one child to hide and the others to seek him or her. *See also* Play Hooky.

PLAY HOOKY *to play hooky.* To skip school or some other scheduled activity. DAE: 1848. Source: CHILDREN'S GAMES (Hide and Seek). To play "hide" (from school) and "seek" (by the truant officer). *See also* Play Hide and Seek; Skip.

PLAY INTO SOMEONE'S HAND *to play (right) into someone's hand.* To do exactly what your opponent wants you to do. Source: CARD GAMES. To play a card that is needed by your opponent, as in gin rummy, or that exhausts your trump cards, as in bridge. CI.

PLAY MONEY Counterfeit money: "funny money." Source: GAMES (Board Games). The money used in board games such as Monopoly.

PLAY MUSICAL CHAIRS *to play musical chairs.* To move from job to job, from place to place, without time to settle down in any one of them. DOC: early 1900s. Source: CHILDREN'S GAMES (Musical Chairs). For a group of children—or adults—to move around a row of back-to-back chairs until the music stops, then try to find an empty chair to sit on. One chair, and consequently one player, is removed after each stop, until only one person remains. DOC; WPO. *See also* Stop the Music.

PLAY-OFF (n)   *the play-off.* The "credits" that are run at the end of a TV show. Source: SPORTS. WNCD: 1895. The competitions that are held after the end of the regular season to determine the overall winner. WPO. *See also* -Off.

PLAY OVER YOUR HEAD   *to play over your head.* To outdo yourself. Source: SPORTS. To perform better than anyone, including yourself, thought you were capable of. *See also* One Hundred and Ten Percent.

PLAY POSSUM   *to play possum.* To play dumb; to play dead. Source: ANIMAL GAMES. DAE: 1822. To roll over and play dead, as a possum does when it is attacked. CI; HTB; WPO. *See also* Roll over and Play Dead.

PLAY SAFE   *to play (it) safe.* To act defensively, avoiding risks. Source: POOL. To shoot the "cue ball" lightly at the rack of balls, rather than at the "object ball," so that the cue ball merely glances off the rack and hits at least one "rail." CI.

PLAY TAG   *My stomach is playing tag with my liver.* My stomach is upset. Source: CHILDREN'S GAMES (Tag). In "tag," the child designated as "It" must catch up with and touch ("tag") another child, to whom the role is passed: "You're It."

PLAY THE FIELD   *to play the field.* To date different members of the opposite sex rather then "go steady" with a particular one: to "free-lance." Source: BETTING. To bet on all of the horses in a race except the favorite(s). NDAS. *See also* Back the Field; Hedge Your Bets.

PLAY THE GAME   *If you want to succeed, you have to play the game.* If you want to succeed, you have to adjust to the conventions of the field. Source: GAMES. SOED: 1889. "It doesn't matter whether you win or lose, it's how you play the game." This is a partial paraphrase of Grantland Rice's paraphrase of the Olympic Creed, written by Pierre de Coubertin, founder of the Modern Olympics, in 1896. *See also* Win or Lose.

PLAY THE MARKET   *to play the (stock) market.* To gamble on the price of stocks. Source: GAMES. To play a game of chance, over which you have no control.

PLAY TO THE GRANDSTAND   *to play to the grandstand.* To show off for the crowd. Source: BASEBALL. To show off for the applause of the fans in the grandstand. HOI; HTB. *See also* Grandstand; Grandstand Play.

PLAY TWENTY QUESTIONS   *to play twenty questions.* To interview someone who evades answering the questions. Source: CHILDREN'S GAMES

(Twenty Questions). To play "Animal, Vegetable, Mineral"—a guessing game that starts with "Is it an animal?" (or "vegetable" or "mineral") and ends when the secret word is identified in no more than twenty questions. *See also* Guessing Game.

PLAY WITH A MARKED DECK   *to play with a marked deck.* To have an unfair advantage over your competition. Source: CARD GAMES. To play with a deck of cards that you have "marked" in advance—on the back, with ink— or cut or bent or shaved or punctured to indicate to you which cards the other players are holding. *Compare* Play with a Stacked Deck.

PLAY WITH A STACKED DECK   *to play with a stacked deck.* To have an unfair advantage over your competition. Source: CARD GAMES. To deal from a deck of cards that you have deliberately arranged in such a way that you will receive a superior hand. *Compare* Play with a Marked Deck.

PLAY WITH HOUSE MONEY   *to play with house money.* To enjoy life at someone else's expense. Source: GAMBLING. To gamble with money won from the gambling establishment (the "house") rather than from your originial "stake."

PLAY WITH LOADED DICE   *to play with loaded dice.* To act unfairly or dishonestly; to have an unfair advantage. Source: CRAPS. To play with dice that are weighted in such a way that a particular number will appear on each one when they are thrown. HTB. *See also* Dice Are Loaded against You; Loaded Question; Load the Dice; Play a Losing Game.

PLAY WITHOUT A HELMET   *to play (too long) without a helmet.* To be punch-drunk, or punchy. Source: FOOTBALL. Said of President Gerald R. Ford, who once played center on the University of Michigan football team. The president had a much-caricatured habit of running or falling into and off of things.

PLAY YOUR CARDS RIGHT   *to play your cards right.* ("If you play your cards right, . . .") To make (all) the right moves. DOC: 1753. Source: CARD GAMES. To play the right cards at the right time. DOC.

PLAY YOUR TRUMP CARD   *to play your trump card.* To use your secret weapon; to fire your big guns. DOC: 1891. Source: CARD GAMES. To take a "trick" in a nontrump suit by playing a low trump card. "Trump" is the suit of the winning bid. It outranks the other three suits for that particular "hand." DOC; CI. *See also* Card; Trumped-up.

PLUNGE IN   *to plunge (right) in.* To begin work on a project at any convenient point. Source: DIVING. To dive into the water at any convenient place and in any convenient fashion. *See also* Dive in; Take the Plunge.

POINT *See* Ahead on Points; Besides the Point; Come to the Point; Have a Point; Jumping-off Point; Make a Point; Make Your Point; Miss the Point; Score Points; Screw Your Courage to the Sticking Point; Stretch a Point; Two Points.

POINT-BLANK *to answer someone point-blank; a point-blank answer.* DA: 1656. Source: SHOOTING. SOED: 1571. "Point blank" (Fren. *point blanc*) was once the white ("blank") center of a firearm target (it is now black). To hit such a small point required a shot at close range: "point-blank range" (q.v.). DPF.

POINT-BLANK RANGE *at point-blank range.* At a very short distance away. Source: SHOOTING. WNCD: 1591. "Point-blank range" was once the distance required to hit the white mark (Fren. *point blanc*), now black, of a target for firearms. At that distance it was not necessary to adjust the firearm for wind or distance. DPF. *See also* Point-blank.

POKER FACE (n) *to have a poker face.* To have an expressionless face. WNCD: 1885. Source: POKER. To have the expressionless face of a serious and skillful poker player who is attempting to conceal the value of their "hand." DOC; SOE. *See also* Poker Faced.

POKER FACED (p.a.) *to be poker faced.* To have an emotionless expression on your face; to be straight faced. DA: 1923. Source: POKER. To have the emotionless face of a serious and skillful poker player. *See also* Poker Face.

POLE POSITION *to have the pole position.* To have the "prime" position at the beginning of a campaign or other competition. Source: CAR RACING. To have the position on the inside of the first row of cars at the start of a race, as at the Indianapolis 500.

POLISH SOMETHING OFF *to polish something off.* To finish something off, such as a six-pack of beer. SOED: 1829. Source: BOXING. To polish off an opponent—to knock them out. CI; SOED. *See also* Wipe the Floor with.

POLITICAL ARENA *the political arena.* The world of politics. Source: ROMAN GAMES. The *arena* (Latin "sand") was the central portion of the "Roman Circus," the site of chariot races, gladiator battles, and other games since the 4th century B.C. THT. SPD: the "boxing" arena. *See also* Arena.

POLITICAL FACTION *a political faction.* A political party. SOED: 1509. Source: ROMAN GAMES. The combatants in a "Roman Circus" were divided into four to six "factions," each of which had its own color. DPF; SOED.

POLITICAL FOOTBALL *a political football.* An issue in a political campaign that is tossed back and forth between the candidates. Source: FOOT-BALL. An inflated "pigskin" that is tossed back and forth—mostly forth—in a game. SPD. The tossing is much more active in rugby than in North American football.

POOPED   *to be pooped (out).* To be totally exhausted. LTA: 1880s. Source: SAILING. SOED: 1727. For a large wave to sweep the "poop deck" at the rear of the ship. NDAS.

POSSUM   *See* Play Possum.

POST TIME   *It's post time.* It's time to get moving/get going. Source: HORSE RACING. WNCD: 1845. It's time for the horses to line up at the starting post—now "the starting gate"—to begin a race.

POTSHOT   *See* Take a Potshot.

POWER PLAY   *to execute a power play.* To take advantage of a competitor's weakness or bad fortune. WNCD: 1947. Source: ICE HOCKEY. To take offensive action toward the goal of an opponent who is shorthanded because of penalties. Earlier, in football, a power play featured a "flying wedge" in front of the runner. WNCD.

PRESS YOUR LUCK   *Don't press (or push) your luck.* Don't expect more success just because you've had a little; don't tempt fate. Source: GAMBLING; BETTING. Don't increase the amount of your bets just because you've won a little money. CI. In GOLF, to "press" is to intensify the betting as a match progresses, especially if you're losing.

PREY ON YOUR MIND   *for something to prey on your mind.* For something troublesome to occupy your thoughts at all times. SOED: 1798. Source: HUNTING. SOED: M.E. For something to prey on your mind as an animal preys on its natural quarry.

PRIDE OF PLACE   *the pride of place.* The top position. WNCD: 1623. Source: FALCONRY. Shakespeare, *Macbeth,* 1606. The highest point reached by a falcon before it starts its dive. CI. *See also* Jumping-off Point.

PRO   *a pro.* An expert; a veteran. Source: SPORTS. SOED: 1848. A professional, as opposed to an amateur, player. *See also* Old Pro.

PSYCHED-UP   *to get psyched-up.* To get yourself mentally prepared for a big event. Source: SPORTS. To get yourself mentally prepared to participate in a sports event.

PULL A BLUFF   *to pull a bluff on someone.* To trick someone. Source: POKER. To bluff your way through a game of poker, betting as if you had an excellent hand. *Also:* "to run a bluff." *See also* Bluff (n); Bluff (v); Bluffing. *Compare* Pull a Scam.

PULL A BONER *to pull a boner*. To make a serious mistake. LTA: 1912. Source: BASEBALL. DA: 1912. To make a stupid (bonehead) play in the field or commit a stupid error as a baserunner. *See also* Boner.

PULL A FAST ONE *to pull a fast one*. To put something over on someone. Source: CRICKET. Early 20th cent. To hurl a fastball. SFS.

PULL A SCAM *to pull a scam on someone*. To swindle someone. Source: CON GAMES. To swindle someone in a "confidence" game. *See also* Scam. *Compare* Pull a Bluff.

PULL NO PUNCHES *Don't pull any punches*. Don't hold anything back. Source: BOXING. LTA: 1934. Don't hold back any of your punches. LOS. *See also* Pull Your Punches. *Compare* Telegraph a Punch.

PULL THE RUG OUT FROM UNDER SOMEONE *to pull the rug out from under someone*. To undercut someone's argument or attack. Source: CHILDREN'S GAMES. To "topple" someone by literally pulling away the rug on which they're standing. CI. *See also* Take the Wind out of Someone's Sails.

PULL UP SHORT *to pull up short*. To stop just before completing an action. Source: RIDING. For a horse to stop short of a jump or hurdle. *See also* Bring Someone up Short.

PULL UP STAKES *to pull up stakes*. To leave a place of residence or business. Source: CAMPING. To pull up the stakes that anchor the ropes of a tent. DPF. (HTB: To pull up "boundary" stakes. DAE: 1640.)

PULL YOUR PUNCHES *to pull your punches*. To hesitate to take an action. Source: BOXING. To fail to complete an intended blow to your opponent's body; to pull back or "telegraph" a punch. CI. *See also* Pull No Punches; Telegraph a Punch.

PULL YOUR WEIGHT *to pull your weight*. To do your fair share. Source: ROWING. For an oarsman to stroke the oar with all their weight behind it. DPF. Often negative: "You're not pulling your weight."

PUMP WOOD *to pump wood*. To chop—or split—wood. (Said by President Reagan at his ranch in California.) Source: WEIGHT LIFTING. To pump *iron*— i.e., to lift weights in body building.

PUNCH *See* Beat Someone to the Punch; One-two Punch; Pull No Punches; Pull Your Punches; Roll with the Punches; Sunday Punch; Telegraph a Punch.

PUNCH-DRUNK *to be punch-drunk*. To be dopey or slow witted. Source: BOXING. LTA: 1915. To be dopey or slow witted as a result of too many blows to the head in too many fights. LOS. *See also* Punchy; Slap-happy.

PUNCHING BAG *to use someone as/for a punching bag*. To beat someone up frequently—especially your spouse. Source: BOXING. WNCD: 1889. To use a stuffed leather bag (a "heavy" bag), about one foot in diameter and four feet long, suspended from the ceiling, to practice throwing punches at. *See also* In There Punching.

PUNCH SOMEONE'S LIGHTS OUT *to punch someone's lights out*. To defeat someone soundly. Source: BOXING. To knock your opponent "out like a light" (q.v.).

PUNCHY *to be punchy*. To be dopey or slow witted. Source: BOXING. LTA: 1942. To be slow witted as a result of too many blows to the head in too many fights: "punch-drunk" (q.v.). LOS.

PUNCH YOUR WAY OUT OF A PAPER BAG *You couldn't punch your way out of a paper bag*. (Usu. neg.) You're a mental weakling. Source: BOXING. You're a physical weakling and an ineffectual fighter. NDAS.

PUNT *If in doubt, punt*. If in doubt, give the responsibility to someone else. Source: FOOTBALL. If there is any doubt about making a first down on the next play (usually the fourth down), kick the ball to the other team. Reminiscent of Panini's "If in doubt, use the genitive." (SOED: *rugby, 1845.*) *Compare* Pass the Buck.

PUSH OFF *to push off*. To leave. SOED: 1726. Source: BOATING. To push a small boat off the land and into the water; to push a boat away from the dock. *See also* Shove Off.

PUSHOVER *a pushover*. An easy task; an easy mark. LTA: 1906. Source: BOXING, WRESTLING. An opponent who can be "floored" by a simple push. CI. *See also* Child's Play; Soft Touch.

PUT A TAIL ON *to put a tail on someone*. To have someone follow ("tail") someone else without being seen by that person. Source: CHILDREN'S GAMES (Pin the Tail on the Donkey). For a blindfolded child to attempt to pin a paper tail in the proper place on a picture of a donkey on the wall. *See also* On Someone's Tail; Tail (v). *Compare* Pin Something on Someone.

PUT-DOWN *a put-down*. A humiliating, degrading, or belittling remark or action. WNCD: 1926. Source: WRESTLING. A "takedown": the taking down of your opponent to the mat. *Compare* Go to the Mat for; Put Someone down.

PUT THE GLOVES ON *to put on the gloves with someone*. To challenge or debate someone. Source: BOXING. LTA: 1847. To box or "spar" with someone. LOS. *Compare* Take Off the Gloves.

PUT OUT *to be/feel put out by something*. To be or feel upset by something. Source: BASEBALL(?). To be thrown out or tagged out by a member of the opposing team. Candles and cats are also "put out," of course.

PUT SOMEONE AWAY *to put someone away.* To knock someone out of the competition. Source: BOXING. To knock out your opponent. (Often negative: "I hit him with everything I had, but I couldn't put him away.") LOS. *See also* Knock Someone for a Loop.

PUT SOMEONE DOWN *to put someone down.* To belittle or degrade someone. Source: WRESTLING(?). To take your opponent to the mat: a "takedown." *See also* Put-down.

PUT SOMEONE THROUGH THEIR PACES *to put someone through their paces.* To make someone show what they can do and how well they can do it. Source: HORSE RACING. To test the quality of a horse by having it demonstrate its various "gaits." CI. *See also* Change of Pace; Keep Pace with; Off the Pace; Pacemaker; Set the Pace. *Compare* Jump through Hoops.

PUT UP OR SHUT UP *Put up or shut up!* Present your evidence or remain silent. DOC: 1878. Source: POKER. Put down your bet or stop bragging about what a terrible hand you have. DOC; SOE. *See also* Put Your Money Where Your Mouth Is.

PUT UP YOUR DUKES *Put up your dukes!* Let's fight! DOC: 1870s. Source: BOXING. Put up your fists and prepare to defend yourself. "Dukes" is Cockney rhyming slang for "Duke of Yorks," which rhymes with "forks" and means fingers or fists.

PUT YOU BEST FOOT FORWARD *to put your best foot forward.* To do your best. Source: TRACK AND FIELD. To put your stronger foot ahead of your weaker one in the starting blocks. DOC; WPO. *See also* Get off on the Right Foot.

PUT YOUR CARDS ON THE TABLE *to put your cards on the table.* To reveal your true intentions. Source: CARD GAMES. To put your winning hand of cards on the table, face up, at the conclusion of a game. CI. *See also* Lay Your Cards on the Table; Showdown.

PUT YOUR MONEY ON THE LINE *to put your money on the line.* To stake your reputation on something. Source: GAMBLING; BETTING. To place your bet on the sideline of a crap game or on the counter of a betting window at the racetrack. DOC. *See also* Lay Something on the Line; Put Your Money Where Your Mouth Is. *Compare* Lay It on the Line.

PUT YOUR MONEY WHERE YOUR MOUTH IS *to put your money where your mouth is.* To back up your boasting with action. DOC: 1930. Source: GAMBLING; BETTING. To back up your bragging—or complaining—with a cash bet. DOC. *See also* Put Up or Shut Up; Put Your Money on the Line.

Q

QUARRY *the quarry*. The thing pursued. SOED: 1615. Source: HUNTING. WNCD: 14th cent. The entrails of a skinned deer (O.Fren. *cuirée*, "skinned"), which were fed to the hunting dogs. DPF; THT. The term is now applied to the entire, usually live, animal (or human).

QUARTERBACK *to quarterback an operation, campaign, drive, etc.* To take charge of a "team" effort. Source: FOOTBALL. WNCD: 1944. To call the offensive signals, receive the ball from the "center," and initiate each offensive play for a football team. *See also* Armchair Quarterback; Monday-morning Quarterback.

QUICK OFF THE MARK *to be quick off the mark*. To be a fast starter; to be a fast actor or thinker. Source: FOOT RACING. To be quick to leave the starting line (the "mark") in a footrace. CI; DOC. *Also:* "to be *first* off the mark." *See also* First out of the Blocks. *Compare* Off the Mark.

QUICK ON THE DRAW *to be quick on the draw*. To be quick to respond. Source: DUELING (Western style). NDAS: mid-1800s. To be quick in getting your revolver out of its holster. DOC.

QUIT WHILE YOU'RE AHEAD *to quit while you're ahead*. To drop out while you still have a profit. Source: GAMBLING. To drop out of a game of chance while you still have more money than you started with—and therefore avoid losing that also.

R

RACE (n) *See* Close Race; Off to the Races; One-horse Race; Rat Race.

RACE IS NOT TO THE SWIFT *"The race is not to the swift."* (Eccl. 9:11). Anything is possible. Source: FOOT RACING. King James Version, 1611. The swiftest runner does not always win the race; e.g., a tortoise can beat a hare. DOC; WPO. *See also* In the Long Run.

RACK UP *to rack up a sale (etc.).* To record a sale (etc.). Source BOWL-ING (?). To set up the bowling pins for another roll. POOL(?). To position the "rack" of balls for a "break." NDAS. FOOTBALL(?). WNCD: 1949. To record a victory.

RAFFLE SOMETHING OFF *to raffle something off.* To sell chances on winning a prize. SOED: 1851. Source: DICE GAMES. THT: late 14th cent. "Raffle" was once a betting game in which each player, in turn, threw three dice, and the winner was the one with the highest total. THT. It was based on an earlier game in France. WNWD. *See also* Hold a Raffle.

RAILBIRD *a railbird.* A determined spectator. Source: HORSE RACING. WNCD: 1892. A spectator at a racetrack who stands at the rail that separates the track from the grandstand. There is also a real bird by this name. SOED.

RAIN CHECK *See* Take a Rain Check.

RAISE SOMEONE'S HACKLES *to raise someone's hackles.* To make someone angry. DOC: 1883. Source: COCKFIGHTING. For a gamecock to display its long neck-feathers when it is angry. CI; DOC.

RAISE THE ANTE *to raise the ante.* To increase the "cost" of something. DA: 1909. Source: POKER. DA: 1838. To increase the amount that every player is required to deposit ("ante") in the "pot." *See also* Ante Up; Up the Ante.

RAISE THE STAKES   *to raise the stakes.* To increase the demands, and therefore the risk. Source: POKER. To raise the amount of the "ante" or to raise the limit on the amount that can be bet at any one time—e.g., a $5 limit—in a given game. *See also* Sweeten the Pot. *Compare* Up the Ante.

RAKE-OFF (n)   *a rake-off.* A share of illegal earnings. Source: GAMBLING. WNCD: 1888. The losings that are "raked off" the gambling table by the croupier and kept by the casino. NDAS; WNWD.

RAMROD   *to ramrod something through.* To force a bill through a legislature (etc.). WNCD: 1940. Source: SHOOTING. DAE: 1757. To ram a ball and wadding down the barrel of a muzzle-loading firearm with a rod. *See also* Stiff as a Ramrod.

RAPTURE   The feeling of being seized and carried away by emotion. WNCD: 1605. Source: FALCONRY. SOED: 1600. The feeling of being seized by a large bird of prey (a "raptor," such as a hawk) and carried high into the sky. Divers sometimes experience the "rapture of the deep" if they go too far *down* in the water.

RAT RACE   *the rat race.* The mad scramble for survival in the big city. DOC: 1939. Immediate Source: RACING. The mad scramble of rats toward food or away from danger—not an organized competition, except perhaps at behavioral psychology "fairs." Ultimate Source: SAILING. A dangerous tidal current—literally a "tide race." CI; DOC. *See also* Like Rats Leaving a Sinking Ship; On a Merry-go-round; Smell a Rat.

RAW DEAL   *to get a raw deal.* To be treated unfairly. WNCD: 1920. Source: POKER. To be dealt a crooked hand. Many other senses of "deal" derive from poker. SOE. *See also* Fair Deal; New Deal.

RAZZ   *to razz someone.* To ridicule or harass someone vocally. Source: BASEBALL. For fans to show their displeasure at the personnel on the field—the manager, the players, the umpires, or all of the above—by producing a "razzberry" (or "raspberry"): a "Bronx Cheer" (q.v.), or interlabial trill. HOI; LOS. *Also:* "give someone the bird." *See also* Razzberry.

RAZZBERRY   *a razzberry (or raspberry).* An interlabial trill: a "bird." LTA: 1918. Source: BASEBALL. A "Bronx cheer" (q.v.), which originated in Yankee Stadium, in the Bronx, New York. *See also* Razz.

REACH A DEADLOCK   *to reach a deadlock.* For negotiations to stall, or reach a stalemate. Source: WRESTLING. For two wrestlers to have equally effective holds on each other. DPF. *See also* Stalemate. *Compare* Reach a Stalemate.

REACH A STALEMATE   *to reach a stalemate.* To come to an impasse. Source: CHESS. For one of the players to be unable to move their "king" without putting it "in check." The result is a "draw." DPF; HF; OL. *See also* Stalemate. *Compare* Reach a Deadlock.

READ 'EM AND WEEP   *Read 'em and weep!* Here comes the *bad* news! (e.g., as presented in a letter or report). Source: POKER. (Said by the dealer while dealing.) See what fate has dealt you! NDAS: Craps.

READY TO DEAL   *to be ready to deal.* To be ready to go, ready to make deals. Source: POKER. To be ready to deal the cards for the next hand. *See also* Deal Me in.

READY WHEN THE BELL RINGS   *to be ready when the bell rings.* To be prepared to act when the time comes. Source: BOXING. To be ready to come out fighting when the bell rings to signal the beginning of a fight or round. LOS.

REAL MCCOY   *the real McCoy.* The genuine article: the real thing. DA: 1924. Source: BOXING. The *real* "Kid McCoy," an American boxing champion near the turn of the century who was so good that when other boxers started to borrow his name he had to remind them that he was the *real* McCoy. DOC; HOI; WPO. The *real* source may be "Real MacKay" scotch whiskey. DA: 1922. DOC; HTB; NDAS.

RECORD-BREAKING (adj.)   *a record-breaking achievement.* An achievement that surpasses all previous ones—e.g., a record-breaking day at the Stock Market. Source: SPORTS. An achievement in sports that surpasses all previous ones—e.g., a record-breaking number of home runs in a season by a rookie. *See also* Break the Record.

RECREATIONAL DRUGS   "Party" drugs, such as marijuana, cocaine, or amphetamines. Source: RECREATION. "Recreational drugs" is an oxymoron, because "recreation" implies activity, in sports and games, which contributes to the *healthy* amusement of the participants.

RED HERRING   *a red herring.* A deliberate distraction or diversion. DOC: 19th cent. Source: FOX HUNTING. A smoked, and therefore "red," herring that was once used to train fox hounds to follow a track—and was also used by opponents of fox hunting to divert the hounds from the fox's track so that they would lose its scent, setting them "at fault" (q.v.). CI; DOC; DPF; SPD; WPO. *See also* Catch Someone Red-handed; Cover Up Your Tracks; See Red; Throw Someone off the Scent; Throw Someone off the Track.

REEL IN   *to reel someone in.* To trick someone into doing something. Source: FISHING. To reel in a fish—i.e., to wind up the fishing line on the reel, thus bringing in the fish. *Compare* Rope Someone in.

REEL OFF   *to reel something off.* To recite something from memory—easily and quickly. LTA: 1840. Source: FISHING. SOED: 1837. For a fishing line to unreel, quickly, when a fish runs away with the lure. CI.

REST ON YOUR LAURELS *to rest on your laurels.* To "ride on your reputation": i.e., to be satisfied with your past achievements. DOC: 1874. Source: OLYMPIC GAMES. To be satisfied with your past victories in the ancient Greek games, where a laurel (or bay) wreath was awarded at the Pythian Games. (An olive wreath was awarded at the Olympian Games.) CI; DOC; DPF. Poets were also awarded wreaths in both ancient Greece and Rome—hence the term "Poet Laureate." *Compare* Rest on Your Oars.

REST ON YOUR OARS *to rest on your oars.* To be satisfied with your past achievements. Source: ROWING; BOATING. To stop rowing and lean on your oar-handles to get some rest. CI; DPF. Not used in "crew," where a rower pulls only *one* oar. *Compare* Rest on Your Laurels.

RHUBARB *a rhubarb.* A heated argument. Source: BASEBALL. LTA: 1915. A bench-emptying brawl on the field: a brouhaha. LOS. Popularized by Red Barber in the 1930s. The word "rhubarb" is spoken by actors playing members of a crowd. NDAS.

RICOCHET ROMANCE *a ricochet romance.* A love affair between two persons who are on the rebound from disappointing alliances. Source: SHOOTING. WNCD: 1769. A "ricochet" is the glancing of a bullet off a hard surface.

RIDE *See* Go along for the Ride; Let It Ride; Roller Coaster Ride.

RIDE A HOBBY-HORSE *to ride a hobby-horse.* To beat a pet theory to death. Source: CHILDREN'S PLAY. To ride a "hobby-horse," a stick with a horse head figure on one end, which soon becomes monotonous and tiring. DPF. *See also* Hobby.

RIDE HIGH IN THE SADDLE *to ride high (or tall) in the saddle.* To enjoy a period of success or prosperity. Source: HORSE RACING. For a jockey to stand up in the stirrups after winning a race. *See also* Riding High; Saddle.

RIDE OUT THE STORM *to ride out the storm.* To tough out a difficult situation. SOED: 1529. Source: SAILING. To turn the bow of the craft into the wind, lower the sails, "batten the hatches," and otherwise try to survive a storm on the water. SOED. *See also* Weather the Storm.

RIDER *a rider.* An attachment to a legal document. SOED: 1669. Source: RIDING. The person on a horse.

RIDE ROUGHSHOD *to ride roughshod over someone.* To treat someone deplorably. SOED: 1688. Source: RIDING; RACING. To ride a horse that is shod with the nails protruding, thus giving the rider an advantage over their competitors. CI; SOED.

RIDE THE CREST OF A WAVE *to ride the crest of a wave.* To enjoy a period of good fortune. Source: SURFING. To maneuver your surfboard nearly parallel to, and on the leeward side of, a large wave. *See also* Catch the Wave.

RIDING FOR A FALL   *to be riding for a fall.* To be heading for trouble. Source: RIDING; RACING (esp. the Steeplechase). HTB: early 20th cent. To be riding a horse in such a reckless manner that a "fall" is inevitable. CI; DPF. *See also* Fall off a Horse. *Compare* Come a Cropper.

RIDING HIGH   *to be riding high.* To be enjoying a period of success or prosperity. Source: RIDING. To be sitting tall in the saddle, erect and confident. CI says that the reference is to the "moon" riding high in the sky. *See also* Ride High in the Saddle.

RIGHT OFF THE BAT   *to happen right off the bat.* To happen suddenly and abruptly. LTA: 1910. Source: BASEBALL. To happen as suddenly as the ball rebounds off the bat. SFS; WPO.

RIGHT ON THE BUTTON   *to be right on the button.* To be right on target. Source: BOXING. LTA: 1928. For a blow to land right on the point of your chin (the "button"). LOS.

RIGHT ON THE MONEY   *to be right on the money.* To be exactly right. Source: GAMBLING; BETTING. For a bet to be exactly right—e.g., an accurate bet on a horse to win, place, or show; an accurate bet in roulette on the number, color, etc.

RIGHT UP YOUR ALLEY   *to be right up your alley.* For something to be perfectly suited for you—e.g., a job or a problem that needs solving. Source: BASEBALL. DAE: 1912. An "alley," or "power alley," is that part of the outfield that lies between the fielders—i.e., left or right of the "center fielder."

RING (n)   *See* At Ringside; Grab the Brass Ring; Have a Ringside Seat; Three-ring Circus; Throw Your Hat in the Ring.

RING A BELL   *to ring a bell.* ("That rings a bell!") To jog the memory. Source: SHOOTING. To hit the target in a shooting gallery, causing the bell to ring. HTB. *See also* Give That Man a Cigar; Shooting Gallery. *Compare* Ring the Bell.

RINGER   *a ringer.* A sucker; an easy mark. Immediate Source: HORSE RACING. WNCD: 1863. A fast horse that is entered in a race under a different name, thus lengthening the odds. WPO. Ultimate Source: HORSESHOES. A "ringer" is a tossed horseshoe that "rings" the stake and makes a "ringing" sound if it also *hits* the stake. *See also* Bring in a Ringer; Close Counts in Horseshoes; Dead Ringer.

RING SOMEONE'S BELL   *to ring someone's bell.* To knock someone out. Source: BOXING. To hit an opponent so hard that they hear bells ringing. LOS. This expression probably originated at a time when a bell was always rung to signal the end of a round. Nowadays, a buzzer is often used.

RING THE BELL *to ring the bell*. To do something for which you are rewarded. DA: 1928. Source: SHOOTING. DA: 1917. To ring the bell in a shooting gallery by hitting the (moving) target. *See also* Shooting Gallery. *Compare* Ring a Bell.

RISE TO THE BAIT *to rise to the bait*. To succumb to temptation. Source: FISHING. For a fish to rise to, or come closer to, the surface of the water to "strike" the baited hook. CI. *See also* Take the Bait.

RIVERBOAT GAMBLE *a riverboat gamble*. A dangerous or risky venture. Source: GAMBLING. A venture as risky as gambling on board one of the paddlewheel boats that plied the Mississippi River in the mid-1800s.

ROCK HOUND *a rock hound*. A person who hunts for and collects beautiful, unusual, or valuable rocks and stones. WNCD: 1915. Source: HUNTING. A "hound"—i.e., the generic hunting dog (O.E. *hund*, "dog"), as in "foxhound," "dachshund," etc. WPO. *See also* On the Rocks. *Compare* Hound (v).

ROCK THE BOAT *Don't rock the boat!* Don't start any trouble! DOC: 1931. Source: BOATING. Don't cause the rowboat to rock from side to side, or it may tip over. DOC.

RODE HARD AND PUT AWAY WET *You look like you've been rode hard and put away wet*. You look a mess. Source: RIDING. You look like a horse that has been ridden hard and then stabled without a hosing off or rubbing down.

ROLLER COASTER RIDE *a roller coaster ride*. An uncontrolled series of sharp rises and falls, e.g., of the Stock Market. Source: ROLLER COASTER. WNCD: 1888. A ride on a roller coaster, in which the passenger car—or "coaster," on "rollers"—negotiates steep climbs and twists and then plunges down sharp inclines at breathtaking speed.

ROLL OF THE DICE *a roll of the dice*. A gamble. Source: CRAPS. A roll of two dice to determine winning or losing. *Also:* a "throw of the dice." *See also* On a Roll.

ROLL OVER AND PLAY DEAD *to roll over and play dead*. To give up completely. Source: ANIMAL GAMES. To roll over on your back and pretend to be dead, as a possum does when it is attacked. *See also* Play Possum.

ROLL WITH THE PUNCHES *to roll with the punches*. To take things in stride, without quitting or complaining. DOC: 1956. Source: BOXING. To reduce the force of your opponent's punch by moving your head and upper body away from it, in the same direction. DOC; FP.

ROOKED *to be rooked*. To be cheated. WNCD: 1590. Source: CHESS. For your chesspiece to be taken by your opponent's "rook," or "castle," which can be moved any number of squares forward or sideways. The ultimate source may simply be the raucous behavior of "rooks," or crows.

ROOM TO SWING A CAT IN *not enough room to swing a cat in.* (Usu. neg.) Not enough room to move around in. Source: ARCHERY. Shakespeare, *Much Ado about Nothing,* 1598. Not enough space in which to hang up a leather sack with a live cat in it and shoot the cat dead with an arrow. DPF; HOI. WPO: *enough* room, above decks, to swing a cat-o'-nine-tails in.

ROOT FOR *to root for someone.* To hope for someone's success, e.g., a political candidate. Source: SPORTS. WNCD: 1889. To hope for the success of a particular team or player—in person or in spirit. WNWD. *See also* Cheerleader; Fan.

ROPE SOMEONE IN *to rope someone into doing something.* To convince someone to do something that they are reluctant to do. SOED: 1848. Source: RODEO. DOC: 1810. To lasso a steer or calf ("calf roping") on the ranch or in a rodeo. CI. *See also* Have Someone on the Ropes; Know the Ropes. *Compare* Reel Someone in.

ROTTEN HAND *Life has dealt me a rotten hand.* Life has been unfair to me. Source: POKER. The dealer ("life") has dealt me a losing hand of cards— again and again.

ROUGH-AND-TUMBLE *a rough-and tumble existence.* A life of scrambling for survival. WNCD: 1832. Source: BOXING. A boxing match without rules, called "rough and tumble." CI. *Compare* No Holds Barred.

ROULETTE *See* Russian Roulette.

ROUND AND ROUND *Round and round she goes, and where she stops nobody knows.* There's no telling how this is going to turn out. Source: WHEEL OF FORTUNE. This incantation is spoken by the operator of a wheel of fortune at a carnival or fair.

ROUND PEG IN A SQUARE HOLE *to be like, or feel like, a round peg in a square hole.* To be or feel totally out of place. Source: CHILDREN'S GAMES. *See also* Square Peg in a Round Hole. *Compare* Like a Fish out of Water.

ROUND THE TURN *to round the turn.* To make progress. Source: HORSE RACING. To negotiate one end of an oval race track. *Also:* "to round the final turn."

ROW WITH ONLY ONE OAR *to be rowing with only one oar.* To be mentally deficient. Source: BOATING. To be using only one of the two oars in a rowboat, causing the boat to go around in circles. *See also* Have Only One Oar in the Water; Not Rowing with Both Oars.

RUBBER CHECK   *a rubber check.* A check that "bounces" because of insufficient funds. WNCD: 1926. Source: BALL GAMES. A check that bounces like a rubber ball. WNWD. *See also* Check (n).

RUBBER-CHICKEN CIRCUIT   *the rubber-chicken circuit.* The series of public appearances of speakers or candidates, the free meals of which always seem to be chicken that has the consistency of rubber. Source: CIRCUS. Rubber chickens are a favorite prop of circus clowns, who pretend to shoot them out of the canvas sky.

RUB OF THE GREEN   *the rub of the green.* The fortunes of life, love, war, etc. Source: GOLF. The direction in which the grass is bent on the putting surface of a "green," which affects the sideways roll (the "break") of the ball. LOS. BILLIARDS; POOL. The nap on the green felt of a billiard table. BOWLING (Lawn Bowling). WNCD: 1586. The unevenness of the bowling green. *See also* There's the Rub.

RULES   *See* Ground Rules; Play by House Rules; Stickler for the Rules.

RUN (n)   *See* End Run; In the Long Run; Make a Run at; No Runs, No Hits, No Errors.

RUN (v)   *to run for something.* To be a candidate for a position or office. Source: FOOT RACING. SOED: 1861. To participate in a race. EOD. *See also* Cut and Run; Take the Ball and Run with It.

RUN AFOUL OF   *to run afoul of the law (etc.).* To get in trouble with the law (etc.). DAE: 1854. Source: SAILING. DAE: 1809. For two ropes to get tangled up with ("run afoul of") each other. *Compare* Hook up with.

RUN A TIGHT SHIP   *to run a tight ship.* To maintain strict control over something. Source: SAILING. To maintain strict control over the crew of a sailing vessel. CI. Probably alluding to the tightness of the ship's ropes. WPO. *See also* Ship of State; Shipshape.

RUN AWAY FROM THE FIELD   *to run away from the field.* To take a commanding lead in a political "race" (etc.). Source: HORSE RACING. For a horse to take a commanding lead in a horse race. *See also* Runaway Victory; Run away with. *Compare* Come back to the Field.

RUNAWAY VICTORY   *a runaway victory.* A decisive victory, as in politics. Source: RACING. SOED: 1895. A victory in which the winner "runs away from the field"—i.e., wins going away. *See also* Run away from the Field; Win Going away.

RUN AWAY WITH   *to run away with something (e.g., an honor or award).* To win something easily; to win going away. Source: RACING. To run away from the rest of the "field" in winning a race. *See also* Runaway Victory; Run away from the Field; Win Going away.

RUN CIRCLES AROUND   *to run circles—or rings—around someone.* To outclass someone completely. Source: FOOT RACING. To be so much faster than your opponent that you could circle them and still win the race. DOC; DPF. *Compare* Skate Circles around.

RUN FOR THE MONEY   *to give someone a run for their money.* To provide ample competition for your opponent. Source: HORSE RACING. For a horse and jockey to give the bettors their money's worth, whether they win or not. CI; DPF.

RUN-IN   *to have a run-in with someone.* To have an unfriendly encounter with someone. Source: RUGBY. To score a touchdown: a "run-in." SOED. *Compare* Make a Run at.

RUN INTERFERENCE FOR   *to run interference for someone.* To clear the way for someone—literally or figuratively. Source: FOOTBALL. LTA: ca. 1900. To "block" opposing players out of the way of your teammate who is carrying the ball.

RUN ITS COURSE   *for something to run its course.* For a fire to burn itself out, an epidemic to run out of victims, a flood to run out of water, etc. DOC: 1576. Source: RACING. For a race to take place on a track ("course") of measured length. DOC. *See also* Course.

RUN LIKE A TOP   *to run like a top.* To operate smoothly and quietly, like a well-tuned engine. Source: CHILDREN'S PLAY (Spinning Tops). To run smoothly and quietly, like a spinning "top"—a wooden cone that is caused to spin on its point. *See also* Sleep Like a Top.

RUNNER-UP   *a runner-up.* A second-place finisher in a contest—e.g., a beauty pageant: first runner-up, second runner-up, etc. Source: DOG RACING. WNCD: 1842. A second-place finisher in a dog race—later, in any race.

RUNNING   *See* Hit the Ground Running; In the Running; Off and Running; Out of the Running.

RUNNING IN PLACE   *to be running in place.* To be making no progress, in spite of your activity. Source: FOOT RACING. To be pumping your legs without moving your body forward—a method of warming up before a race. *Compare* Spin Your Wheels; Tread Water.

RUNNING MATE   *a running mate.* A candidate for a secondary office: e.g., for vice president or lieutenant governor, i.e., on the same "ticket" as the candidate for president or governor. Source: HORSE RACING. WNCD: 1868. A horse that is used to set the pace for a more favored horse from the same stable: a "stablemate." SFS; SPD. *See also* Pacemaker; Pacesetter; Stablemate.

RUNOFF *a runoff.* A final ballot to break a tie. Source: RACING. A final race between winners of preliminary "heats." SFS. The original "runoff" may have been a final race to break a tie.

RUN RIOT *to run riot.* To act uncontrollably, like crabgrass. Source: FOX HUNTING. For the hounds to follow the wrong scent, barking as if it were the right one. CI.

RUN THAT BY ME AGAIN *Would you run that by me again?* Would you explain that to me one more time? Source: FOOTBALL. The metaphor alludes to the seemingly endless instant replays that follow every play of the game, however insignificant. *See also* Instant Replay.

RUN TO THE GROUND *to run someone/something (in)to the ground.* To track someone down; to get to the bottom of something; to solve a knotty problem. Source: FOX HUNTING. For the hounds to run a fox into its den, or hole. CI; DOC; HOI. *Also:* to "run to earth." *See also* Hot on the Trail.

RUN UP THE SCORE *to run up the score.* To defeat someone by a greater margin than is necessary: to pile it on. Source: SPORTS. To score as many points as possible when already far ahead of your opponent. Originally from card games: to "bid up." WNCD.

RUSSIAN ROULETTE *to play Russian roulette.* To take a dangerous or foolish chance. DOC: 1960. Source: ROULETTE (Fren. "little wheel"). WNCD: 1937. The connection to roulette is the cylinder ("little wheel") of a revolver, which is loaded with only one bullet, spun, held to your temple, and fired. If you're lucky—five chances in six—you won't die. The "game" originated among Russian Army officers in World War I. DOC; HF; WPO.

S

SADDLE *to saddle someone with something.* To burden someone with something. SOED: 1693. Source: RIDING. To put a saddle on a horse. *See also* Back in the Saddle Again; Ride High in the Saddle.

SAFETY NET *a safety net.* Protection from financial disaster—e.g., protection of lower-income persons from the extremely high costs of catastrophic illness. Source: CIRCUS. The net that is stretched below the performers on the high wire and trapeze. *See also* Walk a Tightrope.

SAIL (n) *See* Have the Wind Taken out of Your Sails; Take the Wind out of Someone's Sails; Trim Someone's Sails.

SAIL CLOSE TO THE WIND *to sail close to the wind.* To ask for trouble. Source: SAILING. To sail almost directly into the wind. CI.

SAILING *See* Clear Sailing; Smooth Sailing.

SAIL THROUGH *to sail (right) through something.* To perform a task easily and quickly. Source: SAILING. SOED: 1886. To sail through a passage easily and quickly. *See also* Clear Sailing; Smooth Sailing.

SAIL UNDER FALSE COLORS *to sail under false colors.* To misrepresent yourself. Source: SAILING. For a ship to fly the flag (the "colors") of a country that it does not actually represent. WPO.

SANDBAG *to sandbag.* To create the impression that you are less qualified or capable that you really are—e.g., in order to become the underdog in a competition. Source: SPORTS; GAMES. To perform poorly in order to deceive your opponent—e.g., to get them to drop their guard or relax their concentration, as in poker—or to build up a large handicap, as in golf, for future benefit. NDAS. *See also* Hustle; Sandbagger.

SANDBAGGER *a sandbagger.* A person who deliberately creates the impression that they are less qualified or capable than they really are. Source:

SPORTS; GAMES. A person who performs poorly in order to deceive their opponent into dropping their guard or relaxing their concentration or to build up a large handicap for future benefit. *See also* Sandbag.

SAVED BY THE BELL   *to be saved by the bell.* To be rescued from an unpleasant situation in the nick of time. Source: BOXING. To be saved from further punishment—or a possible knockout—by the ringing of the bell (or buzzer) to signal the end of the round, especially the last round, of a fight. CI; FP; LTA. *See also* Come Out Fighting at the Bell.

SAY IT AIN'T SO, JOE   *Say it ain't so, Joe!* Tell me you didn't do it! Source: BASEBALL. Supposedly said by a young boy to Shoeless Joe Jackson after he and other members of the Chicago White Sox were convicted of "throwing" the championship of 1919: the Chicago "Black Sox" scandal. WPO.

SCAM   *a scam.* A "con" game or swindle. WNCD: 1965. Source: CARNI-VAL. "Carny" slang for an illegal game at a carnival. WPO. *See also* Gimmick; Pull a Scam; Skin Game.

SCORE (n)   *See* Doesn't Know the Score; Have a Score to Settle; Know the Score; Run Up the Score.

SCORE (v)   *to score.* To make a sexual conquest; to get a "hit" or "fix" on drugs. Source: SPORTS. To make a "point" in a game. EOD; FP; OL.

SCORE POINTS   *to score points.* ("Did you score any points?") To make a favorable impression on someone. Source: SPORTS. To make "points" in a game. *Compare* Ahead on Points.

SCRATCH (n)   *See* Not up to Scratch; Start from Scratch.

SCRATCH (v)   *to scratch someone from something.* To remove someone from a scheduled event. Source: HORSE RACING. SOED: 1685. To remove ("scratch out") the name of a horse that was scheduled to run a race. DPF; NDAS. *See also* Scratched.

SCRATCHED   *to be scratched.* For someone or something to be removed from a scheduled event. Source: HORSE RACING. For a horse to be removed—i.e., its name "scratched out"—from a scheduled race. *See also* Scratch (v).

SCREWBALL   *a screwball.* An eccentric, unconventional, off-the-wall person: a nut. Source: BASEBALL. WNCD: 1936. A pitch, invented by Carl Hubbell, that has the speed of a fastball but "runs away" from the batter, i.e., moves away at the last moment. NDAS. The name comes from "corkscrew." WPO. *Compare* Flake.

SCREW YOUR COURAGE TO THE STICKING POINT *to screw your courage to the sticking point.* To summon all your courage. Source: ARCHERY. Shakespeare, *Macbeth,* 1606. To crank back the string of a crossbow until it catches on the "dog." Lady Macbeth said "sticking place." *Compare* Let Slip the Dogs of War.

SCRIMMAGE *to scrimmage with someone.* To argue or debate with someone. LTA: 1880. Source: FOOTBALL. To play a practice game against another unit of your own team. Originally from fencing's *skirmish* by way of rugby's *scrummage* (SOED: 1833).

SCUTTLE *to scuttle plans for something.* To abandon plans for something. Source: SAILING. SOED: 1642. To abandon a ship or boat and sink it by drilling or chopping holes in the sides. *Compare* Scuttlebutt (originally a wooden cask that had been drilled into or "tapped").

SCUTTLEBUTT *a scuttlebutt.* A rumor or piece of gossip. NDAS: 1930. Source: SAILING. WNCD: 1805. The sort of gossip and rumors that emanate from conversation around a ship's water keg (the "scuttled butt" or "tapped cask"). WNWD; WPO. *Compare* Scuttle.

SEA *See* All at Sea; Between the Devil and the Deep Blue Sea; Get Your Sea Legs.

SECOND (v) *to second something.* ("I'll second that.") To support a motion or nomination or opinion. Source: DUELING; BOXING. To aid and support one of the participants in a duel (LTA: 1613) or boxing match (LTA: 1897)—as a "second." The noun *second,* meaning "supporter," dates from the 16th cent. SOED: 1588. *See also* Set-to.

SECOND-STRINGER *a second-stringer.* A person in the upper, but not the highest, ranks of an organization. Source: FOOTBALL. A "first reserve," just behind the players in the "starting lineup." *Also:* "second-*string,*" from the extra bowstring carried by an archer. WNCD: 1643.

SECOND TO NONE *to be second to none.* To be as good as, or better than, anyone else. SOED: late M.E. Source: RACING. To finish first. CI; DOC. *Compare* Come Off Second Best.

SECOND WIND *See* Get Your Second Wind.

SEE RED *to see red.* To become suddenly and intensely angry. DOC: 1901. Source: BULLFIGHTING. For the bull to become enraged at the sight of the matador's red cape, though any color would probably cause the same reaction. DOC; WPO. *See also* Red Herring.

SEESAW *to seesaw back and forth.* To vacillate. SOED: 1712. Source: CHILDREN'S PLAY (Seesaw). To ride a seesaw or teeter-totter: a board balanced on a fulcrum so that the rider—and their partner at the other end of the board—rise and fall in turn. Sometimes the board is adjustable to different weights of riders. *See also* Teeter on the Brink.

SEE STARS   *to see stars.* To be stunned by a blow to your head. Source: BOXING. To be knocked on your back in the ring, so that you see either the stars or the lights of the arena above you. CI.

SEE WHICH WAY THE WIND IS BLOWING   *to see which way the wind is blowing.* To delay making a decision until you can find out more about the prevailing conditions. Source: SAILING. To delay plotting a course until you can check out the direction of the wind. CI. *See also* Send Up a Trial Balloon.

SEND SOMEONE TO THE SHOWERS   *to send someone to the showers.* To eliminate someone from the competition. Source: BASEBALL. To remove a player, usually a pitcher, from the lineup, as a result of which they can go take a shower, because baseball players, unlike the players of most other team sports, are not allowed to return to the game once they have been removed. NDAS. *See also* Get Sent to the Showers.

SEND UP A TRIAL BALLOON   *to send up a trial balloon.* To send out feelers to gauge the readiness of the public for a new product or project. Source: FLYING. To send up a small, gas-filled balloon to gauge the strength and direction of the wind. *See also* See Which Way the Wind Is Blowing.

SENT DOWN TO THE MINORS   *to be sent down to the minors.* To be demoted. Source: BASEBALL. To be transferred from a team in the "major" leagues—the American or National leagues—to a team in the "minor" leagues, the "farm" clubs, once classified as *A, B, C,* and *D* but now all classified as certain numbers of *A*'s: *AAA* ("Triple" A), *AA* ("Double" A), and *A* ("Single" A). *See also* Bush (adj.); Bush-league (adj.); Farm Out; Minor-league.

SET A TRAP   *to set a trap for someone.* To attempt to "catch" someone, e.g., a criminal or a mate. Source: TRAPPING. SOED: O.E. To "arm" a trap for snaring any animal that triggers it. *See also* Bait the Trap.

SET 'EM UP IN THE OTHER ALLEY   *Set 'em up in the other alley!* I'm hot, on a roll, on a tear. Source: BOWLING. Set up the ten pins in a 1–2–3–4 triangle at the end of the "alley."

SET THE HOOK   *to set the hook.* To clinch a deal. Source: FISHING. To firm up the hook in a fish's mouth by pulling or jerking up on the line. *See also* Set Your Hooks for.

SET THE PACE   *to set the pace.* To provide the example for others to follow. Source: RACING. To establish the speed of a race by moving to the front at the outset and running at a fast pace for as long as possible. CI; DPF. *See also* Keep Pace with; Off the Pace; Pacemaker; Pacesetter; Put Someone through Their Paces.

SET-TO   *a set-to.* A verbal battle. WNCD: 1743. Source: BOXING. Before boxing rules were codified by the Marquess of Queensberry in 1867, contestants were ''set to'' (brought to) the ''mark'' (a line scratched in the dirt) at the beginning of each round (called a set-to) by their seconds. DPF; LTA. *See also* Not up to Scratch; Second (v).

SET-UP (n)   *a set-up.* A ''trap.'' Source: BOWLING(?). The pins are set up at the end of the alley, ready to be hit. POOL(?). The balls are set up at the end of the table, ready to be hit. NDAS.

SET UP (v)   *to set someone up.* To entrap someone. Source: BOWLING(?). To ''set up' bowling pins to be hit by a bowling ball. POOL(?). To set up pool balls to be hit by the cue ball.

SET YOUR HOOKS FOR   *to set your hooks for someone.* To attempt to ''catch'' a member of the opposite sex. (Object: matrimony.) Source: FISHING. To secure the hook(s) on your fishing line. *See also* Set the Hook.

SET YOUR SIGHTS HIGH   *to set your sights high.* To have high aspirations. Source: SHOOTING. To aim for a distant target, i.e., to aim high, by raising the end of the arrow or barrel above parallel. *See also* Aim High.

SET YOUR SIGHTS ON   *to set your sights on something.* To designate something as your goal or objective. Source: SHOOTING. To aim your firearm at a target. Bows also have ''sights'' now. *See also* Have Something in Your Sights; Have Your Sights Set on Something.

SHADOW BOXING   *to be shadow boxing.* To be attacking an imaginary opponent. Source: BOXING. LTA: 1919. To be ''sparring'' with an imaginary opponent. *Compare* Tilt at Windmills.

SHAKE   *See* Fair Shake; In Two Shakes of a Lamb's Tail; No Great Shakes.

SHAKEDOWN CRUISE   *to take something out for a shakedown cruise.* To test drive a newly overhauled vehicle. Source: SAILING. To take a new or refitted boat out for a trial run. NDAS. *See also* Cruise.

SHAKE-UP   *a shake-up.* A restructuring of an organization or its administration and personnel. WNCD: 1847. Source: DICE GAMES. A shaking of the dice, either in the hand or in a mechanical tumbler. DAE. *See also* Tinhorn.

SHELL GAME   *a shell game.* A scam; a swindle. DAE: 1893. Source: CON GAMES. WNCD: 1890. A ''rigged'' game in which bystanders are encouraged to bet on which of three ''shells'' (English walnut shells or cups) an object, such as a pea, is located under after the shells have been moved out of their original order. A ''shell company'' is a phony business, existing only on paper. *See also* Palm Something off; Play Fast and Loose; Skin Game.

SHIP OF STATE   *the ship of state.* The government. Source: SAILING. The sailing ship as a miniature state, with the captain as "governor" and the crew as the "governed." *See also* Like Rats Leaving a Sinking Ship; Run a Tight Ship; When My Ship Comes in.

SHIPSHAPE   *Everything is shipshape.* Everything is in order. LTA: 1860. Source: SAILING. SOED: 1644. Everything is as neat and orderly as on a ship, where "there is a place for everything, and everything is in its place." CI. *See also* Decked out; Run a Tight Ship.

SHIVER MY TIMBERS   *Well, shiver my/me timbers!* Well, what do you know! Immediate Source: CRICKET. 20th cent. Well, scatter my wickets! Ultimate Source: SAILING. WNWD: 1830s. Well, rack my beams! (An oath attributed to sailors, such as Popeye.)

SHOO-IN   *a shoo-in.* A candidate who is certain to win. WNCD: ca. 1950. Source: HORSE RACING. SPD: 1900. A horse that is certain to win—possibly because the jockeys have all bet on it and are holding their own horses back. FP; NDAS; SPD.

SHOOT FROM THE HIP   *to shoot from the hip.* To speak bluntly and perhaps irreverently. Source: SHOOTING. To shoot a firearm without raising it to eye level or taking aim. NDAS.

SHOOTING CRAPS   *to be shooting craps.* To be taking a wild gamble. Source: CRAPS. DAE: 1898. To be throwing two dice, hoping to get a "natural" (a 7 or 11) or a total other than 2 ("craps" or "snake eyes"), 3, or 12 on the first throw. *See also* Crap Game; Crapshoot.

SHOOTING GALLERY   *a shooting gallery.* A place where heroin addicts can "shoot up" and "crash." Source: SHOOTING; CARNIVAL. WNCD: 1836. A "stand" at a carnival or amusement park where, for a price, and the chance of a prize, you can shoot at tiny moving figures with a BB gun. NDAS. *See also* Ring a Bell; Ring the Bell; Sure as Shooting; Whole Shooting Match.

SHOOT OFF YOUR MOUTH   *to shoot off your mouth.* To speak uninhibitedly or irresponsibly. DAE: 1880. Source: FIREWORKS. To shoot off fireworks, which have poor aim and, once launched, are beyond your control.

SHOOT THE BREEZE   *to shoot the breeze.* To engage in idle conversation. Source: SAILING. To sail "with" the wind.

SHOOT THE DICE   *to shoot the dice.* To take a chance. Source: CRAPS. To throw the dice.

SHOOT THE MOON   *to shoot the moon.* To risk everything. Immediate Source: CARD GAMES. To go for all the tricks (as in bridge), or to try to get as many cards—or get rid of as many cards—as possible. Ultimate Source: SHOOTING. To set your sights as high as possible, even as high as the moon.

There is also a CHILDREN'S GAME called "shoot the moon" that involves trying to roll a steel ball up two steel rods without letting it drop between them.

SHOOT THE WORKS   *to shoot the works.* To risk everything at one time. Source: FIREWORKS. To shoot off all of the fireworks at one time. CRAPS. To bet all of your remaining cash on one final throw of the dice. NDAS.

SHOOT YOUR BOLT   *to shoot your bolt.* To use up all of your resources at one time. Source: ARCHERY. DOC: 13th cent. To shoot your last arrow (or "bolt"). CI. *Compare* Shoot Your Wad.

SHOOT YOUR WAD   *to shoot your wad.* To spend all your money. ("He shot his wad on a new car.") DOC: 1925. Source: SHOOTING. In the case of a muzzle-loader: to propel not only the "ball" but the cloth "wad" that held the ball in place. DOC. *Compare* Shoot Your Bolt.

SHORTSTOP   *to shortstop something.* To intercept a passing dish at a family style dinner. Source: BASEBALL. For the infielder to the left of second base to intercept a batted or thrown ball—i.e., to stop it short of going into the outfield. NDAS. *Compare* Stop Short of Something.

SHORT-SUITED   *to be short-suited.* To be cheated out of your fair share of something; to be short-changed. Source: CARD GAMES. To be dealt a hand of cards from a deck that lacks one or more cards in one or more "suits."

SHOT (n)   *See* Call the Shots; Cheap Shot; Give It a Shot; Give It Your Best Shot; Long Shot; Not by a Long Shot; Take a Shot at It; Take Your Best Shot.

SHOTGUN APPROACH   *a shotgun approach.* A generalized attack, aimed at nothing in particular. Source: HUNTING. The use of a shotgun, which scatters numerous tiny missiles, instead of a rifle, which propels only one larger one. *See also* Take a Potshot.

SHOT IN THE DARK   *a shot in the dark.* A wild guess. Source: HUNTING. A wild shot, in the dark of night, with little chance of finding the target. DOC. *See also* Dark Horse.

SHOULD OF STOOD IN BED   *I should of stood in bed.* I should have stayed home in bed and avoided this disaster. WPO: 1930s. Source: BOXING. This is the sort of thing a manager or trainer might say after watching their boxer get beaten in the ring. WPO.

SHOVE OFF   *to shove off.* To leave. ("I guess I'll shove off now.") Source: SAILING. SOED: O.E. To push a boat away from the beach or dock. CI. *Compare* Push off.

SHOW   *to show.* (Usu. neg.: "She didn't show.") To appear as promised. Source: HORSE RACING(?). To finish third, or at least third, in a horse race. Perhaps just short for "show up." *Compare* No-show.

SHOWDOWN   *a showdown.* A final confrontation. Source: POKER. DAE: 1884. The climax of a poker game, when the remaining players "call" for the highest bettor to "show" their hand by putting the cards (down) on the table, face up, after which the other players do likewise. DPF. *See also* Put Your Cards on the Table; Show Your Hand.

SHOW MUST GO ON   *The show must go on!* Business must proceed as usual, in spite of severe setbacks. DOC: 19th cent. Source: CIRCUS. The activity of the circus must continue—e.g., the band must "play on"—in spite of an injury to a performer or an accident involving one of the animals. The object is to avoid panic. DOC; WPO.

SHOW THE WHITE FEATHER   *to show the white feather.* To display cowardice. Source: COCKFIGHTING. To act like a cowardly gamecock—one that has a white feather in its tail. CI; WPO.

SHOW YOUR HAND   *to show your hand.* To reveal your plans or intentions, unintentionally. Source: CARD GAMES. To reveal your "hand" of cards to your opponent, presumably unintentionally. CI. *See also* Showdown; Tip Your Hand.

SHOW YOUR HOLE CARD   *to show your hole card.* To give away your advantage. Source: POKER. To unintentionally reveal the cards that have been dealt to you face down ("in the hole") in stud poker: the first card in five-card stud; the first, second, or last card in seven-card stud. *See also* Card.

SHUFFLE (n)   *See* Fast Shuffle; Get Lost in the Shuffle.

SHUTOUT (n)   *a shutout.* A decisive victory. Source: BASEBALL. WNCD: 1889. A game that ends with one team scoring at least one run and the other team scoring none at all. LOS; SFS. *Also:* to "pitch a shutout." *See also* Blank; Love Game.

SHUT YOUR TRAP   *Shut your trap!* Shut your mouth! Source: TRAPPING. "Trap" in this metaphor compares the open jaws of a steel trap with the open mouth of a noisy person. NDAS. *Compare* Stow It.

SIDE (n)   *See* Change Sides; Choose Up Sides; Flip Side; On the Flip Side; On the Side; On the Winning Side; Other Side of the Coin; Take Sides with.

SIDELINED   *to be sidelined with a cold (etc.).* To be knocked out of action by a cold (etc.). WNCD: 1943. Source: FOOTBALL. To be confined to the "sidelines" (the boundary makers on the side of the field) during a game, because of illness, injury, etc. LOS. *See also* Sidelines.

SIDELINES   *to watch from the sidelines.* To be a spectator of, instead of a participant in, an event. Source: FOOTBALL. DAE: 1899. For a player to watch from outside the boundaries (the "sidelines") of the field while a game is in progress—because of illness, injury, etc. "Sidelines" are also "hobbles" on the same-side legs of a horse. DAE: 1844. *See also* Sidelined.

SIDESTEP   *to sidestep an issue.* To avoid an issue. Source: FOOTBALL. To step to the side, while carrying the ball, in order to avoid a potential tackler. SFS.

SIDE WITH   *to side with someone.* To take sides with someone. SOED: 1600. Source: SPORTS(?). To play on the same team (to team up) with someone. *See also* Change Sides; Choose Up Sides; One Sided (p. a.); Take Sides with.

SIGHTS   *See* Have Something in Your Sights; Have Your Sights Set on Something; Set Your Sights High; Set Your Sights on.

SIGN HIM/HER UP   *Sign him up! Sign her up!* What a performance! Source: BASEBALL. Baseball players are "signed up"—put under contract—after being "drafted" or "tried out" or otherwise observed or tested.

SIGN OF GOOD BREEDING   *a sign of good breeding.* An indication of "class." Source: HORSE RACING. Evidence of the superior lineage of a horse from former facing champions.

SIMON SAYS   *Simon says, "Clean up your room!"* This is an order! Source: CHILDREN'S GAMES (Simon Says). One child plays "Simon," the leader, and the other children play the followers. When the leader says "Simon says 'Raise your right hand,' " they must do so or be eliminated from the game. When the leader says just "Raise your right hand," the ones who do so are also eliminated from the game—until there is only one child left.

SINK OR SWIM   *It's sink or swim.* It's showdown time, the moment of truth. DOC: 1538. Source: SWIMMING. You're going to drown ("sink") if you don't manage to swim. DOC.

SIT TIGHT   *to sit tight.* To be satisfied with what you have; to choose neither to act nor react. SOED: 1898. Source: POKER. To be satisfied with the hand of cards that you have been dealt and choose not to draw others or initiate a bet. DOC. *See also* Hold a Pat Hand; Stand Pat.

SITTING DUCK   *to be a sitting duck.* To be an easy target—for con artists, thieves, etc. DOC: 1944. Source: HUNTING. For a duck to be an easy target for hunters because it is sitting on the water or land. CI; DOC. *See also* Blow Someone out of the Water; Dead Duck. *Compare* Lame Duck.

SKATE CIRCLES AROUND   *to skate circles around someone.* ("She can skate circles around him when it comes to computer programing.") To have superior ability or potential in relation to someone else. Source: ICE SKATING. To be able to execute the compulsory school figures (e.g., circles and figure eights) better than someone else; to be able to skate so fast that you can circle your opponent and still win the race. *Compare* Run Circles around.

SKATE ON THIN ICE   *to be skating on thin ice.* To be living dangerously, taking unnecessary risks. DOC: 1897. Source: ICE SKATING. To be skating on ice that is barely able to support you. The realization of this fact usually causes you to skate even faster. DOC; DPF; HTB. *See also* Tread on Thin Ice.

SKIN A CAT   *See* More Than One Way to Skin a Cat.

SKIN GAME   *a skin game.* A situation in which you have been set up, so that you have no chance of succeeding. Source: CON GAMES. WNCD: 1868. A "confidence" game in which the player has no chance of winning and is "skinned" of all their money. *See also* Scam; Shell Game.

SKIN OFF MY NOSE   *See* No Skin off My Nose.

SKIP   *to skip something—e.g., school.* To be absent from something—e.g., school—deliberately. Source: CHILDREN'S PLAY. WNCD: 14th cent. To run lightly, with each foot touching the ground twice instead of once. All senses of "skip" derive from this fashion of running. *See also* Hop, Skip, and a Jump; Play Hooky.

SKIPPER   *the skipper.* The boss. Source: SAILING. WNCD: 14th cent. The captain of a sailing vessel.

SKULL SESSION   *a skull session.* A planning session. Source: FOOT-BALL. WNCD: 1937. A review of "plays" by the coaches and players before or during a game. The use of "skull" suggests a mental rather than a physical activity. LOS.

SKUNK   *to skunk someone.* To defeat someone badly. WNCD: 1846. Source: SPORTS; GAMES. To defeat someone completely—preventing them from scoring—in a sport or game. WNWD. *Also:* to be "skunked." *See also* Blank.

SKYROCKET   *Prices have skyrocketed.* Prices have risen dramatically. WNCD: 1890. Source: FIREWORKS. "Skyrockets" are fireworks that are propelled into the air, where they explode in a splash of color.

SKY'S THE LIMIT   *The sky's the limit!* There is *no* limit to our fun, spending, etc. Source: FLYING(?). To the aviator, there seems to be no vertical limit to the sky.

SLACK OFF   *to slack off.* For production, sales, attendance, etc., to decline in quantity. SOED: 1606. Source: SAILING. For the ropes to go slack in the absence of wind. *See also* Take up the Slack.

SLAM DUNK   *to slam dunk someone/something.* To put someone away (e.g., a competitor); to total something (e.g., someone else's car). Source: BASKET-

BALL. LTA: early 1970s. To force the ball directly through the basket, with one or two hands, rather than shoot it in or "lay it up."

SLAP-HAPPY *to be slap-happy.* To be temporarily dazed or stupefied. Source: BOXING. WNCD: 1936. To be permanently dazed or stupefied as a result of too many blows to the head in too many fights. LTA. *See also* Punch-drunk; Punchy.

SLEEP LIKE A TOP *to sleep like a top.* To sleep silently and motionlessly. Source: CHILDREN'S TOYS. SOED: 1854. To sleep as silently and motionlessly as a spinning top (a wooden cone that is caused to twirl on its point). Such a top is said to "sleep." CI; DPF; HOI. *See also* Run Like a Top.

SLINGS AND ARROWS *"the slings and arrows of outrageous fortune."* The "hard knocks" of life. Shakespeare, *Hamlet,* 1601. Source: SLINGSHOT; ARCHERY. Shakespeare is personifying Fortune as a warrior or hunter (of humans). DOC.

SLINGSHOT *to slingshot around the moon.* For a spacecraft to catch the moon's gravity and circle it as if attached to a cord. Source: SLINGSHOT. The old-fashioned slingshot (or "sling") consisted of a piece of leather attached to the loop of a cord. A stone was inserted in the leather pad, the cord was twirled, and one end of the cord was released, thereby releasing the stone.

SLUSH FUND *a slush fund.* An off-the-record accumulation of petty cash; a secret fund for supporting illegal activities. Source: SAILING. WNCD: 1864. A fund accumulated by sailors, for their own use, from the sale of excess grease or fat. WPO.

SMALL FRY Children. Source: FISHING. A catch of small fish, which will "fry up" into a "small" meal. NDAS.

SMART MONEY *The smart money is on X.* The experts say that X is the stock to buy, the candidate to support, etc. WNCD: 1926. Source: GAMBLING; BETTING. The handicappers say that X is the horse to bet on. *See also* Highly Touted.

SMASH HIT *a smash hit.* A show—a movie, a TV series, etc.— that is an instant success. Source: TENNIS. A hard overhand hit of a "lobbed" ball. *See also* Hit (n).

SMELL A RAT *to smell a rat.* To suspect a trick. Source: HUNTING. For a rat terrier to smell the scent of a rat and burrow after it. CI; WPO. *See also* Rat Race.

SMOKE OUT *to smoke someone/something out.* To force someone or something out into the open. SOED: 1608. Source: HUNTING. WNCD: 1605. To force an animal out of its hole by directing smoke into the hole. CI; DOC.

SMOOTH SAILING *to be smooth sailing.* To be trouble free. ("It was smooth sailing during the first few years of their marriage.") Source: SAILING. To be sailing with a gentle breeze and calm seas. SOED. *See also* Clear Sailing; Sail through.

SNAKE EYES *to come up with snake eyes.* To come up with nothing to show for your efforts. Source: CRAPS. To throw "craps": two ones. "Snake eyes" is a losing throw if it is the *first* throw of the dice. It is the *lowest* losing combination—just as the snake is the lowest animal to the ground.

SNATCH DEFEAT FROM THE JAWS OF VICTORY *to snatch defeat from the jaws of victory.* To turn an almost-assured success into a disappointing failure. Source: SPORTS. To turn an almost-assured victory into a stunning defeat, usually at the last minute. This is a sports announcer's takeoff on "snatch victory from the jaws of defeat." *See also* Agony.

SNIFF SOMETHING OUT *to sniff something out.* To uncover something hidden, and usually illegal. SOED: 1864. Source: HUNTING. For a dog to track down a quarry by its scent. CI.

SNOOKER *to snooker someone.* To trick someone. WNCD: 1925. Source: SNOOKER. 1889. To prevent a direct shot by your opponent. Snooker is a variation of pool that is played with fifteen red balls and six others. *See also* Hoodwink; Stymie. *Compare* Euchre.

SNOOKERED *to be snookered.* To be tricked by someone. Source: SNOOKER. To be prevented by your opponent from making a direct shot. *See also* Behind the Eight Ball; Finessed; Stymied. *Compare* Euchred.

SNOWBALL *for something to snowball.* For something to grow rapidly from a small beginning. SOED: 1929. Source: CHILDREN'S PLAY. For a snowball to grow in size as it is rolled through wet snow. RIDING. For snow to "ball up" under a horse's hoof. DAE: 1931.

SNOWBALL'S CHANCE IN HELL *not a snowball's chance in hell.* No chance at all. DOC: 1931. Source: CHILDREN'S PLAY. Snowballs and snowmen are often the last snow in the yard to melt; but even packed snow would melt instantly in the fires of hell. DOC.

SOCK IT TO ME *Sock it to me!* Give me the bad news. Source: BOXING. Hit me with your best shot. CI. (A gag line on the TV show *Laugh In*.)

SOFTBALL-SIZE HAIL Mammoth-size hail. (Formerly called grapefruit-size hail.) Source: SOFTBALL. Hail the size of softballs—approx. 3¾ inches in diameter. *See also* Baseball-size Hail; Golf Ball-size Hail; Marble-size Hail.

SOFTEN SOMEONE UP *to soften someone up.* To weaken someone's defenses in preparation for making a request or asking a favor. Source: BOXING.

To deliver blows to the body, causing your opponent to lower their guard and be more susceptible to a blow to the head. CI. *Compare* Soften the Blow.

SOFTEN THE BLOW   *to soften the blow.* To reduce the shock of some bad news. Source: BOXING(?). To reduce the shock of hard blows by rolling with the punches. *Compare* Soften Someone Up.

SOFT-PEDAL   *to soft-pedal something.* To deemphasize something, such as a political hot potato. Source: CAR RACING(?). SPD indicates that the term is used in car racing for "tread lightly on the gas pedal," but the obvious source is the "soft pedal" on a piano. CI.

SOFT TOUCH   *a soft touch.* A person who is easily taken advantage of, especially when you want to borrow money: a sucker. WNCD: 1939. Source: CON GAMES. An easy mark for a con man (or woman). CI. *See also* Pushover.

SOUTHPAW   *a southpaw.* A left-hander. WNCD: 1892. Source: BASEBALL. LTA: 1885. A left-handed pitcher, so called because in many ballparks the pitcher faces west, so the throwing arm of a left-handed pitcher is on the south side. The term, which was first used in Comiskey Park in Chicago, now applies to all left-handers, not just pitchers. DPF; NDAS; SFS; WPO.

SPAR   *to spar with someone.* To engage in an impromptu debate with someone. SOED: 1698. Immediate Source: BOXING. LTA: 1755. To engage in a practice match with another boxer. Ultimate Source: COCKFIGHTING. SOED: 1570. For two gamecocks to strike at each other with their natural or metal "spurs." *See also* Sparring Partner; Stand the Gaff; Well Heeled (p. a.).

SPARRING PARTNER   *a sparring partner.* A friend with whom you can argue or quarrel without destroying your friendship. Source: BOXING. WNCD: 1908. A teammate with whom you can engage in practice without being killed. CI; LOS. *See also* Spar. *Compare* Verbal Sparring.

SPECTATOR SPORTS   *Life is not a spectator sport.* A modern maxim. Life must be lived actively, not passively. Source: SPORTS. A "spectator sport" is one, like football, that is designed to be performed before an audience that greatly outnumbers the players. "Stadium golf" is turning the professional part of that game into a spectator sport.

SPIN YOUR WHEELS   *to spin your wheels.* To be wasting your time, not making any progress, not getting anywhere. Source: CAR RACING (Drag Racing)(?). For the rear wheels of a drag racer to turn without advancing the vehicle while it is stopped with the brakes on waiting for the green light. The metaphor is more likely based on a passenger car or truck that is stuck in the mud, sand, or snow. *Compare* Head Is Spinning; Running in Place. *Compare* Wheeler-dealer.

SPIRIT OF FAIR PLAY *in the spirit of fair play.* Generously, selflessly. Source: SPORTS. SOED: *fair play*, 1440. According to the highest standards of "sportsmanship" (q.v.). *See also* Play Fair; Sporting Chance.

SPLIT DECISION *a split decision.* Not a unanimous decision. Source: BOXING. WNCD: 1952. A two-to-one decision of the judges in a boxing match that goes the minimum number of rounds without a knockout.

SPOILSPORT *a spoilsport.* Someone who ruins the fun for everyone else— e.g., by bothering them or refusing to take part. WNCD: 1821. Source: SPORTS. A player who spoils the game for the other participants or refuses to play at all. *See also* Make Sport.

SPONGE *See* Throw in the Sponge/Towel.

SPOOF *a spoof of something.* A parody of something. LTA: 1895. Source: GAMES. A nonsensical game invented in the 1880s by a British comedian. WNWD.

SPORT (n) *See* Bad Sport; Contact Sport; Good Sport; Make Sport; Spectator Sport.

SPORT (v) *to sport something new.* To show off a new outfit, a new hairdo, etc. SOED: 1778. Source: SPORTS. To engage in "sport," i.e., organized play.

SPORTING CHANCE *to have a sporting chance.* To have—or give someone—a reasonable opportunity to succeed. SPORTS. To have—or give someone—a fair chance to play or win, according to the "spirit of fair play" (q.v.).

SPORTING GESTURE *a sporting gesture.* A generous or selfless act. Source: SPORTS. An act of fairness or kindness to your opponent.

SPORTSMANSHIP *good sportsmanship.* Fairness, generosity, and respect for your opponents. Immediate Source: SPORTS. WNCD: 1745. The spirit of fair play, by which you must respect both the "spirit" and the "letter" of the rules. FP. Ultimate Source: GAMBLING; BETTING. DAE: 1740. The quality of a good "sportsman," i.e., a "horseplayer" or gambler on horse races. *See also* Gamesmanship; Spirit of Fair Play.

SPOT (n) *See* Hit the Spot; Knock the Spots off; On the Spot.

SPOT SOMEONE A LEAD *to spot someone a lead.* To give someone a time advantage. Source: RACING. To give someone a handicap, such as a "head start" (q.v.). *See also* Lead from Start to Finish.

SPRINGBOARD *for something to serve as a springboard to something else.* For something to enable you to reach greater heights. Source: DIVING. SOED: 1866. A "springboard" is a diving board equipped with a spring that can elevate a diver to great heights. Used also in ACROBATICS, or "tumbling."

SQUARE OFF   *to square off with someone.* To engage in verbal battle with someone. Source: BOXING. LTA: 1837. For boxers to get into position to start fighting at the beginning of a match or round. This "position" was at the "scratch line" in the center of the ring of spectators—from ancient Greek times until the rules of boxing were codified in 1867. SOED. *See also* Get Squared away.

SQUARE ONE   *See* Back to Square One.

SQUARE PEG IN A ROUND HOLE   *to be—or feel like—a square peg in a round hole.* To be or feel totally out of place. DOC: 19th cent. Source: CHILDREN'S GAMES. This game consists of a board with round and square holes, into which round and square "pegs" are to be inserted properly. DOC. *See also* Round Peg in a Square Hole.

SQUEAKER   *a squeaker.* A narrow escape. Source: SPORTS. A win by the narrowest of margins. NDAS. The source of "squeak" is probably the thin, small, high-pitched sound of a mouse or hinge. WNWD.

SQUEEZE PLAY   *a squeeze play.* A development of pressure from both sides, as of a high pressure system and a low pressure system coming together at a particular location. Immediate Source: BRIDGE. SOED: 1928. A strategy that forces your opponent to play what would otherwise become a winning card. Ultimate Source: BASEBALL. LTA: 1905. A play that features a runner on third base breaking for home plate in anticipation of a bunt attempt by the batter. A "suicide squeeze" is a dash for home plate regardless of what the batter does. DA. *See also* Force Someone's Hand.

STABLEMATE   *a stablemate.* A member of the same ticket: a running mate. Source: HORSE RACING. WNCD: 1926. A horse from the same "stable" (farm) as another horse: a "running mate" (q.v.).

STAKE   *See* At Stake; Have a Stake in; High-stakes; Play for High Stakes; Pull up Stakes; Raise the Stakes.

STAKES ARE HIGH   *The stakes are high.* The risks are great. Source: POKER. The bets are high, and the "pot" is large.

STAKE YOUR LIFE ON SOMETHING   *to stake your life—or reputation (etc.)—on something.* To be so certain of the outcome of something that you are willing to risk your life or reputation (etc.) on it. Source: GAMBLING; BETTING. To bet everything you have on a "sure thing" (q.v.). *See also* You Bet Your Life.

STALEMATE   *to reach a stalemate.* To reach an impasse, or standoff. Source: CHESS. SOED: 1765. For a situation to develop in which a player can't move their king without putting it "in check," thus leading to a "draw." The literal meaning of "stalemate" is "place" *(stall)* of "death" *(māt)*. DPF; HF; OL. *See also* Checkmate; No-win Situation; Reach a Deadlock; Reach a Stalemate.

STALKING HORSE *a stalking horse.* A decoy or false front for an action or activity (SOED: 1579); a political candidate put forth to divide the opposition (SOED: 1612). Source: HUNTING. SOED: 1519. A horse which the hunter dismounts from and walks behind—i.e., on the side opposite the quarry—in order to approach the quarry without being seen. DOC; HF; SPD; WPO.

STAND BY *to stand by.* To be prepared to make an appearance on radio or television. Source: SAILING. To be prepared to weigh anchor and set sail. LTA.

STANDOFF *a standoff.* A situation in which neither side can win without losing. DA: 1950. Source: POKER. DA: 1843. A situation in which neither of two players chooses to "call" without "raising." *See also* Standoffish.

STANDOFFISH *to be standoffish.* To be aloof or unfriendly. WNCD: 1860. Source: SAILING. To be like a sailing vessel that is "standing off" (staying clear of) the shore. CI. *See also* Standoff.

STAND PAT *to stand pat.* To be satisfied with what you have, and choose neither to act nor react. DAE: 1882. Source: POKER. To be satisfied with the hand you have been dealt (in five-card "draw"), and to choose not to draw any cards as replacements. HF; SPD. *See also* Hold a Pat Hand; Sit Tight.

STAND THE GAFF *to be unable to stand the gaff.* To be a coward. DOC: 1900. Source: COCKFIGHTING. For a gamecock to die as a result of being speared by the metal "gaffs" on its opponent's spurs. WPO. *See also* Spar.

START *See* False Start; Fast Starter; Gentlemen, Start Your Engines; Get off to a Flying Start; Get off to a Good/Bad Start; Good for Starters; Head Start; Jackrabbit Start; Lead from Start to Finish; Out of the Starting Gate.

START FROM SCRATCH *to start from scratch.* To start from the beginning, with nothing. Immediate Source: BOXING. SOED: 1778. For boxers to return to the starting line ("scratch") after a knockdown. Ultimate Source: FOOT RACING. To start a race from the line scratched in the dirt, as in the ancient Greek Games and modern "sandlot" races. CI; DOC; DPF; HTB; NDAS; SFS. *Compare* Not up to Scratch.

STAY AHEAD OF THE GAME *to be or stay ahead of the game.* To survive; to keep your head above water. Source: GAMBLING. To have won more money than you have lost. *Compare* Ahead on Points.

STAY ON AN EVEN KEEL *to stay on an even keel.* To remain calm and steady. Source: SAILING. For a sailing boat or ship to stay upright and level. *Compare* Keel Over.

STAY THE COURSE   *to stay the course.* To remain in an activity until it is finished. Source: RACING. To finish a race—i.e., to complete the "course" (q.v.). CI.

STICKING POINT   *See* Screw Your Courage to the Sticking Point.

STICKLER FOR THE RULES   *a stickler for the rules.* A person who respects the "letter," to the exclusion of the "spirit," of the rules or laws. SOED: 1644. Source: SPORTS. SOED: 1538. An official, like a modern referee or umpire, whose job it once was to interpret and enforce the rules of sport. DOC.

STICKS AND STONES   *Sticks and stones can break my bones, but words can never hurt me.* Name-calling doesn't affect me in the least. Source: CHILDREN'S PLAY. This is the incantation of a child who has just been called "names" by another child and is at a safe distance when he or she says it. WPO. Also: "will break" (etc.)

STICKY WICKET   *a sticky wicket.* A difficult or awkward situation. WNCD: 1926. Source: CRICKET. SOED: 1888. A wet ("sticky") infield ("wicket"), causing tricky footing and strange bounces of the ball. CI; DOC; DPF.

STIFF AS A RAMROD   *to stand stiff as a ramrod.* To stand stiff as a poker. DAE: 1904. Source: SHOOTING. DAE: 1757. A "ramrod" was once used to "ram" the ball and "wadding" down the barrel of a muzzle-loading firearm. *Also:* "straight as a ramrod." *See also* Ramrod.

STONE'S THROW   *a stone's throw from here.* Only a short distance from here. WNCD: 1581. Source: CHILDREN'S PLAY. As far as you can throw a stone.

STONEWALL   *to stonewall.* To obstruct justice; to cover up information: to refuse to testify. WNCD: 1889. Source: CRICKET. To bat defensively—protecting the wicket rather than trying to score. CI; DOC; DPF; EOD; NDAS; SFS; SPD. The metaphorical use first occurred in Australia with the meaning "to filibuster"; the sense of "coverup" first appeared at the 1974 Watergate hearings. "Stonewall" as a noun derives from the nickname of Confederate General Thomas J. Jackson, who held his ground at the First Battle of Bull Run in the Civil War (1862). LTA. *Compare* Lay Your Cards on the Table.

STOOL PIGEON   *a stool pigeon.* An informer for the police. DAE: 1850. Source: HUNTING. DAE: 1836. A pigeon that was once tied to a stool and used as a decoy to attract other pigeons into the net. CI; HF; NDAS. The decoy was also called a "flutter pigeon" (1794), a "stool-crow" (1811), and a "stool-bird" (1841). DAE. *See also* Clay Pigeon; Pigeon.

STOP SHORT OF SOMETHING   *to stop short of something.* To refuse to go beyond the limits of your personal standards or values. Source: RACING;

RIDING. SOED: 1530. To pull up short of a barrier or hurdle. CI. *Compare* Cross the Line; Shortstop.

STOP SOMETHING DEAD IN ITS TRACKS *to stop something dead in its tracks.* To put a sudden halt to something; to shut something down completely. Source: HUNTING. DAE: 1845. To stop a moving quarry by shooting it dead with one shot. *Also:* to "stop someone dead in their tracks."

STOP THE MUSIC *Stop the music!* Stop what you're doing! Source: CHILDREN'S GAMES (Musical Chairs). This is a signal to stop the live or recorded music in a game of musical chairs, at which time all but one of the participants are able to find a chair to sit on. It was a favorite expression of Jimmy Durante. *See also* Play Musical Chairs.

STOWAWAY *a stowaway.* A nonpaying passenger on an airplane (etc.): a freeloader. Source: SAILING. SOED: 1854. An unlisted or nonpaying passenger on a ship, "stowed away" in a remote part of the vessel. *See also* Stow It.

STOW IT *Stow it!* Shut up! Source: SAILING. Put it in storage! WNWD. *See also* Stowaway. *Compare* Shut Your Trap.

STRAIGHT-ARM *to straight-arm a problem.* To keep a problem at arm's length. Source: FOOTBALL. WNCD: 1928. To keep an opposing tackler at arm's length, with your hand on their helmet.

STRAIGHT FROM THE HORSE'S MOUTH *to get it straight from the horse's mouth.* To get information directly from the highest authority. DOC: 20th cent. Source: HORSE RACING. To get a "tip" directly from the racehorse itself(!). CI; HOI; WPO. *Compare* Don't Look a Gift Horse in the Mouth.

STRAIGHT FROM THE SHOULDER *to speak straight from the shoulder.* To speak directly and bluntly. Source: BOXING. DOC: 1856. To deliver a straight blow, as opposed to a "hook" or an "uppercut."

STRANGLEHOLD *to have a stranglehold on someone.* To have someone in a position from which they can't escape. Source: WRESTLING. SOED: 1890. To have your arm bent around your opponent's neck, from behind, with the elbow below the Adam's apple and the fingers clenched over the shoulder.

STRENGTHEN YOUR HAND *to strengthen your hand.* To improve your position. Source: CARD GAMES. To "draw" cards that will improve the "hand" that you were originally dealt.

STRETCH (n) *See* Down the Stretch; Fade in the Stretch.

STRETCH A POINT *to stretch a point.* To broaden an interpretation, extrapolate a claim, liberalize a rule. Source: SHOOTING(?). To interpret the target liberally, granting a "point" that would ordinarily be rejected. The target is imagined to be like a balloon, which expands when inflated. *See also* Down the Stretch.

STRIDE *See* Hit Your Stride; Make Great Strides; Off Stride; Take Something in Stride.

STRIKE OUT *to strike out.* To fail in an attempt to get a job, a date, etc. Source: BASEBALL. To fail to hit a pitched ball that is in the "strike" zone in your final chance—two strikes on you already—in a particular turn at bat. *Compare* Have Two Strikes against You.

STRING SOMEONE ALONG *to string someone along.* To encourage someone to believe in you even though your intentions may be less than honorable: to toy with someone. LTA: 1913. Source: FISHING(?). To "reel" someone in. CHILDREN'S GAMES(?). To pull a string attached to a wallet in order to keep it just out of the grasp of a "finder." *See also* Finders Keepers, Losers Weepers.

STROKE OF GOOD LUCK *a stroke of good luck.* An occurrence of good fortune. Source: POOL. An accidentally good shot: a "fluke" (q.v.). *Also:* a "stroke of good fortune."

STRONG SUIT *your strong suit.* Your strength, strong point, forte, specialty. Source: CARD GAMES. SOED: 1862. Your large number of cards—especially "high" cards—in a single suit, promising a high bid and multiple points. *See also* Long Suit.

STUMP *to stump someone.* To baffle or perplex someone. LTA: 1812. Source: CRICKET. SOED: 1744. For a wicket-keeper to knock down a "bail" or "stump" of the wicket and put the batter out. DPF. *See also* Stumped; Stumper.

STUMPED *to be stumped.* To be baffled or perplexed. DAE: 1812. Source: CRICKET. To be "put out" in a cricket match when the bowled ball knocks down a "bail"—or "stump" (q.v.)— of the "wicket." DPF. *See also* Stumper. *Compare* Stymied.

STUMPER *a stumper.* A knotty problem. DA: 1807. Source: CRICKET. SOED: 1776. A wicket-keeper who knocks down a "bail," or "stump" (q.v.) of the wicket and puts the batter out. *See also* Stumped.

STYMIE *to stymie someone.* To block someone's actions. WNCD: 1857. Source: GOLF. To hit your ball on the green between your opponent's ball and the hole, which blocks your opponent's putt. The rule was changed in the early 1950s to permit "marking" of the ball that is closer to the hole. DPF; LOS; NDAS; SFS. *See also* Behind the Eight Ball; Snooker; Stymied.

STYMIED *to be stymied.* To be prevented from taking a desired action. LTA: 1902. Source: GOLF. LTA: 1857. For an opponent's ball to be on the green between yours and the hole. The rule was changed, in the early 1950s; so while you can still be "metaphorically" stymied, you can no longer be "literally" stymied. *See also* Behind the Eight Ball; Finessed; Snookered; Stymie. *Compare* Stumped.

SUCKER *a sucker.* A pigeon, a dupe, an easy mark. DA: 1831. Source: FISHING. DA: 1769. A fish, the "sucker," which feeds off the bottom of the river or lake by sucking up its food. *See also* Never Give a Sucker an Even Break; There's a Sucker Born Every Minute.

SUDDEN DEATH A run-off election—or drawing of lots, or flipping of a coin—to determine a winner between two candidates tied for office. One survives; the other "dies." Immediate Source: SPORTS. An "overtime" competition between tied opponents. The first to score wins the game (football) or match (golf). LOS. Ultimate Source: GAMBLING. A final toss of the dice or coin to determine an overall winner. WPO. There may also be a connection with cockfighting or dog fighting.

SUIT *See* Follow Suit; Long Suit; Short-suited; Strong Suit.

SUIT UP *to suit up for something.* To get ready to engage in some kind of activity. Source: FOOTBALL. To put on the "pads' (equipment) and uniform before a football game.

SUNDAY PUNCH *to throw a Sunday punch.* To attack someone or something with your biggest "weapons." Source: BOXING. WNCD: 1932. To throw a knockout punch—and end someone's week? LOS. *See also* Swing from the Heels.

SURE AS SHOOTING *It's going to happen, sure as shooting.* It's a certainty. WPO: 1851. Source: SHOOTING. It's as sure as the flight of an arrow or bullet. *See also* Shooting Gallery.

SURE-FIRE *a sure-fire deal, plan, scheme, etc.* A can't-miss deal or plan or scheme: a sure thing. Source: SHOOTING. A sure-fire weapon: one that can be counted on to fire when the trigger is pulled. *Compare* Hang Fire.

SURE THING *a sure thing.* A guaranteed success. DA: 1867. Source: GAMBLING; BETTING. DA: 1836. A sure bet—one that can't lose.

SURFACE *for the facts to surface.* For the facts to become evident. Source: SWIMMING. For a swimmer to rise to the surface of the water in order to get a breath of air. *See also* Come up for Air; Surface for Air.

SURFACE FOR AIR *to surface for air.* To pause in the midst of a long (spoken) sentence in order to catch your breath. Source: SWIMMING. To come to the surface of the water for a breath of air. *See also* Come up for Air; Surface.

SURF IS UP *The surf is up!* It's party time! Source: SURFING. The waves are just right for surfing. (This is a California term.)

SWEEPSTAKES *to win the sweepstakes.* To win the lottery or other such promotion. Source: HORSE RACING. SOED: 1862. To win a bet on a "stakes" race, such as the (former) Irish Sweepstakes. The "stakes" were originally put up by the horses' owners and awarded to ("swept by") the owner of the winning horse. DPF; HF. The term probably came into horse racing from gambling—the "lottery." *See also* Win the Sweepstakes.

SWEEP THE BOARDS *to sweep the boards.* To win all the honors, offices, awards, etc. Source: GAMBLING; BETTING. To win all of the prize money. In horse racing, to cash in for all three finishes: "win," "place," and "show." In poker, to "sweep" all of the winnings from the table (the "board"). CI; DPF.

SWEETEN THE POT *to sweeten the pot.* To increase the rewards—and also the risks. Source: POKER. To "raise the stakes" (q.v.). HTB.

SWEPT AWAY *to be swept away.* To be overcome (carried away) by emotion. Source: SAILING. To be swept overboard by a wave. *See also* Go by the Boards; Go Overboard; Swept off Your Feet.

SWEPT OFF YOUR FEET *to be swept off your feet by someone/something.* To be overcome (carried away) by emotion, e.g., love. Source: SAILING. To be knocked down—or swept overboard—by a wave. *See also* Go by the Boards; Go Overboard; Swept away.

SWIM *See* In the Swim; Sink or Swim.

SWING *See* Come Out Swinging; Free Swinger; Get into the Swing of Things; In Full Swing; Room to Swing a Cat in; Take a Swing at Something.

SWING FROM THE HEELS *to swing from the heels.* To give it everything you've got. Source: BOXING. For a boxer to put everything he/she has behind a punch. *See also* Come Out Swinging; Sunday Punch.

T

TABLE (n) *See* Lay Your Cards on the Table; Put Your Cards on the Table; Time to Put Your Chips on the Table; Turn the Tables; Under the Table; Under-the-Table.

TABLES ARE TURNED *The tables are turned.* The situation is now reversed: the shoe is on the other foot. Source: GAMES (Board Games). The table has literally been turned, so that each opponent's position is reversed. *See also* Turn the Tables.

TACK *See* Take a Different Tack.

TACKLE *to tackle a problem.* To attempt to solve a problem. Source: FOOTBALL. SOED: 1847. To seize the ball carrier and throw him to the ground. LTA. The original source may be wrestling. WNCD.

TAIL (n) *See* Heads I Win, Tails You Lose; On Someone's Tail; Put a Tail on; Turn Tail.

TAIL (v) *to tail someone.* To follow someone without being seen by that person. Source: HUNTING. For a hunter to follow a quarry by keeping its tail in sight. *See also* On Someone's Tail; Put a Tail on.

TAKE A BAD BOUNCE *for things to take a bad bounce.* For events to take a turn for the worse. Source: BASEBALL. For a batted ball to bounce erratically—"take a bad hop"—because of the unevenness of the field. FP. *See also* Bounce Back.

TAKE A BREATHER *to take a breather.* To take a break. Source: SPORTS. To take a rest after strenuous exercise.

TAKE A DIFFERENT TACK *to take a different tack.* To change your strategy. Source: SAILING. To head the boat at a different angle into the wind. "Tacking" results in a zigzag course. LTA. *See also* On the First/Last Leg of a Journey.

TAKE A DIVE   *to take a dive.* To lose a competition deliberately—perhaps for financial or political gain. Source: BOXING. LTA: 1930. To throw a fight— i.e., to lose a fight intentionally and for profit. LOS; NDAS. The ultimate source is obviously diving. *See also* Dive in. *Compare* Take a Fall; Take a Nosedive.

TAKE A FALL   *to take a fall.* To take the blame for someone: to be a scapegoat. Source: BOXING. To pretend to be knocked down or out in a boxing match—for profit. The metaphor is probably not from wrestling, despite the use of the word "fall": it takes *two* falls to lose a wrestling match. *See also* Fall Guy; Take the Rap. *Compare* Take a Dive.

TAKE A FLYER   *to take a flyer (or flier) on something.* To take a chance on something, such as the Stock Market. SOED: 1886. Source: GYMNAS-TICS; ACROBATICS. To take a flying leap. NDAS. The expression is also used to describe a fall on the ice.

TAKE A GIANT STEP   *to take a giant step.* To make a major advance. Source: CHILDREN'S GAMES (Mother, May I?). To receive permission from the leader of the game ("Mother") to take a long step forward.

TAKE A HIKE   *Take a hike!* Get lost! Source: HIKING. Take a leisurely walk, especially off the beaten path. The twenty-mile hike in military "basic training" is not so leisurely, though it *is* usually off the beaten path.

TAKE AIM   *to take aim at something.* To focus all of your efforts and attention on achieving a goal. Source: SHOOTING. Shakespeare, *Midsummer Night's Dream,* 1595. To aim a bow or firearm at a target. *See also* Aim High.

TAKE A NOSEDIVE   *to take a nosedive; to nose-dive.* To take a sharp drop— e.g., in temperature or in value. Immediate Source: FLYING. For a plane to head for the ground "nose first." BOXING. For a boxer to fall to the canvas. NDAS. Ultimate Source: DIVING. To dive into the water "nose first." *Compare* Take a Dive.

TAKE A POTSHOT   *to take a potshot at something.* To make a random or generalized attack on something or someone. Source: SHOOTING. SOED: 1858. To take a random shot at an animal—a "pothunter's shot," for the cooking pot—rather than a careful shot at a target. CI; NDAS. *See also* Give it a Shot; Shotgun Approach.

TAKE A POWDER   *to take a powder.* To leave in a hurry. Source: SHOOT-ING. To leave as fast as an explosion of gun powder.

TAKE A RAIN CHECK   *to take a rain check.* To decline or postpone an invitation; to get a guarantee of the current price for the future purchase of an item that is temporarily out of stock. LTA: 1930s. Source: BASEBALL. LTA:

1884. To get a ticket stub that guarantees entry to a future game if the present one is rained out. DOC; DPF; LOS. *See also* Check (n).

TAKE A SHOT AT IT   *to take a shot at it.* ("Take a shot at it!") To give something a try, but with no promises of success. Source: HUNTING. To take a shot at something with a bow or firearm, just to see what happens. *See also* Give It a Shot; Take a Swing at Something.

TAKE A SWING AT SOMETHING   *to take a swing at something.* To give something a try. Source: BASEBALL. To swing the bat at a pitched ball, hoping to get a hit. LOS. *See also* Take a Shot at It.

TAKE A WALK   *Take a walk!* Get lost! Source: BASEBALL. Take your base! (i.e., first base)—an instruction from the home plate umpire to a batter who has just been issued a "walk" by the pitcher.

TAKE IT ON THE CHIN   *to take it on the chin.* To experience a setback without giving up. Source: BOXING. LTA: 1920s. To take a full blow to the chin, the most vulnerable part of the upper body, without going down. FP.

TAKEN ABACK   *to be taken aback.* To be surprised or shocked. Source: SAILING. For a sailing vessel to be slowed because the wind is blowing the sails against the mast. DPF; WPO.

TAKEOFF (n)   *to do a takeoff on something/someone.* To do a parody of something; to make a caricature of someone. WNCD: 1846. Source: FLYING. For an aircraft—or a bird—to "lift off" from the ground. *See also* Get Something off the Ground; Take Off (v).

TAKE OFF (v)   *for something to (really) take off.* For something to (really) catch on—e.g., a new product, fashion, dance, etc. Source: FLYING. For a plane—or a bird—to leave the ground and become airborne. NDAS. *See also* Takeoff (n).

TAKE OFF THE GLOVES   *to take off the gloves.* To get tough; to play hardball. LTA: 1928. Source: BOXING. To fight bare-knuckle, as in the 19th century, rather than with the customary boxing gloves. LTA suggests that the "gloves" may be "dress" gloves. *Compare* Put the Gloves on.

TAKE ON ALL COMERS   *to take on all comers.* To go against all challengers, as in a political primary. Source: BOXING; WRESTLING. LTA: 1880s. To compete against all challengers in a boxing or wrestling match, as at a 19th-century country fair.

TAKE SIDES WITH   *to take sides with someone.* To ally yourself with someone. Source: SPORTS(?). To play on the same side as someone. The ultimate source may be military: to fight on the same side as someone. *See also* Change Sides; Choose up Sides; Side with.

TAKE SOMEONE DOWN A PEG   *to take someone down a peg (or notch).*
To humble someone deservedly. HTB: late 1500s. Source: CRIBBAGE. To
beat someone decisively. The "peg" is used for keeping score. A cricket
"stump" is also called a "peg." SOED: 1909. Pegs have various uses on a
sailing ship. WPO.

TAKE SOMEONE DOWNTOWN   *to take someone downtown.* To give
someone a severe setback. Source: BASEBALL. To take the pitcher downtown—i.e., to hit a homerun off them. In Wrigley Field in Chicago, it is not
unusual for a ball to clear the fences at the top of the bleachers and land
"downtown" on Waveland Avenue or Sheffield Avenue.

TAKE SOMEONE ON   *to take someone on.* To challenge someone for office or engage them in debate. Source: BOXING; WRESTLING. To challenge
someone in the ring.

TAKE SOMEONE TO THE CLEANERS   *to take someone to the cleaners.*
To clean someone out—of money, property, etc. Source: GAMBLING. DOC:
1812. For a gambler to cheat a sucker out of all their money. HTB. *Also:* to
be "taken to the cleaners."

TAKE SOMETHING IN STRIDE   *to take something in stride.* To take
something calmly—e.g., bad news. Source: FOOT RACING. To maintain your
normal pace and rhythm when jumping a hurdle or being jostled by another
competitor. CI. *See also* Make Great Strides.

TAKE THE BAIT   *to take the bait.* To fall for a trick or scam. Source:
FISHING. For a fish to "bite"—i.e., to close its jaws on a baited hook. *See
also* Rise to the Bait.

TAKE THE BALL AND RUN WITH IT   *to take the ball and run with it.*
To assume leadership or responsibility. Source: FOOTBALL. To catch, recover, or be handed the ball—and to run for the goal with it. FP. This expression could also apply to rugby, but not to soccer. *See also* Run (v).

TAKE THE BULL BY THE HORNS   *to take the bull by the horns.* To
attack a difficult problem head on. DOC: early 1700s. Immediate Source: RO-
DEO. To wrestle a steer (a former "bull calf") to the ground by grasping its
horns, from the side or back, and twisting its neck: "bulldogging." FP. Pen-
ultimate Source: BULLFIGHTING. For a matador to seize the horns of a mor-
ibund bull and twist it to the ground. DOC. Ultimate Source: BULL VAULT-
ING. For a Minoan bull vaulter to grasp the bull's horns from the front and
somersault over its back. DPF; HOI.

TAKE THE FIGHT OUT OF SOMEONE   *to take the fight out of someone.*
To wear down, or neutralize, an opponent. Source: BOXING. LTA: 1812. To
slow down an opponent, especially with blows to the body.

TAKE THE LEAD *to take the lead.* To become the front-runner in a political campaign or other competition. Source: RACING. SOED: mid-1800s. To become the front-runner in a race. *See also* Lead from Start to Finish.

TAKE THE LONG COUNT *to take the long count.* To die. Source: BOXING. To be knocked unconscious for more than the count of ten. *See also* Down for the Long Count; Go down for the Long Count.

TAKE THE PLUNGE *to take the plunge.* To take a major step in your life: to get married. Source: DIVING. To throw caution to the wind and dive into unfamiliar waters. CI. *See also* Plunge in.

TAKE THE RAP *to take the rap for someone.* To take the blame for something that you aren't solely—or at all—responsible for. Source: BOXING(?). To take a sharp blow to the body or head. The source could just as well be "fighting." *See also* Fall Guy; Take a Fall.

TAKE THE WIND OUT OF SOMEONE'S SAILS *to take the wind out of someone's sails.* To block someone's plans or ambitions; to burst someone's bubble; to take someone down a peg. LTA: 1901. Source: SAILING. To sail your craft on the windward side of, and close to, another. CI. *See also* Pull the Rug out from under Someone.

TAKE UP THE SLACK *to take up the slack.* To tighten up a procedure; to find other work for employees during a "slow" period. Source: SAILING(?). To increase the tension on a rope. *See also* Slack off.

TAKE YOUR BEST SHOT *Take your best shot!* Give it your best effort. Immediate Source: BOXING. Hit me with your best punch! Ultimate Source: HUNTING; SHOOTING. Take your best shot at an animal or target. *See also* Give It Your Best Shot.

TAKE YOUR LUMPS *to take your lumps.* ("Get in there and take your lumps!") To chalk up experience in the School of Hard Knocks. Source: BOXING. To take the punches thrown by your opponent, some of which will develop into lumps by the next morning.

TALLY HO *Tally Ho!* Here we go! There they go! Source: FOX HUNTING. SOED: 1772. The "huntsman's" cry that signals the sighting of a fox. DPF.

TARGET (v) *to target someone for something.* To single someone out for attention, e.g., to target children for an advertising campaign. WNCD: 1837. Source: SHOOTING. To make something the object of your aim (with a bow or firearm). *See also* Dead on Target; Off Target; On Target.

TARGET LANGUAGE *a target language.* The language that you are attempting to learn or into which you are translating something. WNCD: 1953. Source: SHOOTING. A "target" is the object that you are attempting to hit.

TEAM EFFORT   *a team effort.* An accomplishment by the entire organization rather than by any single member of it. Source: SPORTS. An accomplishment by an entire team rather than by any single player on it. ''Team'' alone derives from the name for two or more animals hitched together to pull a wagon (etc.) *See also* First Team; Function as a Team.

TEAM PLAYER   *a team player.* An employee who puts the interests of the organization before their own. Source: SPORTS. A player who puts the interests of the team before their own. FP; SFS. The source is probably football. *See also* Make the Team.

TEED OFF   *to be teed off.* To be angry at someone. LTA: 1940s. Source: GOLF. For the ball to be struck off the wooden or plastic ''tee'' on the ''teeing'' area of a hole. LOS; NDAS. *See also* Tee It up.

TEE IT UP   *Let's tee it up!* Let's get started!. Source: GOLF. Let's start the round. To ''tee up'' a golf ball is to place it on a wooden or plastic peg— originally a small pile of dirt or sand—from which it is struck down the fairway. The wooden tee was introduced in the 1920s in the United States. LTA. *See also* Teed Off; Tee Off.

TEE OFF   *to tee off on someone.* To attack someone verbally. Source: GOLF. SOED: 1673. To strike the ball off the wooden or plastic ''tee'' on the ''teeing'' area (also called a ''tee'') of a hole. LOS; NDAS. A three-footed ''tee'' is used in football to hold the ball for kickoffs. LTA: 1948. A three-foot high ''tee'' is used to hold the baseball for batting practice or for a children's game called T-Ball or Tee Ball. NDAS. *Also:* ''to tee someone off.'' *See also* Tee It up.

TEETER ON THE BRINK   *to teeter on the brink.* To flirt with disaster. Source: CHILDREN'S GAMES (Teeter-Totter). SOED: 1846. To teeter-totter, i.e., to sit on one end of a board that is balanced on a fulcrum and has another child on the other end, the two of you taking turns going up and down. The child's first ride on a teeter-totter, especially when the child's end of the board goes up, must feel like being on the ''brink of disaster.'' *See also* Seesaw.

TELEGRAPH A PUNCH   *to telegraph a punch.* To advertise your intentions, unintentionally. Source: BOXING. To signal your intention, unintentionally, to throw a punch. LOS. *See also* Pull Your Punches. *Compare* Pull No Punches.

TENNIS ANYONE   *Tennis, anyone?* (On bumper stickers: 10S–NE1.) Would anyone like to change the subject? WPO: 1940s. Source: TENNIS. Would anyone like to play tennis? The word ''tennis'' is from the French *tenez*, ''Hold!'' (meaning ''Watch out! Here it comes!''). Tennis originated as ''court tennis'' in France then moved quickly to England, where it was mentioned by Chaucer in the 14th century and was played by Henry VIII in the 16th century. Oxford University still has a "court tennis" building. *See also* From Pillar to Post.

TEN TO ONE *Ten to one, something will or will not happen!* I'm certain that something will happen/will not happen. Source: GAMBLING; BETTING. I'll give you odds of ten to one—you get $10 for a $1 bet—if I'm wrong about this.

TEST THE WATERS *to test the waters.* To measure the readiness for a new idea or product; to send up a trial balloon. Source: SWIMMING. To dip your toes in the water to discover its temperature.

THAT'S THE WAY THE BALL BOUNCES *That's the way the ball bounces!* That's life; those are the breaks. Source: BALL GAMES. DOC: 1950s. The ball bounces in funny ways in all sports that use one, but a football probably bounces the most erratically because of its elliptical shape. NDAS. Based on this expression are many others, including "That's the way the Mercedes-Benz." *See also* Bounce Back.

THERE'S A SUCKER BORN EVERY MINUTE Attributed to P.T. Barnum, 1850s. WPO. You can fool some of the people all of the time; there's a buyer for everything. Source: CIRCUS. No sideshow, or freakshow, at the circus is too absurd to draw customers and make money. *See also* Sucker.

THERE'S THE RUB *There's the rub!* Shakespeare, *Hamlet*, 1601. There's the problem! Source: BOWLING (Bowls). In the game of "bowls" (or "bocce ball"), a "rub" is any obstruction that impedes the roll of the ball. DOC. *See also* Rub of the Green. *Compare* Hog on Ice.

THREE OF A KIND *to have three of a kind.* To have three things that have something in common: e.g., three sons, three daughters, or triplets. Source: POKER. To have three cards of the same "value" (e.g., three kings or three queens) in your hand. *See also* Four of a Kind.

THREE-RING CIRCUS *a three-ring circus.* ("It was a three-ring circus in there.") A madhouse. WNCD: 1920. Source: CIRCUS. A *major* circus with activity going on in three large circles ("rings") at once. The word "circus" is from the Latin *circus,* as in "Circus Maximus," the Roman version of the Greek *amphitheatre.*

THREE SHEETS TO THE WIND *to be three sheets to the wind.* To be roaring drunk. LTA: 1821. Source: SAILING. To be under full sail: "three sheets." NDAS. The British "three sheets *in* the wind" has a slightly different nautical meaning: three *loose* sails. WPO.

THREESOME *See* Twosome.

THREE STRIKES AND YOU'RE OUT *Three strikes and you're out!* Three chances are all you get! (Or, as a warning: One more failure and you're finished!) Source: BASEBALL. A batter is "out" after three "swinging" or "called" strikes in any given trip to the plate.

THROW (v)   *to throw a contest.* To cause a contest to be lost deliberately, and possibly for profit. Source: SPORTS. LTA: 1860s. For an athlete to cause a game (or match or event) to be lost by the team they represent—deliberately, and for profit. The expression probably originated in boxing.

THROW A NET OVER   *to throw a net over something.* To stifle something. Source: HUNTING. To throw (or "fire") a net over birds on the ground. *Also:* "to throw a net around something." *See also* Net (v).

THROWBACK   *a throwback.* A reversion to earlier times. SOED: 1856. Source: FISHING(?). A fish that is caught and then thrown back into the water, to be caught again another day.

THROW DOWN THE GAUNTLET/GLOVE   *to throw down the gauntlet/ glove.* To challenge someone to something. Source: DUELING (medieval style). To challenge another knight to a duel. If the other knight picked up the gauntlet—later, a glove—the duel was on. DPF; WPO.

THROW IN THE SPONGE/TOWEL   *to throw in the sponge/towel.* To admit defeat; to give up; to die. Source: BOXING. LTA: 1860. For the trainer or corner person or second to throw a sponge—later, a towel—into the ring to signal to the referee that their boxer has had enough. CI; DPF; EOD; FP; HTB; WPO. Brit.: "throw up the sponge." SOED. *Compare* Cry Uncle; Throw In Your Chips; Throw In Your Hand.

THROW IN YOUR CHIPS   *to throw in your chips.* To give up; to quit. Source: POKER. To throw in all of your remaining chips in the process of anteing, betting, seeing, calling, raising, or withdrawing from the game. *Compare* Throw In the Sponge/Towel; Throw In Your Hand.

THROW IN YOUR HAND   *to throw in your hand.* To concede defeat; to give up. Source: POKER. To "fold"—i.e., to withdraw from the game by placing your hand of cards on the table. CI; SOE. *Compare* Throw In the Sponge/Towel; Throw In Your Chips.

THROW OF THE DICE   *a throw of the dice.* A gamble. Source: CRAPS. A throw of two dice to determine winning or losing. *Also:* "a roll of the dice."

THROW SOMEONE A CURVE   *to throw someone a curve.* To behave unexpectedly toward someone; to give someone some startling news. Source: BASEBALL. For a pitcher to throw a batter a ball that curves (a "curve ball"), rather than one that flies straight (a "fastball").

THROW SOMEONE OFF THE SCENT   *to throw someone off the scent.* To deliberately mislead or misinform someone so that they will search in the wrong place or for the wrong thing. Source: HUNTING. For the scent of another animal to distract the dogs from the trail of the original quarry. CI. *See also* Red Herring; Throw Someone off the Track.

THROW SOMEONE OFF THE TRACK   *to throw someone off the track.* To mislead someone. Source: HUNTING. For a hunted animal, such as a fox, to mislead the hunter or the dogs by circling back, running in a stream, etc. *See also* Red Herring; Throw Someone off the Scent.

THROW SOMEONE TO THE LIONS   *to throw someone to the lions.* To put someone in a no-win situation. Source: ROMAN GAMES. For the Romans to put prisoners, e.g., Christians, in the "circus" to be attacked by lions or other wild animals. CI.

THROW SOMETHING IN   *to throw something in.* To make a suggestion or observation; to contribute an idea. Source: BASKETBALL; SOCCER. To throw a ball in from out of bounds.

THROW YOUR HAT IN THE RING   *to throw your hat in the ring.* To declare your candidacy for political office. Source: BOXING. To throw your hat in the "ring" of spectators to signal your intention to challenge the current champion. The expression originated in the United States in the early 19th century in connection with boxing matches at country fairs. It was popularized in the early 20th century during the 1912 campaign of Teddy Roosevelt. CI; DOC; DPF; SFS. It was later also applied to wrestling matches. Brit.: "toss your hat in the ring." *See also* Make a Bid for Something.

THRUST   *the thrust of an argument.* The main point, or force, of an argument. SOED: 1668. Source: FENCING. WNCD: 1586. A forward stroke with a sword or foil. *See also* Make a Pass at. *Compare* Parry.

THUMBS-UP/-DOWN   *Thumbs-up; thumbs-down.* Approval (WNCD: 1922); disapproval (WNCD: 1889). *Also:* positive or negative, okay or not okay, Go! or No go! Source: ROMAN GAMES. Spare! (thumbs-up); Kill! (thumbs-down). These were the signs given by the spectators at a Roman circus to the victorious gladiator—to convince him to spare or kill his vanquished opponent. CI; DPF; HOI.

TIE UP SOME LOOSE ENDS   *to tie up some loose ends.* ("First, I'll have to tie up some loose ends.") To take care of some (minor) unfinished business. Source: SAILING. To insert the loose ends of a spliced rope in between the strands of the rope itself. WNWD.

TILT   *Tilt!* Foul! Source: PINBALL. "Tilt!" is the sign that appears on a pinball machine when a player is guilty of lifting or bumping it, in an illegal manner, in order to improve their score, in which case the game is lost, and so is the quarter. OL.

TILT AT WINDMILLS   *to tilt at windmills.* To attack imaginery opponents. Source: JOUSTING. To "tilt" is to "joust." The "windmills" are from Cervantes' *Don Quixote* (early 17th century), whose hero thought they were giants and attacked them. (They attacked back.) CI; DOC; DPF; HTB; OL; WPO. *See also* At Full Tilt; Go Full Tilt; Shadow Boxing.

TIME (1)   *See* In the Nick of Time; Make Up for Lost Time; Play for Time; Post Time.

TIME (2)   *Time!/Time out!* Stop it! Hold on a second! Immediate Source: SPORTS. This is the call of an official (especially in baseball, where there are no whistles) to stop the progress of a game—or the call of a player to the official (in most sports) to request same. Ultimate Source: BOXING. LTA: 1812. "Time!" was once the announcement of the referee that the thirty seconds had run out for the knocked-down fighter to get back to the "scratch" line at the center of the ring.

TIME FOR A CHANGE   *It's time for a change.* It's time for new leadership. Source: CHESS(?). The "clock" has run out on player A, and it is now player B's turn to move. At one time, it was at this point that the position of the board was changed so that each player had the same perspective when moving. *See also* Change of Pace; Turn the Tables.

TIME TO PUT YOUR CHIPS ON THE TABLE   *It's time to put your chips on the table.* It's time to make a decision. Source: POKER. It's time to decide how much to bet (or *not* to bet, to "fold"). *See also* Fold.

TINHORN   *a tinhorn.* A pretender; a fraud. WNCD: 1885. Source: GAMBLING. HTB: ca. 1850. A small-time gambler who operated a "chuck-a-luck" game, in which three dice were shaken in a metal ("tin") tumbler ("horn"). NDAS; WNWD; WPO. *See also* In Two Shakes of a Lamb's Tail; No Great Shakes; Shake-up.

TIP (n)   *a tip.* Advice on investing money. WNCD: 1567. Source: HORSE RACING. A "tip" on the horses, i.e., advice on betting on a horse race. This advice is given—and taken—voluntarily. The ultimate origin of "tip" is probably card games: to "tip your hand," which is involuntary.

TIP-OFF (n)   *the tip-off.* The hint or clue. WNCD: 1923. Source: BASKETBALL. WNCD: 1922. The batting away of a "jump ball" to a member of your own team. *See also* Tip Off (v).

TIP OFF (v)   *to tip someone off.* To warn someone about something. Source: CARD GAMES. To inadvertently lower your cards so that your opponent can see what is in your hand. *See also* Tip-off (n).

TIP YOUR HAND   *to tip your hand.* To give away your plans or intentions—inadvertently and prematurely. NDAS: early 1900s. Source: CARD

GAMES. To hold your hand of cards in such a way that your opponent can see them. DPF; NDAS. *See also* Show Your Hand.

TIT FOR TAT *Quid pro quo.* This for that: payment in kind. SOED: 1556. Source: BOXING. Blow for blow. CI; DOC; EOD; HOI; WPO. Originally "tip for tap," 15th century.

TOE THE LINE *to toe the line (or mark).* To follow orders, obey rules. LTA: 1840s. Sources: FOOT RACING. HTB: 1813. To have the toes of one foot on the starting line of a race. DOC; DPF; NDAS; OL. All races started this way at one time (a "standing start"), but now only the longer ones do. The shorter races start in "starting blocks." BOXING. LTA: 1840. For boxers to move up to the "scratch line" at the start of a match or after a knockdown, as in the ancient Greek games. *See also* Get a Toehold; On Your Toes.

TOE-TO-TOE *to go at it toe-to-toe.* For two persons to shout in each other's face. Source: BOXING. WNCD: 1925. For two boxers to fight without backing off. LOS. *See also* Go Toe-to-toe with.

TOO CLOSE TO CALL *for something to be too close to call.* For candidates to be too evenly matched for anyone to predict an eventual winner. Source: HORSE RACING. For two or more horses to be so evenly matched that it is impossible to predict which one will win the race. Also used in boxing and many other sports. *See also* Close Call; Call 'Em as You See 'Em; Hard Call; Hard to Call; Judgment Call; Tough Call.

TOP *See* At the Top of Your Game; Off the Top; Run Like a Top; Sleep Like a Top.

TOP DOG *the top dog.* The leader; the boss. WNCD: 1900. Source: DOG FIGHTING. The winning dog in a dogfight—the one on top. WPO. *Compare* Underdog.

TOP-RANKED CONTENDER *a top-ranked contender.* A candidate who is among the few who have a legitimate chance to win. Source: BOXING. A boxer who is ranked among the top ten in their weight class. *See also* Contender.

TOP-SEEDED *the top-seeded candidate; to be top seeded.* The candidate who is expected to win. Source: TENNIS. The player—the "number one seed"—who is expected to win the tournament. The top players are "seeded" 1 to 16, then assigned to two different groups, odd numbers in one group and evens in the other, so that the best players do not eliminate each other in the first round. This 20th-century innovation is an improvement over the "battle royal" (q.v.).

TOPSY-TURVY *Everything is topsy-turvy.* Everything is upside-down. WNCD: 1528. Source: CHIDREN'S TOYS. Everything is turned *(turv)* upside *(top)* down, like a tumbling top that has lost its momentum. HF. *See also* Head Is Spinning.

TORCH IS PASSED   *The torch is passed.* The reins of leadership have been passed on to a successor; the knowledge of scholars has been passed on to their students. Source: OLYMPIC GAMES. The torch, lit in Athens, Greece, has been passed on to the next runner on its way to the site of the next Modern Olympiad or Winter Games. This tradition has existed only since the 1936 games in Berlin. DPF; SPD. The Greeks also carried a torch, rather than a baton, in their relay races. *See also* Carry a/the Torch; Pass the Torch.

TOSS SOMETHING AROUND   *to toss an idea around.* To suggest solutions to a problem: to brainstorm. Source: BASEBALL(?). To toss a baseball around before the start of a game or inning. *See also* Bat an Idea around.

TOSS-UP (n)   *a toss-up.* A draw; a tie. Source: COINS. A toss of a coin, in which case each side has an even chance (50–50) of turning up. CI; NDAS. *See also* Win the Toss.

TO THE BITTER END   *to see something through to the bitter end.* To see something through to the very end—happy or unhappy. LTA: 1800. Source: SAILING. For a mooring rope to be "paid out" to its very end, which encircles the wooden "bits" on a drum, presumably because the vessel has drifted or the tide is unusually high. CI; HTB; SOED; WPO. *See also* At the End of Your Rope.

TO THE POINT Pertinent and relevant. Source: SHOOTING. In the center of the target. *See also* Come to the Point.

TOUCH ALL THE BASES   *to touch all the bases.* To take every precaution; to receive every necessary approval. Source: BASEBALL. To touch first, second, and third base and home plate after hitting a home run. (Otherwise, it doesn't count!) NDAS. *See also* Cover All the Bases; Touch Base with Someone.

TOUCH AND GO   *It's touch and go.* It's anybody's guess how things will turn out. SOED: 1815. Source: CHILDREN'S GAMES(?). It's "Touch and Run," a game like hide and seek. SOED. SAILING(?). It's touch rocks and go backward: to "back and fill." HTB.

TOUCH BASE WITH SOMEONE   *to touch base with someone.* To consult with or seek approval from someone. Source: BASEBALL. To touch first, second, and third base, in that order, upon getting a hit or being advanced by another batter. NDAS; OL; SFS. *See also* Cover All the Bases; Touch All the Bases.

TOUCHÉ   *Touché!* You've got a point. Source: FENCING. WNCD: 1921. You've scored a hit (Fren. *touché,* "touched") on your opponent and have won a point.

TOUGH CALL   *a tough call.* A political race that is so close that it's difficult to predict a winner. Source: HORSE RACING. A horse race that is difficult to predict a winner in because two or more of the horses are at the same "odds." Also used in many other sports. *See also* Hard to Call; Too Close to Call.

TOUGH SLEDDING   *to be tough sledding.* To be difficult. Source: CHILDREN'S PLAY (Sledding)(?). To be as difficult as pulling a sled through deep or heavy snow.

TOUT   *to tout the virtues of someone/something.* To extol the virtues of someone or something. WNCD: 1926. Source: HORSE RACING. To "tout" is to sell tips—or solicit bets—on the horses, which are then said to be "highly touted" (q.v.). The original meaning was to "spy" on horses in order to get information worth selling. SOED: 1812.

TOWEL   *See* Crying Towel; Throw in the Sponge/Towel.

TOY WITH AN IDEA   *to toy with an idea.* To mull an idea over in your head. SOED: 1842. Source: CHILDREN'S TOYS. SOED: 1529. To turn an idea over and over the way a child does with a new toy.

TOY WITH SOMEONE'S AFFECTIONS   *to toy with someone's affections.* To trifle with someone's emotions. SOED: 1550. Source: CHILDREN'S TOYS. SOED: 1529. To treat someone like a toy.

TRACK (n)   *See* Cover Up Your Tracks; Have the Inside Track; Keep Track of; Lose Track of; Make Tracks; On the Right Track; On the Track of; On the Wrong Track; Stop Something Dead in Its Tracks; Throw Someone off the Track.

TRACK DOWN   *to track someone/something down.* To pursue someone or something until you find them. Source: HUNTING. To trail an animal by following its "tracks": its footprints or other evidence. *Compare* Backtrack.

TRACK RECORD   *to have a good/bad track record.* To have a history of successes or failures. WNCD: 1952. Source: HORSE RACING. For a racehorse to have a good/bad record of wins at the racetrack. The "track record" of horses is one of the bases for their handicapping in a race—and for the wagers by serious bettors. DOC; NDAS. CI and WNCD believe that the "records" are in the sport of "track and field."

TRAIL THE FIELD   *to trail the field.* To come in last in a political "race." Source: RACING. To come in last in a physical race—behind all of the other runners (the "field").

TRAP (n)   *See* Death Trap; Mind Like a Steel Trap; Set a Trap; Shut Your Trap.

TRAPPED   *to be trapped*. To be caught, as in an elevator, and unable to escape. Source: TRAPPING. SOED: M.E. For an animal to be caught in a hunter's trap and unable to escape. All senses of "trap" derive from trapping animals.

TREAD ON THIN ICE   *to tread on thin ice*. To live dangerously. Source: FISHING (Ice Fishing). To walk ("tread") on ice that is likely to break at any moment. *See also* Skate on Thin Ice.

TREAD WATER   *to tread water*. To make no progress. Source: SWIM-MING. To "swim" in a vertical position, head barely above water, making no forward progress but managing to stay afloat. *Compare* Running in Place.

TRICK   *See* Every Trick in the Book; Never Miss a Trick.

TRIGGER-HAPPY   *to be trigger-happy*. To be in the habit of speaking or acting without thinking. Source: SHOOTING. WNCD: 1943. To be in the habit of shooting prematurely or irresponsibly. *Compare* Itchy Trigger Finger.

TRIM SOMEONE'S SAILS   *to trim someone's sails*. To put someone in their place—a lower place; to take someone down a notch or two. Source: SAILING. To adjust the sails according to the force and direction of the wind. To "trim" is not necessarily to "furl"—or "roll up"—the sails, as the metaphor implies.

TRIPLE THREAT   *a triple threat*. A person who is accomplished in three different fields. Source: FOOTBALL. WNCD: 1924. An offensive player who can run, pass, and kick—all three. LOS.

TROT OUT   *to trot something out*. To produce something to show off. Source: HORSE RACING. WNCD: 1838. To put a horse through its paces.

TROTS   *to have the trots*. To have a case of diarrhea—the runs. Source: RACING. In foot racing, a "trot" is somewhere between a "jog" and a "run." In horse racing, a "trot" is a diagonal "gait."

TRUMPED-UP   *a trumped-up charge*. A false accusation. WNCD: 1728. Source: CARD GAMES. To "trump up" is take a trick in a nontrump suit by playing a "trump" card, usually a low one. *See also* Hold the Trump Card; Play Your Trump Card.

TRYING TO STAY AFLOAT   Trying to survive, to stay solvent, to stay in office, etc. Source: BOATING; SWIMMING. Trying not to capsize or drown.

TRY YOUR LUCK AT SOMETHING   *to try your luck at something*. To give something a try, without any guarantee of success. SOED: 1838. Source: GAMBLING. To gamble on something, e.g., a game of chance. CI.

TUG OF WAR   *a tug of war*. A contest in which the lead keeps changing hands. WNCD: 1677. Source: TUG OF WAR. A game in which the team at each end of a rope attempts to pull the middle of the rope over a certain point. *See also* Anchorman; War Games.

TURN INTO A SIDESHOW *for something to turn into a sideshow.* For something to become ridiculous. Source: CIRCUS; CARNIVAL. DAE: 1855. For something to turn into the kind of entertainment that is found in the booths on the "midway" that leads to the "big top" of a circus or to the grandstand of a carnival or fair: i.e., a "freakshow."

TURN-OVER (n) *a turn-over.* A change in the holders of particular jobs or offices. Source: FOOTBALL. An involuntary surrendering of the ball to the opposing team because of a fumble, a blocked kick, etc. Also used in basketball and many other sports.

TURN TAIL *to turn tail.* To give up and run away. Source: FALCONRY. For the hawk to abandon its prey and fly away—i.e., to "turn its tail" to its prey. SOED.

TURN THE TABLES *to turn the tables on someone.* To reverse the conditions of your relationship with someone. DOC: 1612. Source: GAMES (Board Games). To literally turn the chess, checkers, backgammon, or other game table so that the opponent's position is reversed. DOC; DPF. The motivation for this action is not clear, because the reversal would *improve* the opponent's perspective. CI indicates that the source is a medieval game called "tables," HOI "card games," and HTB "backgammon." *See also* Tables Are Turned; Time for a Change.

TURN TURTLE *to turn turtle.* To go out of business, go bankrupt. Source: SAILING. For a vessel to capsize and roll over like a turtle, which, placed on its back, is helpless. NDAS. *See also* Go Belly Up; Go under; Overhaul.

TWENTY QUESTIONS *See* Play Twenty Questions.

TWO CAN PLAY THIS GAME *Two can play this game!* I can be just as "offensive" as you can! Source: GAMES. I can match your skills in the game that you're playing. Brit.: "two can play at this game," mid-19th cent.

TWO DOWN, ONE TO GO Two tasks accomplished, one remaining. Source: BASEBALL. Two batters "out" in the inning, with one more to retire.

TWO OF A KIND *to have two of a kind.* To have two things of the same sort: e.g., two sons or two daughters—or twins. Source: POKER. To have two cards of the same number or picture in your hand: e.g., two fives or two queens. *See also* Four of a Kind.

TWO POINTS *Two points!* Good shot! (A wadded-up piece of paper has found the wastebasket that it was aimed at.) Source: BASKETBALL. A "field goal," which, if it is under 21 feet in the NBA, or under 19 feet 9 inches in the NCAA, scores two points. A field goal longer than these distances scores three points, so we should expect the exclamations in "wastebasketball" to change accordingly.

TWOSOME   *a twosome.* A pair of persons engaged in the same activity together: a "couple." WNCD: 14th cent. Source: GOLF(?). Two golfers who are playing a "round" together and are possibly matched against each other. LOS. *Also:* "threesome," 1839; "foursome," 14th cent. "Fivesomes" are usually not permitted.

U

UNCLE   *See* Cry Uncle.

UNDERDOG   *an underdog*. A person with little chance of succeeding; a candidate who is not expected to win. WNCD: 1887. Source: DOG FIGHTING. The losing dog—the one on the bottom—in a dogfight. *See also* Dark Horse. *Compare* Top Dog.

UNDERHANDED   *to use underhanded methods*. To use dishonest or unscrupulous methods. WNCD: 1834. Source: CRICKET. To "bowl" (pitch) with the hand below the shoulder and under the ball. SOED.

UNDER PAR   *to be feeling under (or below) par*. To be feeling below average. Source: GOLF(?). In golf, to be "under par" is a *good* thing, not a *bad* thing. The term is probably not from golf at all but from the Stock Market, where a stock is traded above or below its face value: "par." DPF. *See also* Par for the Course. *Compare* Up to Par.

UNDER-THE-TABLE (adj.)   *an under-the-table deal*. A dishonest business transaction. WNCD: 1948. Source: POKER. A substitution of a hidden card, under the table, to replace one of lesser value. *See also* Under the Table.

UNDER THE TABLE   *to do business under the table*. To conduct business dishonestly or unethically. Source: POKER. To hold your "hand"—and hands—under the table, where hidden cards can be substituted for cards of lesser value. *See also* Aboveboard; Under-the-table (adj.). *Compare* Open and Aboveboard.

UNDER THE WEATHER   *to be under the weather*. To be sick. NDAS: mid-1800s. Source: SAILING. To be sailing in bad weather. NDAS; WPO. *See also* Weather the Storm.

UNDER THE WIRE   *to just make it under the wire*. To barely show up on time or on schedule. DAE: 1887. Source: HORSE RACING. To beat another horse to the "finish line": a wire strung across the finishing point of the race,

high above the horses. HOI. The wire is there to aid the photographer of a
"photo finish" (q.v.). *See also* Dead Heat, Go down to the Wire; Lead from
Wire to Wire. *Compare* In the Nick of Time.

UP *to be up.* ("You're up!") To be next to perform. Source: BASEBALL.
To be "up to bat" next in the batting order. LOS. *Compare* On Deck.

UP A TREE *to be up a tree.* To be in a predicament. DOC: 1825. Source:
HUNTING. For a hunted animal to be treed and therefore without any way out
of its difficulty. DOC. *Compare* Out on a Limb.

UP/DOWN *the computer is up/down.* The computer is working or not working. Source: ROMAN GAMES. These senses of "up" (alive) and "down"
(dead) are probably derived from the "thumbs-up" and "thumbs-down" signals from spectators at a Roman Circus to a victorious gladiator: "Spare!" or
"Kill!" They do not seem to have the same origin as the "up" and "down"
in expressions such as the market is "up" or "down."

UP IN THE AIR *for something to be up in the air.* For something to remain
unsettled or uncertain. Source: JUGGLING. For a juggled object to seem always to be "up in the air" rather than in the juggler's grasp at regular intervals. *See also* Juggle; Juggle the Books.

UPSHOT (n) *The upshot of all this is . . .* The significance—or result—of
all this is . . . WNCD: 1604. Source: ARCHERY. SOED: 1531. The "upshot" was once the concluding event in an archery tournament. CI.

UPSIDE (n) *The upside is . . . On the upside.* The good news is . . . On
the rise. Source: WHEEL OF FORTUNE. The "upside" of the medieval Wheel
of Fortune was the "good" side, the one that indicated rising fortune. *Compare*
Downside.

UPSIDE-DOWN (adj.) *to be upside down.* To be in disarray, with everything topsy-turvy. SOED: mid-1500s. Source: COINS (Flipping Coins)(?). For
the "heads" side of the coin to be "down" (hidden) and the "tails" side to
be "up" (showing). CHILDREN'S PLAY (Spinning Tops). WNCD: 14th cent.
For a top to be topsy-turvy, i.e., turned *(turv)* upside *(top)* down. *See also*
Heads I Win, Tails You Lose.

UP THE ANTE *to up the ante.* To increase the demands. Source: POKER.
To raise the amount that must be deposited in the "pot" before you can receive
cards for the next "hand." NDAS; SOE. *See also* Ante Up; Raise the Ante.
Compare Raise the Stakes.

UP THE CREEK *to be up the creek without a paddle.* To be in serious
trouble, without any means of helping yourself. Source: CANOEING. To be
going upstream without a paddle—an impossible situation for a canoe. HTB:
"up Salt Creek," 1880s.

UP TO PAR   *not feeling up to par.* Not feeling or performing as well as usual. Source: GOLF(?). A golfer tries to play *down* to par (Lat. "equal"), not *up* to par. In golf, as in racing and swimming, it is the *low* score that counts. DOC; SFS; WPO. *See also* Par for the Course. *Compare* Under Par.

UP TO SPEED   *to get up to speed.* To attain your usual level of performance. ("It usually takes me about half an hour to get up to speed.") Source: CAR RACING. To achieve full racing speed at the beginning of the race or after a "pit stop."

UP TO YOUR EARS   *to be up to your ears in something.* To be almost inundated with something, e.g., work. Source: SWIMMING. To be up to your ears in water, and you can't swim. *See also* Keep Your Head above Water. *Compare* Up to Your Eyeballs; Up to Your Neck.

UP TO YOUR EYEBALLS   *to be up to your eyeballs in something.* To be almost inundated with work, bills, problems, etc. Source: SWIMMING. To be in water up to your eyeballs, and you can't swim. *See also* Keep Your Head above Water. *Compare* Up to Your Ears; Up to Your Neck.

UP TO YOUR NECK   *to be up to your neck in trouble.* To be almost inundated with work, bills, debts, etc. Source: SWIMMING. To be up to your neck in water, and you can't swim. CI. *See also* Keep Your Head above Water; Neck and Neck. *Compare* Up to Your Ears; Up to Your Eyeballs.

UP YOUR SLEEVE   *See* Ace up Your Sleeve; Have a Card up Your Sleeve; Have Something up Your Sleeve.

V

VANISH WITHOUT A TRACE *to vanish without a trace.* To disappear completely. Source: HUNTING. For a hunted animal to disappear without leaving a track or trail.

VAULT *to vault over something.* To overcome an obstacle. SOED: 1884. Source: GYMNASTICS; TRACK AND FIELD. WNCD: 1538. To leap over a "vaulting horse"; to leap over a high bar, using a pole—the "pole vault." *See also* Vaulting Ambition.

VAULTING AMBITION Excessive or unrealistic ambition. Source: GYMNASTICS; TRACK AND FIELD. SOED: *vaulting,* 1531. To "vault" is to leap over something with the aid of equipment, as with the "vaulting horse" and the "pole vault." *See also* Vault.

VERBAL FENCING Dueling with words as weapons. Source: FENCING. Dueling with "swords" (foils, epées, sabres) according to the rules of fencing.

VERBAL SLUGFEST *a verbal slugfest.* A heated debate. Source: BOXING. A "slugging" match rather than a "boxing" match. LOS.

VERBAL SPARRING Restrained argument or debate. Source: BOXING. Restrained boxing—for practice, not for blood. *Compare* Sparring Partner.

VESTIGE *a vestige of something.* A trace of something that has long since disappeared. WNCD: 1545. Source: HUNTING. A footprint (literally) or some other track or trace of a quarry that has passed by earlier. THT. *See also* Investigate.

VIE FOR *to vie for something.* To compete for something, such as a political office. WNCD: 1577. Source: CARD GAMES. To bid or bet on the strength of the cards in your hand. Orig.: "to challenge an opponent at cards." THT.

W

WADE IN *to wade (right) in.* To attack a difficult problem head on. Source: SWIMMING. To walk (''wade'') into cold or treacherous waters without hesitation.

WAIT TILL NEXT YEAR *Just wait'll next year!* Next year is bound to be better than this one. Eternal optimism. Source: BASEBALL. This season may have been a disaster, but next year we all start out even, so we have as good a chance as anybody else to win the title.

WALK A FINE LINE *to walk a fine line.* To take a big risk, barely staying out of trouble. Source: CIRCUS. To walk a tightrope or tightwire or high wire, any one of which looks like a ''fine line'' from the ground. *See also* Walk a Tightrope.

WALK A TIGHTROPE *to walk a tightrope.* To live close to the edge. Source: CIRCUS. SOED: *tightrope,* 1801. To walk on a tightly strung wire (originally a rope), with or without a balancing pole, and with or without a net below. *See also* Safety Net; Walk a Fine Line.

WALKOVER *See* Win in a Walkover.

WALL *See* Drive Someone up the Wall; Hit the Wall; Off-the-wall (adj.); Off the Wall (p. a.).

WAR GAMES Simulated war, as an exercise. WNCD: 1942. Source: GAMES. War play, as opposed to the real thing. *See also* Let Slip the Dogs of War; Tug of War.

WASHED UP (p. a.) *to be (all) washed up.* To be a (total) failure. WNCD: 1923. Source: SAILING. For a sailing vessel to be washed up on the shore: a ''shipwreck.'' CI. *See also* On the Rocks.

WATCH SOMEONE LIKE A HAWK *to watch someone like a hawk.* To keep a close watch on someone. Source: FALCONRY. To watch someone as closely as a falcon, or hawk, watches its prey far below on the ground. *Also:* "to keep an eagle eye on someone."

WATER *See* Com'on in—The Water's Fine; Dead in the Water; Fish in Troubled Waters; Have Only One Oar in the Water; In Deep Water; Keep Your Head above Water; Like a Fish out of Water; Muddy the Water; Not Have Both Oars in the Water; Test the Waters; Tread Water.

WAVE (n) *See* Catch the Wave; Make Waves; Ride the Crest of a Wave.

WEATHER THE STORM *to weather the storm.* To survive a period of extreme difficulty. Source: SAILING. SOED: 1655. To "ride out the storm" (q.v.). *See also* Keep a Weather Eye Open; Under the Weather.

WEIGH ANCHOR *to weigh anchor.* To leave. Source: SAILING. SOED: M.E. To haul up the anchor in preparation for setting sail. WPO. *See also* Anchorman. *Compare* Cut and Run.

WELCOME ABOARD *Welcome aboard!* Welcome to your new job! DAE: 1837. Source: SAILING. Welcome on board the ship or boat. *See also* All Aboard; On Board.

WELL HEELED (p. a.) *to be well heeled.* To be well-to-do. WNCD: 1897. Source: COCKFIGHTING. HTB: 18th cent. For a gamecock to be equipped with a sharp pair of artificial "spurs" for a cockfight. *See also* Spar.

WE WUZ ROBBED *We wuz robbed!* We were cheated of success! Source: SPORTS. We deserved to win, but Fate—or the referee—cheated us out of it.

WHAT GOES AROUND, COMES AROUND Things even out eventually. Source: WHEEL OF FORTUNE. Today's losers are tomorrow's winners. *See also* Come Full Circle.

WHAT THE DEUCE *What the deuce!* What's going on? Source: CRAPS. SOED: *deuce,* 1651. This is an expression of exasperation at throwing "snake eyes" ("craps": two ones), the lowest losing total, on the first throw of the dice. THT; WNWD.

WHEELER-DEALER *a wheeler-dealer.* A super salesman. WNCD: 1954. Source: GAMBLING. A casino operator who operates both a roulette wheel and a card game. NDAS; WPO. *See also* Dealer's Choice; Wheeling and Dealing. *Compare* Spin Your Wheels.

WHEELING AND DEALING *to be wheeling and dealing.* To be doing a brisk business in sales, honest or otherwise. Source: GAMBLING. To be spinning the roulette wheel and dealing cards, though not at the same time. CI. *See also* Dealer's Choice; Wheeler-dealer.

WHEN MY SHIP COMES IN   *When my ship comes in I'm going to . . .* When I make my fortune I'm going to . . . WPO: 19th cent. Source: SAIL-ING. When my ship comes to port with its cargo. . . . *See also* Ship of State.

WHEN THE CAT'S AWAY, THE MICE WILL PLAY   *When the cat's away, the mice will play.* A proverb. When the boss is gone, the employees goof off. Source: ANIMAL GAMES. When their arch-enemy, the cat, is absent, the mice do whatever they please. CI. *Compare* Cat and Mouse Game.

WHEN THE CHIPS ARE DOWN   In a time of crisis. DOC: 1930s. Source: POKER. When you have made your bet and your poker chips are in the "pot" and cannot be withdrawn. CI; DOC; DPF; SOE.

WHISTLE-BLOWER   *a whistle-blower.* A person who "exposes" someone else, usually a superior, for violating the law. WNCD: 1970. Source: SPORTS(?). An official who "blows the whistle" to signal that a player has violated the rules. *See also* Blow the Whistle.

WHITE ELEPHANT   *a white elephant.* Something you own that you can't get rid of because nobody wants it. Source: CIRCUS. WPO: 1850s. The story goes that P. T. Barnum whitewashed a gray elephant in order to "top" another promoter who was exhibiting a *real* white elephant, which then became (un)expendable. *See also* One-upmanship.

WHITE FEATHER   *See* Show the White Feather.

WHOLE NEW/'NOTHER BALL GAME   *a whole new/'nother ball game.* An entirely different matter. Source: BASEBALL. A turn of events in a game whereby the team behind becomes the team ahead. DOC; OL. *See also* Ball Game. *Compare* Horse of a Different/Another Color.

WHOLE NINE YARDS   *to get/want the whole nine yards.* To get or want everything at once, e.g., all of the available options on a new car. Source: FOOTBALL(?). To get or want (almost) the entire number of yards necessary for a first down on one play. However, the required number is ten, not nine, so we suspect another source, such as tailoring. *Compare* Whole Shooting Match.

WHOLE SHOOTING MATCH   *the whole shooting match.* Everything: the works. NDAS: late 1800s. Source: SHOOTING. All of the prizes at the shooting match. WPO. *See also* Shooting Gallery. *Compare* Hook, Line, and Sinker; Lock, Stock, and Barrel; Whole Nine Yards.

WHO'S ON FIRST   *Who's on first?* The situation is confused/confusing. Source: BASEBALL. This is the title of an Abbott and Costello routine. "First" refers to "first base."

WICKET   *See* Sticky Wicket.

WIDE OF THE MARK *to be wide of the mark.* To be totally wrong. Source: SHOOTING. For your shot to be wide of the target (off the mark). DPF.

WILD CARD *a wild card.* An unknown variable. Immediate Source: FOOTBALL. WNCD: 1970. A team that fails to win a division championship but is added to the playoffs by virtue of their record. NDAS. Ultimate Source: POKER. A card that can assume any value desired by the player who holds it. For example, a "deuce" can represent an ace or any other card in the variation of poker called deuces wild. NDAS; SOE.

WILD-GOOSE CHASE *a wild-goose chase.* A futile effort or search. WNCD: 1592. Source: HUNTING. Samuel Johnson's *Dictionary,* 1755. An endeavor as futile as trying to catch a wild goose with your bare hands. DPF; LTA. RIDING. Shakespeare, *Romeo and Juliet,* 1595. A 16th-century game, on horseback, in which the object was for the riders to "follow the leader" (q.v.) and do exactly what the leader did. CI; DOC; HOI; LTA.

WIN (v) *See* Can't Win for Losing; Heads I Win, Tails You Lose; No-win Situation; You Can't Win 'Em All.

WIN A FEW, LOSE A FEW *Win a few, lose a few! C'est la vie!* That's life! Source: SPORTS; GAMES. You can't win 'em all! (Said by someone who "can't win *any* of 'em"). *See also* Can't Win for Losing; You Can't Win 'Em All.

WIN BY A KNOCKOUT *to win by a knockout.* To win decisively. Source: BOXING. To win by rendering your opponent unconscious, or at least unable to rise before the count of ten: a "K.O." or "kayo." SFS. *See also* Knockout.

WIN BY A NOSE *to win by a nose.* To win by the slightest margin in a very close "race," e.g., political. Source: HORSE RACING. For a horse to win a race by the length of its nose. (That's at least *two* feet long.)

WIND (n) *See* Get Your Second Wind; Have the Wind Taken out of Your Sails; Sail Close to the Wind; See Which Way the Wind Is Blowing; Take the Wind out of Someone's Sails; Three Sheets to the Wind.

WING IT *to wing it.* To improvise. Source: FLYING. To fly without a flight plan, or perhaps even a planned destination. *See also* Fly by the Seat of Your Pants; Flying Blind.

WIN GOING AWAY *to win going away.* To win by a large margin. Source: RACING. To be moving away from the rest of the "field" at the finish line. *See also* Runaway Victory; Run away with; Win Hands down.

WIN HANDS DOWN *to win hands down.* To win easily. Sources: HORSE RACING. DOC: 1867. For a jockey to win a race so easily that he or she is able to cross the finish line with hands lowered and the reins relaxed. CI; DPF.

BOXING. To win a boxing match without lifting a glove. NDAS. *See also* Win Going away.

WIN IN A WALKOVER *to win in a walkover.* To win easily, perhaps without even trying. SOED: 1902. Source: FOOT RACING. SOED: 1838. To win by simply walking over the course, because there are no other competitors. DPF. The term is now used in many other sports, some of which do not even involve walking. *Also:* "win in a walk." *See also* No Contest.

WIN, LOSE, OR DRAW *win, lose, or draw.* Regardless of what happens. Source: BOXING. Win the fight, lose the fight, or tie the fight (a "draw"). SFS. *See also* Draw (n); Win or Lose.

WIN ONE FOR THE GIPPER *to win one for the Gipper.* To sacrifice everything to achieve a goal. Source: FOOTBALL. To win a football game for George Gipp (the "Gipper"). This was supposedly said by Notre Dame coach Knute Rockne before a game with Army to inspire his football team to win the game for their former teammate, George Gipp—at least according to the 1940 film starring Ronald Reagan as "the Gipper." LTA.

WIN OR LOSE *win or lose.* Regardless of what happens. Source: SPORTS. Win the game or lose the game (we'll still be proud of you). *See also* Play the Game; Win, Lose, or Draw.

WIN THE LOTTERY *to win the lottery.* To come into a lot of money. Source: LOTTERY. To win the organized drawing of "lots" called a "lottery." The lottery goes back to Roman times, but it was not introduced into England—from Italy (Ital. *lotteria*)—until 1567. It came to America in 1620 with the pilgrims.

WIN THE SWEEPSTAKES *to win the sweepstakes.* To win the lottery or other such promotion. Source: LOTTERY. To win the lottery, for which numerous persons buy tickets (establishing the size of the "pot"), lots are drawn, and the winner "sweeps" away all of the "stakes" or bets. DPF; HF. *See also* Sweepstakes.

WIN THE TOSS *to win the toss.* To beat out someone else for a job (etc.). Source: FOOTBALL. To correctly call the "heads" or "tails" of a coin, flipped by an official before the start of the game, to determine which team gets the choice of kicking off or receiving the ball. The winner of the toss gets to make this choice. The loser of the toss then gets to choose which goal to defend. *See also* Toss-up (n).

WIPE THE FLOOR WITH *to wipe the floor with someone.* To defeat someone badly. Source: BOXING; WRESTLING. To treat an opponent as if they were a mop for wiping up the floor. CI; NDAS. *See also* Floor; Polish Something Off.

WIRE *See* Go down to the Wire; Lead from Wire to Wire; Under the Wire.

WITHOUT A NET *to perform without a net.* To operate without any protection or backup. Source: CIRCUS. To perform on the high wire or trapeze without a safety net below.

WITH THE GLOVES OFF *to debate someone with the gloves off.* To debate someone without inhibition or restraint. Source: BOXING. To fight someone without boxing gloves: bare fisted or bare knuckled. DPF. *See also* Gloves Are off.

WORLD-CLASS *a world-class performance, achievement, production, etc.* A performance that ranks with the best in the world. WNCD: 1968. Source: SPORTS. An athletic performance at the annual World Games that ranks with the best in the world. NDAS. *Compare* Olympic-class.

WRESTLE AWAY *to wrestle something away from someone.* To win a struggle for something with someone: for power, position, etc. Source: WRESTLING. To take the title away from someone in a wrestling match. The expression probably results from a confusion with the verb *wrest,* which is not sports related.

WRESTLE WITH *to wrestle with something.* To struggle for a solution to something: a problem, a decision, a matter of conscience, etc. FP. Source: WRESTLING. SOED: M.E. To wrestle with someone.

Y

YOU BET   *You bet!* Certainly! Absolutely! Source: GAMBLING; BETTING. You can bet on that! SOED. *See also* Bet the Ranch.

YOU BET YOUR LIFE   *You bet your life!* Absolutely! The outcome is so certain that you should be willing to risk your life on it. Source: GAMBLING; BETTING. You should bet everything you have on this. It's a sure bet (or sure thing). *See also* Bet the Ranch; Stake Your Life on Something.

YOU CAN'T TELL THE PLAYERS WITHOUT A PROGRAM   *You can't tell the players without a program!* The performers are so numerous, and they all look so much alike, that it's difficult to tell them apart. Source: FOOTBALL. Because all of the players on a given team wear the same uniforms, which formerly omitted the names, the only way you can tell them apart is to buy a program, look up their number, and find their name. This warning is shouted by program "hawkers" at various sporting events.

YOU CAN'T WIN 'EM ALL   *You can't win 'em all!* A modern maxim. It is impossible to succeed all of the time. (Probably said to cheer up someone who can't seem to win *any* of 'em.) DOC: 1940. Source: SPORTS. You can't win *all* of your games or matches; at least nobody ever has. DOC suspects an origin in poker, but this sounds too much like a (Yogi) Berraism or (Casey) Stengalism to us. *See also* Can't Win for Losing; Win a Few, Lose a Few.

YOUR BALL GAME   *It's your ball game.* It's your show. You're in charge. You make the rules. Source: BALL GAMES. You organized the game; you set the ground rules. *See also* Ball Game. *Compare* My Ball.

YOUR MOVE   *It's your move.* It's your turn to act. Source: CHESS; CHECKERS. SOED: 1656. It's your turn to move a chesspiece or checker. *See also* Move.

YOUR NUMBER IS UP You are about to die. Source: LOTTERY. Your losing number has just been displayed on the board. CI. *See also* Numbers Game.

YOU WANNA BET *You wanna bet?* You can't be serious! Source: GAMBLING; BETTING. I'd be happy to take your bet on that. The odds on your winning are extremely low. *See also* Bet the Ranch.

YO-YO (n) *X is a yo-yo.* X is unstable. Source: YO-YO. WNCD: 1916. X is like a yo-yo, a spool that spins at the end of a string and then returns to the hand when the string is snapped. *See also* Yo-yo (v), Yo-yoish.

YO-YO (v) *to yo-yo.* To vacillate. WNCD: 1967. Source: YO-YO. To behave like a yo-yo, going up and down. *See also* Yo-yo (n), Yo-yoish.

YO-YOISH *X is yo-yoish.* X is unpredictable or unstable. Source: YO-YO. X is like a yo-yo, experiencing ups and downs. *See also* Yo-yo (n), Yo-yo (v).

Z

ZERO IN ON   *to zero in on something.* To focus all of your attention on one thing. Source: SHOOTING. To set the sights of your rifle for a particular spot on a target. CI.

ZIG WHEN YOU SHOULD HAVE ZAGGED   *to zig when you should have zagged.* To be in the wrong place at the wrong time; to turn the wrong way in an automobile accident. Source: BOXING. LTA: 1939. To move the wrong way in the ring, thereby running into the fist of your opponent. Said by a boxer who had just been beaten by Joe Louis. LTA.

CLASSIFICATION OF ENTRIES ACCORDING TO ACTIVITY

ACROBATICS

See Gymnastics

ANIMAL GAMES

Cat and Mouse Game
Play Cat and Mouse
Play Possum
Roll over and Play Dead
When the Cat's away, the Mice Will Play

ARCHERY

Beside the Point
Come Unstrung
Drawback
Fall Short of the Mark/Target
High-strung
Hit the Bull's-eye
Let Slip the Dogs of War
Off-color
Room to Swing a Cat in
Screw Your Courage to the Sticking Point
Shoot Your Bolt
Slings and Arrows
Upshot

ATHLETICS

Athlete's Foot

BADGER-BAITING

Badger

BADMINTON

Keep It up

BALL GAMES

Bounce Back
Rubber Check
That's the Way the Ball Bounces
Your Ball Game

BANDY

See Ice Hockey

BASEBALL

Ball Game
Ballpark
Ballpark Figure
Baseball-size Hail
Bat an Idea around
Bat Cleanup
Batting a Thousand
Batting Average
Bean (v)
Bench
Benched
Big-league
Blank
Bleachers
Boner
Bronx Cheer
Bush
Bush-league
Call 'Em as You See 'Em
Caught Napping
Caught off Base
Chalk Something up to Experience

Change of Pace
Charley Horse
Choke
Close Call
Clutch
Clutch-hitter
Come off the Bench
Come out of Left Field
Cover All the Bases
Designated
Designated-hitter
Doubleheader
Draw the Collar
Fan
Farm Out
Fast out of the Box
Field (v)
Flake
Flaky
Friendly Confines
Game of Inches
Gamer
Get Sent to the Showers
Get to First Base
Get Your At-bats
Get Your Turn at Bat
Go into Extra Innings
Good in the Clutch
Goose Egg
Go the Route
Go to Bat for
Grandstand
Granstand Play
Ground Rules
Hang Up Your Spikes
Hardball Tactics
Hard Call
Have a Good Lineup
Have a Lot of Clout
Have a Lot of Moxie
Have a Lot on the Ball
Have an Off Day
Have Someone in the Bullpen
Have Something on the Ball
Have the Book on Someone
Have Two Strikes against You
Hit-and-run
Hot Dog (n)

Hotdog (v)
Hot Streak
In a Slump
In the Ballpark
In the Catbird Seat
In the Clutch
In the Lineup
In There Pitching
In the Wrong League
Iron Man
It Ain't Over Till It's Over
Judgment Call
Knock out of the Box
Lay Down Some Ground Rules
Let's Play Ball
Major-league
Make a Hit
Make the Right Call
Meal Ticket
Minor-league
Minor-leaguer
Muff
My Ball
Nice Guys Finish Last
No Runs, No Hits, No Errors
Not in the Same League with
Off at the Crack of the Bat
Off-base (adj.)
Off Base (p. a.)
0 for April
On Deck
One down, Two to Go
One Hundred and Ten Percent
On the Ball
On the Fly
Out in Left Field
Out-of-bounds
Out of the Box
Out of Your League
Pinch Hit
Play Ball
Play-by-play
Play Hardball
Play to the Grandstand
Pull a Boner
Put out
Razz
Razzberry

Rhubarb
Right off the Bat
Right up Your Alley
Say It Ain't So, Joe
Screwball
Send Someone to the Showers
Sent down to the Minors
Shortstop
Shutout
Sign Him/Her up
Southpaw
Squeeze Play
Strike Out
Take a Bad Bounce
Take a Rain Check
Take a Swing at Something
Take a Walk
Take Someone Downtown
Three Strikes and You're Out
Throw Someone a Curve
Toss Something around
Touch All the Bases
Touch Base with Someone
Two down, One to Go
Up
Wait Till Next Year
Whole New/'Nother Ball Game
Who's on First

BASKETBALL

Go into Overtime
Mount a Full-court Press
One-on-one
On the Rebound
Slam Dunk
Throw Something in
Tip-off (n)
Two Points

BETTING

See Gambling

BILLIARDS

Carom (n)
Carom (v)
Debut
English
Fluke

Kiss (n)
Kiss (v)
Make a Miscue
Miscue
Rub of the Green

BINGO

Bingo

BOATING

All in the Same Boat
Bail out
Go under
Have Only One Oar in the Water
Hit a Snag
In Someone's Wake
In the Wake of
Mainstream
Make Waves
Not Have Both Oars in the Water
Not Rowing with Both Oars
Push off
Rest on Your Oars
Rock the Boat
Row with Only One Oar in the Water
Trying to Stay Afloat

BOOMERANG

Boomerang

BOWLING (Bowls, Duckpins)

Bowl Someone over
Have All Your Ducks in a Row
Kingpin
Knock into a Cocked Hat
Rack Up
Rub of the Green
Set 'Em Up in the Other Alley
Set-up (n)
Set Up (v)
There's the Rub

BOXING

Ahead on Points
Answer the Bell
At Ringside
At the Drop of a Hat
Backpedal

Bare-knuckle
Beat Someone to the Punch
Beat the Count
Bigger They Are
Blizzard
Blow-by-blow
Bout
Boxer Shorts
Catch Someone Off Guard
Cheap Shot
Come off Second Best
Come Out Fighting at the Bell
Come Out Smoking
Come Out Swinging
Come to Your Senses
Counterpuncher
Coup
Cover-up (n)
Cross the Line
Don't Count Me out
Down and out
Down but Not out
Down for the Count
Down for the Long Count
Drop Your Guard
Evenly Matched
Fall Guy
Fighting Chance
Floor
Floored
Free-for-all
Free Swinger
Get Up and Fight Like a Man
Get up off the Canvas
Give It Your Best Shot
Gloves Are off
Go Down for the Long Count
Go Head-to-head
Go the Distance
Go Toe-to-toe with
Go Up against
Grudge Match
Hang in There
Hang Up Your Gloves
Hard-nosed
Have a Glass Jaw
Have a Go at Something
Have a Ringside Seat

Have Someone in Your Corner
Have Someone on the Ropes
Haymaker
Head-to-head
Heavyweight
Hit below the Belt
Hit on
Hit the Deck
Infighter
Infighting
In There Punching
Kayo
Knock-down-drag-out
Knock 'Em Dead
Knockout
Knockout Blow
Knockout Drops
Knock Someone Cold
Knock Someone for a Loop
Knock the Spots off
Knock the Stuffings out of
Knock Yourself out
Laid Low
Lay a Glove on
Lead with Your Chin
Let Down Your Guard
Lightweight
Low Blow
Lower the Boom
Main Event
Make a Clean Break
Make a Comeback
Matchup
Meet Your Match
Mismatch
Mix It up
No Skin off My Nose
Not up to Scratch
Not up to the Mark
One-two Punch
On Guard
On the Ropes
On Your Guard
On Your Toes
Out (1)
Out Like a Light
Out on Your Feet
Overtrained

Pack a Wallop
Palooka
Pinned in a Corner
Polish Something off
Pull No Punches
Pull Your Punches
Punch-drunk
Punching Bag
Punch Someone's Lights out
Punchy
Punch Your Way out of a Paper Bag
Pushover
Put On the Gloves
Put Someone away
Put Up Your Dukes
Ready When the Bell Rings
Real McCoy
Right on the Button
Ring Someone's Bell
Roll with the Punches
Rough-and-tumble
Saved by the Bell
Second (v)
See Stars
Set-to
Shadow Boxing
Should of Stood in Bed
Slap-happy
Sock It to Me
Soften Someone up
Soften the Blow
Spar
Sparring Partner
Split Decision
Square Off
Start from Scratch
Straight from the Shoulder
Sunday Punch
Swing from the Heels
Take a Dive
Take a Fall
Take a Nosedive
Take It on the Chin
Take Off the Gloves
Take On All Comers
Take Someone on
Take the Fight out of Someone
Take the Long Count

Take the Rap
Take Your Best Shot
Take Your Lumps
Telegraph a Punch
Throw In the Sponge/Towel
Throw Your Hat in the Ring
Time (2)
Tit for Tat
Toe the Line
Toe-to-toe
Top-ranked Contender
Verbal Slugfest
Verbal Sparring
Win by a Knockout
Win Hands down
Win, Lose, or Draw
Wipe the Floor with
With the Gloves off
Zig When You Should Have Zagged

BRIDGE

Bid
Dummy
Finesse (1)
Finesse (2)
Go Someone One Better
In Spades
Make a Bid for Something
Never Miss a Trick
Overplay Your Hand
Pass (v)
Squeeze Play

BULLFIGHTING (Bull Vaulting)

Mano a Mano
Moment of Truth
See Red
Take the Bull by the Horns

BULL VAULTING

See Bullfighting

BURLING

As Easy as Falling off a Log

CAMPING

Pull Up Stakes

CANOEING

Go with the Flow
Paddle Your Own Canoe
Up the Creek

CARD GAMES

Aboveboard
Ace
Ace up Your Sleeve
Card
Carte Blanche
Close to the Vest
Cut a Deal
Discard
Euchre
Euchred
Every Trick in the Book
Fast Shuffle
Follow Suit
Force Someone's Hand
Get Lost in the Shuffle
Have a Card up Your Sleeve
Have Something up Your Sleeve
Holding All the Cards
Hold the Trump Card
Kibitz
Kibitzer
Knock on Wood
Layout
Lay Your Cards on the Table
Leave in the Lurch
Left in the Lurch
Long Suit
Not According to Hoyle
Not in the Cards
Not Many Cards Left to Play
Not Playing with a Full Deck
Open and Aboveboard
Play into Someone's Hand
Play with a Marked Deck
Play with a Stacked Deck
Play Your Cards Right
Play Your Trump Card
Put Your Cards on the Table
Shoot the Moon
Short-suited
Show Your Hand
Strengthen Your Hand

Strong Suit
Tip Off (v)
Tip Your Hand
Trumped-up
Vie for

CARNIVAL (Amusement Park)

Ballyhoo
Close, but No Cigar
Gimmick
Give That Man a Cigar
Grab Bag
Grab the Brass Ring
Hanky-panky
On a Merry-go-round
Scam
Shooting Gallery
Turn into a Sideshow

CAR RACING

Flat-out
Gentlemen, Start Your Engines
Get Nowhere Fast
Go Flat out
Hot-rodder
Life in the Fast Lane
On the Bubble
Pit Stop
Pole Position
Soft-pedal
Spin Your Wheels
Up to Speed

CHECKERS

All the Right Moves
Checkered Past
Make Your Move
Move
Your Move

CHESS

All the Right Moves
At Odds
Check (n)
Check (v)
Checkmate
Gambit
Game of Chess

Hold in Check
In Jeopardy
Make a Play for
Make Your Move
Move
Opening Gambit
Pawn (n)
Reach a Stalemate
Rooked
Stalemate
Time for a Change
Your Move

CHILDREN'S GAMES (Play, Toys)

As Easy as Falling off a Log
At Sixes and Sevens
Booby Prize
Bring Home the Bacon
Build Sand Castles
Burst Someone's Bubble
Catch On
Chatterbox
Child's Play
Choose Up Sides
Coast
Cry Uncle
Dibs
Doll
Dolled Up
Double Dare
Double Dutch
Drag Your Feet
Draw the Line
Finders Keepers, Losers Weepers
Follow the Leader
Get into the Swing of Things
Guessing Game
Have a Chip on Your Shoulder
Have a Field Day
Head Is Spinning
Hobby
Home Free
House of Cards
Jack-in-the-box
Knock It off
Knock on Wood
Knock the Stuffings out of
Leapfrog

Left Holding the Bag
Like Catching a Greased Pig
Mudslinging
Piggyback
Pin Something on Someone
Play Doctor
Play Hide and Seek
Play Hooky
Play Musical Chairs
Play Tag
Play Twenty Questions
Pull the Rug out from under Someone
Put a Tail on
Ride a Hobby-horse
Round Peg in a Square Hole
Run Like a Top
Seesaw
Shoot the Moon
Simon Says
Skip
Sleep Like a Top
Snowball
Snowball's Chance in Hell
Square Peg in a Round Hole
Sticks and Stones
Stone's Throw
Stop the Music
String Someone along
Take a Giant Step
Teeter on the Brink
Topsy-turvy
Touch and Go
Tough Sledding
Toy with an Idea
Toy with Someone's Affections
Upside Down

CIRCUS

Bozo
Dog and Pony Show
Get on the Bandwagon
Jump through Hoops
Rubber-chicken Circuit
Safety Net
Show Must Go on
There's a Sucker Born Every Minute
Three-ring Circus
Turn into a Sideshow

Walk a Fine Line
Walk a Tightrope
White Elephant
Without a Net

CLIMBING

At the End of Your Rope
Get a Foothold
Get a Toehold
Hang by Your Fingertips

COCKFIGHTING

Battle Royal
Cockeyed
Cockfight
Cock of the Walk
Cockpit
Cocksure
Cocky
Crestfallen
Game (adj.)
Pit against
Pitted against
Raise Someone's Hackles
Show the White Feather
Spar
Stand the Gaff
Well Heeled (p. a.)

COINS (Flipping, Matching, Tossing)

Can't Make Heads or Tails
Flip Side
Heads I Win, Tails You Lose
Odd Man out
On the Flip Side
Other Side of the Coin
Toss-up (n)
Upside-down (adj.)

CON GAMES

Buy a Pig in a Poke
Easy Mark
Let the Cat out of the Bag
Palm Something off
Play Fast and Loose
Pull a Scam
Shell Game

Skin Game
Soft Touch

CRAPS

Crap Game
Crap Out
Crapshoot
Dicey
Game of Craps
Have a Point
Hazard a Guess
High Roller
I've Got You Covered
Loaded Question
Make a Point
Make No Bones about It
Make No Bones about Something
Make No Bones about Wanting to Do Something
Make Your Point
Natural
No Dice
On a Roll
Only Game in Town
On the Side
Play with Loaded Dice
Roll of the Dice
Shooting Craps
Shoot the Dice
Shoot the Works
Snake Eyes
Throw of the Dice
What the Deuce

CRIBBAGE

Bilk
Take Someone down a Peg

CRICKET

Bowl Someone over
Butterfingers
Hat Trick
Hit It off
Hold Up Your End
Lay an Egg
Muff
Not Cricket
Play for Time

Pull a Fast One
Shiver My Timbers
Sticky Wicket
Stonewall
Stump
Stumped
Stumper
Underhanded

CROQUET

Finessed

CURLING

Hog on Ice

CYCLING

Backpedal
Bicycle

DICE GAMES

At Sixes and Sevens
Dice Are Loaded against You
Dicey
Die Is Cast
Fair Shake
High Jinks
Hold a Raffle
Hubbub
In Two Shakes of a Lamb's Tail
Load the Dice
No Great Shakes
Not Fit to Hold a Candle to
Raffle Something off
Shake-up

DIVING

Dive in Head First
Dive Right in
Go off the Deep End
Jumping-off Point
Jump in with Both Feet
Make a Splash
Plunge in
Springboard
Take a Dive
Take a Nosedive
Take the Plunge

DOG FIGHTING

At Each Other's Throats
Dogfight (n)
Pit Bull Terrier
Top Dog
Underdog

DOG RACING

Let Slip the Dogs of War
Runner-up

DOMINOES

Domino Effect
Domino Theory

DRAWING LOTS

Draw
Draw a Blank
Get the Short End of the Stick
Lot
Luck of the Draw

DUELING

Beat Someone to the Draw
Get the Drop on
In Full Swing
Quick on the Draw
Second (v)
Thrown down the Gauntlet/Glove

FALCONRY

Get Your Hooks into
Haggard
Hoodwink
Hoodwinked
In One Fell Swoop
Lure (n)
Lure (v)
Pride of Place
Rapture
Turn Tail
Watch Someone Like a Hawk

FENCING

Catch Someone Off Guard
Cross Swords
Hit (n)

Let Down Your Guard
Make a Pass at
Nip and Tuck
Off Guard
On Guard
On Your Guard
Parry
Thrust
Touché
Verbal Fencing

FIREWORKS

Fireworks
Fizzle Out
Shoot off Your Mouth
Shoot the Works
Skyrocket

FISHING

Backlash
Bait the Hook
Barb
Bite (v)
Bobbing along
Can of Worms
Cast about
Dead as a Mackerel
Dragnet
Drink like a Fish
Fish (v)
Fishing Expedition
Fish in Troubled Waters
Fish or Cut Bait
Fish Out
Fish Story
Fishtail
Fishy
Get a Bite
Get a Nibble
Get Hooked on
Get off the Hook
Get Your Hooks into
Give Someone Some Line
Go Belly Up
Good Catch
Hand Someone a Line
Have Other Fish to Fry
Hook (v)
Hook, Line, and Sinker

Hook Up
Hook Up with
In the Swim
Junket
Keeper
Kettle of Fish
Land (v)
Let Someone off the Hook
Like a Fish out of Water
Loaded to the Gills
Lure (n)
More Fish in the Ocean
Muddy the Water
Net (v)
Network
Off the Hook
On Your Own Hook
Out of Season
Reel in
Reel off
Rise to the Bait
Set the Hook
Set Your Hooks for
Small Fry
String Someone along
Sucker
Take the Bait
Throwback
Tread on Thin Ice

FLYING

Bail out
Dogfight (n)
Fly by the Seat of Your Pants
Flying Blind
Fly in the Face of
Get Something off the Ground
Give It the Gun
Golden Parachute
Send Up a Trial Balloon
Sky's the Limit
Take a Nosedive
Takeoff (n)
Take Off (v)
Wing It

FOOTBALL

All-American
Armchair Quarterback

Bench-warmer
Blindside (v)
Blindsided
Bragging Rights
Call the Signals
Carry the Ball
Catch Someone Flat-footed
Chalk Something up to Experience
Chalk Talk
Cheap Shot
Cheerleader
Deke
Earn a Letter
End Run
Fake Out
First-stringer
Game Plan
Get a Handle on
Get a Kick out of
Go for It
Hold the Line
Huddle (n)
Huddle (v)
Instant Replay
Ivy League
Juke
Kickoff (adj.)
Kick Off (v)
Letter
Level the Playing Field
Make a Run at
Monday-morning Quarterback
My Ball
No Pain, No Gain
Offsides
Old College Try
One Leg at a Time
Play without a Helmet
Political Football
Punt
Quarterback
Rack Up
Run Interference for
Run That by Me again
Scrimmage
Second-stringer
Sidelined
Sidelines
Sidestep

Skull Session
Staight-arm
Suit Up
Tackle
Take the Ball and Run with It
Triple Threat
Turn-over (n)
Whole Nine Yards
Wild Card
Win One for the Gipper
Win the Toss
You Can't Tell the Players without a Program

FOOT RACING

Anchorman
Cut Corners
Dropout (n)
Drop Out (v)
False Start
Fast Starter
First out of the Blocks
From the Word Go
Front-runner
Get a Head Start
Get Off to a Flying Start
Get Set
Get the Jump on
Get Your Second Wind
Go the Extra Mile
Have a Go at Something
Have Legs
Hit the Wall
Hit Your Stride
In the Long Run
Jump the Gun
Make Up for Lost Time
Make Up Ground
Marathon
No Go
Off Stride
On the Go
Out of the Blocks
Quick off the Mark
Race Is Not to the Swift
Run (v)
Run Circles around
Running in Place
Start from Scratch

Take Something in Stride
Toe the Line
Win in a Walkover

FOX HUNTING

At Fault
Break Cover
Call Off Your Dogs
Close on the Heels
Cover Up Your Tracks
Crazy Like a Fox
Drive Someone up the Wall
Foxhole
Fox-trot
Hark Back
Hot to Trot
Hound (v)
In at the Death
In at the Kill
In Full Cry
In Hot Pursuit
In the Hunt
On Someone's Tail
Outfox
Red Herring
Run Riot
Run to the Ground
Tally Ho

GAMBLING (Betting)

Across-the-board (adj.)
Across the Board (adv.)
Against All Odds
All Bets Are off
At Stake
Back the Field
Back the Wrong Horse
Beat the Odds
Bet the Ranch
Bet Your Bottom Dollar
Break Even
Break the Bank
By All Odds
Calculated Risk
Call In a Marker
Can't Win for Losing
Cash In on
Cut Your Losses
Debt of Honor

Don't Bet on It
Down on Your Luck
Even Money
Five Will Get You Ten
Gamble Away
Game of Chance
Get the Upper Hand
Go for Broke
Good Bet
Hard Call
Have a Lot Riding on
Have a Stake in
Hedge Your Bets
Hustle
Lay It on the Line
Lay Odds
Lay Something on the Line
Long Odds
Long Shot
Make Book on
Not Worth the Gamble
Numbers Game
Odds
Odds Are against
Odds Makers
Odds-on Favorite
Off the Top
On a Winning Streak
Out of Luck
Outside Chance
Parlay
Payoff (n)
Pay Off (v)
Piece of the Action
Play a Hunch
Play by House Rules
Play the Field
Play with House Money
Press Your Luck
Put Your Money on the Line
Put Your Money Where Your Mouth Is
Quit While You're ahead
Rake-off
Right on the Money
Riverboat Gamble
Smart Money
Sportsmanship
Stake Your Life on Something
Stay ahead of the Game

Sudden Death
Sure Thing
Sweep the Boards
Take Someone to the Cleaners
Ten to One
Tinhorn
Try Your Luck at Something
Wheeler-dealer
Wheeling and Dealing
You Bet
You Bet Your Life
You Wanna Bet

GAMES

At Loggerheads
Beat Someone at Their Own Game
Come into Play
Fun and Games
Game Is up
Game of Life
Gamesmanship
Hot
Name of the Game
Not All Fun and Games
No-win Situation
On a Winning Streak
On Your Game
Play along with
Play a Losing Game
Play a Waiting Game
Play Chicken
Play Fair
Play Games
Play Money
Play the Game
Play the Market
Sandbag
Sandbagger
Spoof
Tables Are Turned
Turn the Tables
Two Can Play This Game
War Games
Win a Few, Lose a Few

GOLF

Chicanery
Duffer
Golf Ball-size Hail

Hacker
Make the Cut
Nineteenth Hole
One-upmanship
One Up on
Par for the Course
Press Your Luck
Rub of the Green
Stymie
Stymied
Teed Off
Tee It up
Tee Off
Twosome
Under Par
Up to Par

GYMNASTICS (Acrobatics, Tumbling)

Bend over Backwards
Flip
Head over Heels
Land on Your Feet
Mental Gymnastics
More Than One Way to Skin a Cat
Springboard
Take a Flyer
Vault
Vaulting Ambition

HANDBALL

On the Rebound

HIKING

Not out of the Woods Yet
Take a Hike

HOPSCOTCH

Back to Square One
Hopscotch

HORSE RACING

Also-ran
At the Drop of a Hat
Bring in a Ringer
Break out of the Pack
Break Something/Someone in
Carry a Lot of Weight
Come a Cropper

Come Back to the Field
Dark Horse
Dead Heat
Dead Ringer
Derby
Disc Jockey
Don't Look a Gift Horse in the Mouth
Down the Stretch
Eat Someone's Dust
Fade in the Stretch
Finish out of the Money
Free-for-all
Get Someone's Goat
Go down to the Wire
Handicap (n)
Handicap (v)
Hard to Call
Have the Inside Track
Heavy Going
Highly Touted
Hold Your Horses
Homestretch
Horse of a Different/Another Color
Horse Race
Horses for Courses
Hot to Trot
In a Lather
In the Homestretch
In the Money
In the Running
Jock
Jockey for Position
Know Your Oats
Lead from Wire to Wire
Left at the Post
Long in the Tooth
Make a Killing
Neck and Neck
Nip and Tuck
Nose Someone out
No-show
Off and Running
Off to the Races
One-horse Race
On the Nose
Out of the Running
Out of the Starting Gate
Overcome Long Odds

Photo Finish
Post Time
Put Someone through Their Paces
Railbird
Ride High in the Saddle
Ringer
Round the Turn
Run away from the Field
Run for the Money
Running Mate
Scratch (v)
Scratched
Shoo-in
Show
Sign of Good Breeding
Stablemate
Straight from the Horse's Mouth
Sweepstakes
Tip
Too Close to Call
Tough Call
Tout
Track Record
Trot out
Under the Wire
Win by a Nose
Win Hands down

HORSESHOES

Bring in a Ringer
Close Counts in Horseshoes
Dead Ringer
Ringer

HUNTING

Backtrack
Bag (v)
Bark up the Wrong Tree
Beat around the Bush
Beat the Bushes
Bird Dog (n)
Bird-dog (v)
Bird in the Hand
Blow Someone out of the Water
Cast about
Catch Someone Red-handed
Coldcock
Come away Empty-handed

Corduroy
Dachshund
Dead Duck
Dead Set on
Decoy
Dog
Double Back
Draw a Blank
Duck Soup
Fair Game
Ferret Out
Flush Out
Fortune Hunter
Get Your Bearings
Give It to Someone with Both Barrels
Gun-shy
Happy Hunting Ground
Hard on the Heels of
Hightail It
Hit Home
Hit-or-miss (adj.)
Hit or Miss (adv.)
Hold at Bay
Hot on the Trail
Hunt Down
Hunting Ground
In the Bag
Investigate
Jackrabbit Start
Juke
Keep Track of
Keep Your Ear to the Ground
Kill Two Birds with One Stone
Lame Duck
Let Someone Have It with Both Barrels
Lie Low
Loaded for Bear
Look What the Cat Dragged in
Lose Track of
Make Tracks
Mixed Bag
Not out of the Woods Yet
On a Cold Trail
One-shot Deal
On the Right Track
On the Track of
On the Wrong Track
Open Season

Out of Season
Out on a Limb
Pigeon
Pit Bull Terrier
Pitfall
Prey on Your Mind
Quarry
Rock Hound
Shotgun Approach
Shot in the Dark
Sitting Duck
Smell a Rat
Smoke out
Sniff Something out
Stalking Horse
Stool Pigeon
Stop Something Dead in Its Tracks
Tail (v)
Take a Shot at It
Take Your Best Shot
Throw a Net over
Throw Someone off the Scent
Throw Someone off the Track
Track Down
Up a Tree
Vanish without a Trace
Vestige
Wild-goose Chase

ICE HOCKEY (Bandy)

Bandy about
Bandy-legged
Bandy Words
Face-off (n)
Face Off (v)
Get on the Stick
Hat Trick
Hockey Puck
Keep the Ball Rolling
Power Play

ICE SKATING

Cut No Ice
Cut Quite a Figure
Skate Circles around
Skate on Thin Ice

JOUSTING

At Full Tilt
Carousel
Carry the Day
Enter the Lists
Go Full Tilt
Tilt at Windmills

JUGGLING

Hocus-pocus
Juggle
Juggle the Books
Up in the Air

KITE FLYING

Go Fly a Kite
High as a Kite
Higher Than a Kite

LOTTERY

Cast In Your Lot
Draw a Blank
Win the Lottery
Win the Sweepstakes
Your Number Is up

MARBLES

Go for All the Marbles
Knuckle down
Knuckle under
Lose Your Marbles
Marble-size Hail
Not Have All Your Marbles
Pick Up Your Marbles and Go Home
Play for Keeps

MOTORCYCLE RACING

Go Flat Out

OLYMPIC GAMES

Agony
Carry a/the Torch
Go for It
Go for the Gold
Let the Games Begin
Marathon
Olympic-class

Pass the Torch
Rest on Your Laurels
Torch Is Passed

PALL-MALL

Mall
Pell-mell

PINBALL

Pinball
Pinballed
Tilt

POKER

Ace in the Hole
Ante Up
Bank on
Bargaining Chip
Bet Your Boots
Blue-chipper
Blue-chip Stock
Bluff (n)
Bluff (v)
Bluffing
Buck
Buck Passer
Buck Sheet
Buck Stops Here
Call Someone's Bluff
Cards Are Stacked against You
Cash in Your Chips
Chip In
Count Me in
Count Me out
Cut Me in
Dealer's Choice
Deal Me in
Deal Me out
Dealt out
Deal Yourself in
Double-dealer
Double-dealing
Down and Dirty
Draw to an Inside Straight
Fair Deal
Fair Dealing
Fill an Inside Straight
Fold

Four-flusher
Four of a Kind
Full House
Good for Openers
Good for Starters
High-stakes
Hit the Jackpot
Hold a Pat Hand
Holdout
Hot Hand
In
In Hock
In the Chips
In the Hole
Kick in
Kitty
Like Drawing to an Inside Straight
Like Trying to Fill an Inside Straight
Luck of the Draw
New Deal
Only Game in Town
Out (2)
Outbluff
Pass the Buck
Penny Ante
Play Both Ends against the Middle
Play for High Stakes
Poker Face
Poker-faced
Pull a Bluff
Put Up or Shut Up
Raise the Ante
Raise the Stakes
Raw Deal
Read 'Em and Weep
Ready to Deal
Rotten Hand
Showdown
Show Your Hole Card
Sit Tight
Stakes Are High
Standoff
Stand Pat
Sweeten the Pot
Three of a Kind
Throw In Your Chips
Throw In Your Hand
Time to Put Your Chips on the Table

Two of a Kind
Under-the-table (adj.)
Under the Table
Up the Ante
When the Chips Are down
Wild Card

POLO

Come a Cropper
On the Ball

POOL

Behind the Eight Ball
Call the Shots
Chalk Something up to Experience
Dirty Pool
Get a Break
Good/Bad Break
Make a Run at
Never Give a Sucker an Even Break
Oddball
On the Spot
Play Safe
Rack Up
Rub of the Green
Set-up (n)
Set Up (v)
Stroke of Good Luck

RACING

Break away
Bring Someone up Short
Catch Up
Close Race
Come-from-behind (adj.)
Come from behind (v)
Come in First
Course
Cross the Finish Line
Get Off to a Good/Bad Start
Get Started
Hard on the Heels of
Head Start
In the Lead
Keep Pace with
Lead from Start to Finish
Make Great Strides
Make Someone Eat Your Dust

Off the Pace
Pacemaker
Pacesetter
Rat Race
Ride Roughshod
Riding for a Fall
Runaway Victory
Run away with
Run Its Course
Runoff
Second to None
Set the Pace
Spot Someone a Lead
Stay the Course
Stop Short of Something
Take the Lead
Trail the Field
Trots
Win Going away

RACQUETBALL (Squash)

Off-the-wall (adj.)
Off the Wall (p.a.)

RECREATION

Recreational Drugs

RIDING

Back in the Saddle Again
Bring Someone Up Short
Carrot-and-stick
Cinch
Fall off a Horse
Get off Your High Horse
Get on Your High Horse
Get out of Hand
Give Someone Free Rein
Give Someone Their Head
Go along for the Ride
Hightail It
In a Lather
In Hand
Leg Up
Pull Up Short
Rider
Ride Roughshod
Riding for a Fall
Riding High

Rode Hard and Put away Wet
Saddle
Snowball
Stop Short of Something
Wild-goose Chase

RODEO

Hit the Ground Running
Rope Someone in
Take the Bull by the Horns

ROLLER COASTER

Roller Coaster Ride

ROMAN GAMES

Agony
Arena
Champion
Championship Performance
Desultory
Political Arena
Political Faction
Throw Someone to the Lions
Thumbs-Up/-Down
Up/Down

ROULETTE

Let It Ride
Russian Roulette

ROWING

Not Rowing with Both Oars
Pull Your Weight
Rest on Your Oars

RUBGY

Carry the Ball
Get a Handle on
Run-in

SAILING

All Aboard
All at Sea
Anchorman
A-number One
Any Port in a Storm
At the End of Your Rope
At the Helm

Bearing Down on
Between the Devil and the Deep Blue Sea
Break the Ice
Broad in the Beam
By and Large
Chart a Course
Chock-full
Clear Sailing
Come in with Flying Colors
Cruise
Cut and Run
Dead in the Water
Deck (v)
Decked
Decked Out
Deep Six
Devil to Pay
Drift
From Stem to Stern
Get a Fix on
Get Squared away
Get Your Bearings
Get Your Sea Legs
Give a Wide Berth
Give Someone Some Leeway
Go by the Boards
Go Overboard
Go under
Hand over Fist
Hard-and-fast
Hard Up
Have the Wind Taken out of Your Sails
Headline
High and Dry
Hit the Deck
How the Land Lies
In Someone's Wake
In the Wake of
In Tow
Keel Over
Keep a Weather Eye Open
Know the Ropes
Lay of the Land
Leading Light
Lifesaver
Like Rats Leaving a Sinking Ship
Like the Cut of Someone's Jib
Loom Large

Lose Your Bearings
Lower the Boom
Mainstay
Make Headway
On Board
On Deck
On the First/Last Leg of a Journey
On the Rocks
Overhaul
Pilot
Pilot Light
Pooped
Rat Race
Ride out the Storm
Run Afoul of
Run a Tight Ship
Sail Close to the Wind
Sail through
Sail under False Colors
Scuttle
Scuttlebutt
See Which Way the Wind Is Blowing
Shakedown Cruise
Ship of State
Shipshape
Shiver My Timbers
Shoot the Breeze
Shove off
Skipper
Slack off
Slush Fund
Smooth Sailing
Stand by
Standoffish
Stay on an Even Keel
Stowaway
Stow It
Swept away
Swept off Your Feet
Take a Different Tack
Taken Aback
Take the Wind out of Someone's Sails
Take Up the Slack
Three Sheets to the Wind
Tie Up Some Loose Ends
To the Bitter End
Touch and Go
Trim Someone's Sails

Turn Turtle
Under the Weather
Washed-up
Weather the Storm
Weigh Anchor
Welcome Aboard
When My Ship Comes in

SHOOTING

Aim High
Blizzard
Call the Shots
Come to the Point
Dead on Target
Double-barreled
Draw a Bead
Flash in the Pan
Get a Bead on
Give It a Shot
Give It Your Best Shot
Go Off Half-cocked
Hang Fire
Have Something in Your Sights
Have Your Sights Set on Something
Hit the Spot
Itchy Trigger Finger
Knock the Spots off
Like Shooting Fish in a Barrel
Lock, Stock, and Barrel
Long Shot
Make a Point
Make Your Mark
Make Your Point
Miss by a Country Mile
Miss Is as Good as a Mile
Miss the Point
Miss Your Mark
Not by a Long Shot
Off Target
Off the Mark
One-shot Deal
On Target
Point-blank
Point-blank Range
Ramrod
Ricochet Romance
Ring a Bell
Ring the Bell

Set Your Sights High
Set Your Sights on
Shoot from the Hip
Shooting Gallery
Shoot the Moon
Shoot Your Wad
Stiff as a Ramrod
Stretch a Point
Sure as Shooting
Sure-fire
Take Aim
Take a Potshot
Take a Powder
Take Your Best Shot
Target (v)
Target Language
To the Point
Trigger-happy
Whole Shooting Match
Wide of the Mark
Zero in on

SKEET

Clay Pigeon

SKIING

Hang a Left/Right
On the Edge

SLINGSHOT

Slings and Arrows
Slingshot

SNOOKER

Snooker
Snookered

SOCCER

Get a Kick out of
Get the Ball Rolling
In the Nick of Time
Keep the Ball Rolling
Kick an Idea around
Kick in
Level the Playing Field
On the Ball
Throw Something in

SOFTBALL
Softball-size Hail

SPORTS
Abet
At the Top of Your Game
Bad Sport
Blow the Whistle
Body English
Break the Record
But Who's Counting
Come into Play
Contact Sport
Contender
Cry Foul
Crying Towel
Deadhead (n)
Deadhead (v)
Doesn't Know the Score
First-string
First Team
For a Lark
Franchise
Free Agent
Function as a Team
Gate
Get Up for the Game
Goal
Good Sport
Hail the Size of
Hall of Famer
Hang It up
Hang Loose
Have a Lark
Have a Score to Settle
Hot
How about That, Sports Fans
Jock
Keep Your Eye on the Ball
Know the Score
Lose Your Touch
Make Sport
Make the Cut
Make the Team
Name of the Game
No Contest
No Pain, No Gain
No-show

Number One
-Off
Off Your Game
Old Pro
On a Winning Streak
One Hundred and Ten Percent
One Sided (p. a.)
On the Winning Side
On Your Game
Palooka
Perfect Ten
Play along with
Play Catch-up
Play Fair
Play-off
Play over Your Head
Pro
Psyched-up
Record-breaking (adj.)
Root for
Run Up the Score
Sandbag
Sandbagger
Score (v)
Score Points
Side with
Skunk
Snatch Defeat from the Jaws of Victory
Spectator Sport
Spirit of Fair Play
Spoilsport
Sport (v)
Sporting Chance
Sporting Gesture
Sportsmanship
Squeaker
Stickler for the Rules
Sudden Death
Take a Breather
Take Sides with
Team Effort
Team Player
Throw (v)
Time (2)
We Wuz Robbed
Whistle-blower
Win a Few, Lose a Few
Win or Lose

World-class
You Can't Win 'Em All

SURFING

Catch the Wave
Hang a Left/Right
Hang Ten
Ride the Crest of a Wave
Surf Is up

SWIMMING

Above Your Head
Come Up for Air
Com'on in—The Water's Fine
Duck
Get Your Feet Wet
Grasp at Straws
In Deep Water
In over Your Head
Keep Your Head above Water
Lifesaver
Out of Your Depth
Over a Barrel
Sink or Swim
Surface
Surface for Air
Test the Waters
Tread Water
Trying to Stay Afloat
Up to Your Ears
Up to Your Eyeballs
Up to Your Neck
Wade in

TABLE TENNIS

Ping-Pong Diplomacy
Ping-Ponged

TENNIS

Ace a Test
Ball Is in the Other Court
Ball Is in Your Court
Bandy about
Change Sides
From Pillar to Post
High-strung
Lob
Love Game

On Center Court
Smash Hit
Tennis, Anyone
Top-seeded

TRACK AND FIELD

Get off on the Right Foot
Get off on the Wrong Foot
Hop, Skip, and a Jump
Hurdle (n)
Hurdle (v)
Jumping-off Point
Jump to a Conclusion
Put Your Best Foot forward
Vault
Vaulting Ambition

TRAPPING

Bait the Trap
Coldcock
Death Trap
Mind Like a Steel Trap
Set a Trap
Shut Your Trap
Trapped

TUG OF WAR

Anchorman
Dig in Your Heels
Tug of War

TUMBLING

See Gymnastics

WEIGHT LIFTING

Dumbbell
Heavyweight
Pump Wood

WHEEL OF FORTUNE

Come Full Circle
Downside
Round and Round
Upside (n)
What Goes around, Comes around

WRESTLING

Catch as Catch Can
Come off Second Best
Come to Grips with
Fall Guy
Foiled
Free-for-all
Get a Grip on Yourself
Get a Toehold
Get Someone down
Go to the Mat for
Grudge Match
Hard to Pin down
Headlock
Heavyweight
Lose Your Grip

No Holds Barred
Pin down
Pushover
Put-down
Put Someone down
Reach a Deadlock
Stranglehold
Take On All Comers
Take Someone on
Wipe the Floor with
Wrestle away
Wrestle with

YO-YO

Yo-yo (n)
Yo-yo (v)
Yo-yoish

About the Authors

ROBERT A. PALMATIER is Professor of Linguistics, Department of Languages and Linguistics, Western Michigan University. His two previous books dealt with the topics of transformational grammar and syntax.

HAROLD L. RAY is Professor, Department of Health, Physical Education, and Recreation, Western Michigan University. He is currently working on biographies of George (Potsy) Clark, the first coach of the Detroit Lions, and James Hayes, sportsman and hosteler.

	DATE DUE	